Thundering Zeus

HELLENISTIC CULTURE AND SOCIETY

General Editors: Anthony W. Bulloch, Erich S. Gruen,
A. A. Long, and Andrew F. Stewart

Thundering Zeus

The Making of Hellenistic Bactria

Frank L. Holt

UNIVERSITY OF CALIFORNIA PRESS
Berkeley · Los Angeles · London

University of California Press
Berkeley and Los Angeles, California

University of California Press, Ltd.
London, England

© 1999 by

The Regents of the University of California
Printed in the United States of America

Library of Congress Cataloging-in-Publication data

Holt, Frank Lee.
    Thundering Zeus : the making of Hellenistic
Bactria / Frank L. Holt.
        p.   cm. — (Hellenistic culture and
society ; 32)
    Includes bibliographical references and index.
    ISBN 0-520-21140-5 (alk. paper)
    1. Bactria—History.   2. Bactria—
History—Study and teaching.   3. Greeks—
Bactria—History.   4. Coins, Greek—Bactria.
5. Numismatics.   I. Title.   II. Series.
DS374.B28H66   1999
939'.6—dc21   98-6098
                                                        CIP

Printed in the United States of America

08   07   06   05   04   03   02   01   00

9   8   7   6   5   4   3   2

The paper used in this publication meets the minimum
requirements of ANSI/NISO Z39.48-1992 (R 1997)
(*Permanence of Paper*). ∞

For Stanley Mayer Burstein

Contents

Illustrations

PLATES

Plates 1, 2, and 23: Courtesy of Dr. Paul Bernard; Cover and plates 3–22 and 24–25: Courtesy of The American Numismatic Society, New York; plates 26–27: Courtesy of Dr. Viktor Sarianidi.

MAPS

FIGURES

Preface

There should be some unknown regions preserved as
hunting-grounds for the poetic imagination.

> *George Eliot,* Middlemarch

Of all the frontiers of the ancient world, none has endured so long in the
poetic imagination as the kingdom of Bactria. In those distant haunts of
the Hindu Kush, nearly three thousand miles east of Athens, the early
Greeks imagined a never-never land untouched by civilization. Rivers of
honey oozed on the Bactrian frontier; fierce griffins guarded the precious
gold mined by giant ants; people had ears the size of an elephant's, ate
their parents, and lived for centuries. As on the early maps of European
explorers, Greek geographers dealt with places such as Bactria by crowd-
ing the edges of the known world with sinister warnings: "Beyond this
lie sandy wastes filled with monsters" (or "trackless swamps," or
"Scythian snows," or "ice-bound seas").

To reach the Bactrian frontier at all was a boast worthy of the bravest
adventurers. This hero list included Herakles, Prometheus, Dionysus,
Semiramis, Sardanapoulus, Alexander the Great, and even Shelley's poetic "Ozymandias." When the Roman poet Propertius imagined the ends
of the earth, he thought naturally of Bactria. Centuries later, Marco Polo
met these notions again on his celebrated travels. Even the muses of Boccaccio and Chaucer thrilled to the ancient echoes of this exotic land. In the
"Knight's Tale" we find one of the Greek kings of Bactria, Demetrius I,
imagined as a man like Mars—a heroic young warrior-prince wearing
gold, rubies, pearls, and silk, bearded and with a voice like thunder.
Chaucer dared even to imagine the color of the king's eyes, hair, freckles,

and skin. Later writers such as Viscount Mersey tracked in verse the feats and features of other heroes, in this case Alexander:

> From Bactria he entered Sogdiana
> Across the fertile pastures of Ferghana,
> The hunting lands of arrow, spear and sabre,
> Of Genghis Khan and Tamerlane and Baber.
> His Macedonian coins still come to hand
> In Merv, Bukhara and in Samarkand.
>   V. Mersey, *Alexander of Macedon*
>   (London: J. Murray, 1946), p.v.

These "remote" places rang with danger and romance, and the relics there inspired such local leaders as Shah Sikander ("Alexander") Khan to imagine his direct descent from the ancient Greeks on the basis of his resemblance to their portraits on coins. Bactria, then, has long been just the place that poets would have us preserve as hunting grounds for the unbridled imagination.

This book, like my *Alexander the Great and Bactria,* intends to tug this romanticized region a little closer to the light of history. Poetic imagination is certainly a great human treasure, but so is the search for truth. Without robbing Bactria of its romance, this work tries to rescue what we can of the actual people, places, and events that have inspired so many writers for so many generations. It examines in detail the story of Bactria's first independent Greek rulers, the restless father-son duo of Diodotus I and II, in the turbulent aftermath of Alexander the Great's demise. This has been deemed one of the most difficult historical problems in all of ancient studies. To solve it, information has been gleaned from ancient texts, modern archaeology, and especially numismatics—the study of coinages. These pages offer the first modern history ever devoted to the important but elusive dynasty of the Diodotids of Bactria.

I have tried, perhaps foolishly, to make this book all things to all people. It is a history, a numismatic handbook, and an introduction to Hellenistic civilization. For experts in the fields of history, archaeology, and numismatics, I have included as much documentation and argumentation as possible. This book breaks new ground, and I mean for it to be useful to specialists. At the same time, I have tried to make the text very readable for nonspecialists. All research methodologies have been explained and each point set into its larger context. The appendices provide access to all of the source materials any reader should need, and the glossary offers assistance to those unfamiliar with the terminology. By incorporating all of these features into the book I hope that every reader may find what he or she desires, and I ask both the specialist and the general reader to indulge me in my efforts to accommodate the other.

I would naturally have liked to take the book further, but it has already occupied vast stretches of time over the past sixteen years. This work was conceived before I had written my Ph.D. dissertation and actually begun before my other books were published. As I wrote on other matters and engaged in full-time teaching, I never let go of this important project. For years I collected the necessary numismatic data and tried to sort it out in some scientific manner. I knew that Hellenistic Bactria could never make sense to us until we had solved the mystery of the kingdom's origins under Diodotus I and II. By 1995 I knew I had made enough key discoveries to set them down in a book-length manuscript, which I submitted to the University of California Press. I have done what I could to keep the work up-to-date since its acceptance for publication. Even so, there are still more museums to visit, archaeological sites to see, and books to read. That will never change, and I present here my findings with full knowledge that the next museum, excavation, or book that I examine might alter everything. If that were not true, the subject would not be nearly so exciting for us to consider. It is time, in any case, to do all we can to *remove* Bactria from the realm of the unknown.

Houston, Texas
August 1997

Acknowledgments

This book has been a long but never lonely travail. Many individuals and institutions have assisted me over the years, and they all deserve credit for any lasting value this work may have. I begin with my family, whose enthusiasm has sustained me from start to finish. My wife, Linda, has typed this manuscript many times without complaint, and she has shared daily the thrill of discovery as we pored over these sources and problems together. My daughter, Laura, has lived graciously with this consuming project and offered much valuable assistance over the years. I appreciate their patience during all my travels and the longer hours "away" at my desk.

My department and university have provided the time and tools needed to get this job done. I am particularly grateful to the University of Houston's Office of Sponsored Programs for a Research Initiation Grant in 1984, a Limited Grant-in-Aid in 1985, and a Faculty Development Leave in 1991. The University of Houston Department of History provided a Pratt Grant for travel abroad in 1992 and funds for additional travels, computer software, photography, and so forth. The University of Houston College of Humanities, Fine Arts, and Communication awarded me a Faculty Development Summer Grant in 1994. In 1989 I received a Summer Research Stipend from the National Endowment for the Humanities. I also benefited from a National Endowment for the Humanities Summer Institute Stipend in 1987.

For much assistance, encouragement, and correction, I express sincere gratitude to many fine colleagues around the world. These generous intellectuals include W. Lindsay Adams, Carmen Arnold-Biucchi, U. P. Arora, Paul Bernard, Osmund Bopearachchi, Eugene Borza, Pierre Briant, Paul Bucherer-Dietschi, K. Butcher, Frank Campbell, Elvira Clain-Stefanelli, Susan Downey, Youri Dioukov, Jean-Claude Gardin, Dominique Gerin, Peter Green, Carla Grissmann, Hakim Hamidi, Adrian Hollis, Arthur Houghton, O. P. Kejariwal, Michael Kordosis, Frank and Renee Kovacs, Brian Kritt, Amélie Kuhrt, Frank Lenoir, Pierre Leriche, Mariusz Mielczarek, A. K. Narain, Valerii Nikonorov, I. R. Pichikyan, Ivan Prinsep, Edvard Rtveladze, H.-D. Schultz, Robert Senior, Ioannis Touratsoglou, Gail Trail, Demetrius Velissaropoulos, and the late Martin Price. These scholars have been especially kind in sending offprints and books many of which I might otherwise have missed. Since finishing the manuscript, in fact, I have received two important articles (from S. Kovalenko and J. Wieshöfer) of which I have been able to make only partial use in my notes. These articles show the quality and quickening pace of Diodotid research, and I am grateful to their authors for sharing this work with me. I hope that I shall continue to be the beneficiary of so much collegial kindness.

To all of the museums and libraries that have accommodated my research, I express deep gratitude. I owe much to the University of California Press, its editors and outside readers, and particularly Mary Lamprech for the publication of this book. Most of all, I thank the person to whom this book is dedicated—my friend and mentor, Stanley Mayer Burstein. He has guided my steps with patience and wisdom since 1981, and I have never been able to thank him enough. I hope that this book, in some small way, will make those efforts seem worthwhile.

CHAPTER I

The Hellenistic Background

SILENCE AT BABYLON

On a sweltering June day in Babylon by the banks of the Euphrates River, Alexander the Great died as he had lived—unpredictably, mysteriously, momentously. His last breath opened a chasm in history, separating in 323 B.C. one phase of Western civilization from all that was to follow. Without Alexander, the world could not be the same, a compelling fact that stunned his contemporaries and still fascinates us.[1] Those hardened veterans who surrounded Alexander's deathbed had turned back a million fears. They had won epic battles, besieged grim fortresses, survived withering ambuscades, suffered strange ailments and alien environments, buried their comrades in places never to be seen again, and endured the Achillean wrath of Alexander himself at Opis and the Hyphasis.[2] But Alexander dead was more terrifying than Alexander—or any enemy—alive. Without an able successor to the Macedonian throne, what was the army to make of that awkward silence at Babylon? Who was to bridge the chasm, and how?

1. There have been many good biographies of Alexander, but the best now is that of Alan B. Bosworth, *Conquest and Empire: The Reign of Alexander the Great* (Cambridge: Cambridge University Press, 1988). Also recommended are Peter Green, *Alexander of Macedon, 356–323 B.C.: A Historical Biography* (Berkeley: University of California Press, 1991); J. R. Hamilton, *Alexander the Great* (Pittsburgh: University of Pittsburgh Press, 1973); and E. N. Borza's edition of Ulrich Wilcken, *Alexander the Great* (New York: Norton, 1967).

2. At the Hyphasis River in India (326 B.C.) and the city of Opis in Babylonia (324 B.C.), Alexander faced down "mutinies" of his soldiers by emulating the warrior hero Achilles, whose wrath was the theme of Homer's *Iliad*.

The crisis produced an unlikely hodgepodge of solutions, an unwieldy set of contradictions that only proved how much the leadership of Alexander would be missed. There was division and defection in the ranks at Babylon, mutiny on the Bactrian frontier, and ill-considered rejoicing among some of the Greek city-states. The forceful personality of Alexander the Great had masked a great many problems in the Greek and Persian worlds. Many Greek cities, Athens among them, still resented their loss of freedom to such kings as Alexander and his "barbarian" father, Philip II.[3] Only military force had kept these old Greek city-states (poleis) in line as Alexander waged on their behalf his Pan-Hellenic ("All-Greek") crusade against Persia. Throughout those campaigns, tensions between Greeks and Macedonians continued to build, complicated further by their ill will toward the Persians. The lightning speed of Alexander's conquests left little opportunity to build a common bond between old adversaries. The military that had won the war remained at odds over how to conduct the peace. In fact, many soldiers left behind in places such as Bactria and India were insistent upon leaving their far-flung posts even before the death of their king.[4] Now these volcanic forces threatened to blow the leaderless empire asunder unless another Alexander could be found.

At first, the uneasy army could not agree upon a single successor to the Macedonian throne, so two were chosen: one the debilitated half-brother of Alexander, the other a son yet unborn of the conqueror himself.[5] And then there emerged a third. Unhappy with the incomparable Alexander's incompetent kin, some chose to put the dead king back on his throne. For men like Eumenes, Alexander's chief secretary, the only way to bridge this rift in history was to deny the awful reality of what had happened to the world at Babylon. A royal tent was set up for the ghost of Alexander, complete with his old throne, diadem, and scepter. The invisible, invincible conqueror was made to reign again. Meanwhile, across the empire, Alexander's royal coins continued to be minted by the million. The king's mummified remains became a great prize for those who lacked the potent relics of Eumenes's traveling royal tent. An entire

3. On the rise of Macedonia and the politically motivated charge that Philip was a barbarian, see N. G. L. Hammond, *Philip of Macedon* (Baltimore: Johns Hopkins University Press, 1994); R. M. Errington, *A History of Macedonia* (Berkeley: University of California Press, 1990); and E. N. Borza, *In the Shadow of Olympus: The Emergence of Macedon* (Princeton: Princeton University Press, 1990).

4. See, for example, F. L. Holt, *Alexander the Great and Bactria* (Leiden: Brill, 1988).

5. For a reliable narrative of these complex events, see R. M. Errington, "From Babylon to Triparadeisos: 323–320 B.C." *JHS* 90 (1970): 49–77.

generation was avowing that Alexander was not only alive and well but ruling the world again.[6] For a multitude of personal and political reasons, most of Alexander's anxious contemporaries did not wish to let him go. Frightened and frustrated, they tried to keep one foot in the old world while reaching for the new. Some were torn apart by the effort, some fell back into the oblivion of the era past, while the strongest (to whom Alexander on his deathbed allegedly bequeathed his empire) finally jumped into the future. These were the men who would be kings in the new Hellenistic Age.[7] The true heirs of Alexander were neither his inept and ill-fated kin, all of whom—men, women, and children—were eventually murdered, nor the desperate dreamers who held council around an empty throne. His successors were the men and women who finally dared to bury Alexander and to build a brave new world.[8] Such intrepid souls rose from the ranks to found new kingdoms and foster new dynasties; they explored new frontiers, constructed new cities, expanded trade, patronized the arts,

6. A convenient survey of Alexander's *Nachleben* (afterlife) in the early Hellenistic Age may be found in R. M. Errington's "Alexander in the Hellenistic World," pp. 137–179 in E. Badian, ed., *Alexandre le Grand: Image et realité* (Geneva: Fondation Hardt, 1976). See also P. Goukowsky, *Essai sur les origines du mythe d'Alexandre*, vol. 1 (Nancy: Université de Nancy, 1978); Ursula Hackl, "Alexander der Grosse und der Beginn der hellenistischer Zeitalters," pp. 693–716 in W. Will and J. Heinrichs, eds., *Zu Alexander der Grosse* [Festschrift G. Wirth], vol. 1 (Amsterdam: Hakkert, 1988); and the important study by Andrew Stewart, *Faces of Power: Alexander's Image and Hellenistic Politics* (Berkeley: University of California Press, 1993). For the problem of the Alexander posthumous coinage, consult M. J. Price, *The Coinage in the Name of Alexander the Great and Philip Arrhidaeus*, 2 vols. (Zurich and London: Swiss Numismatic Society and British Museum Press, 1991).

7. Standard general reference works on the Hellenistic Age include F. Walbank, A. Astin, et al., eds., *The Cambridge Ancient History*, 2d ed., vols. 7 and 8 (Cambridge: Cambridge University Press, 1984 and 1989); E. Will, C. Mosse, and P. Goukowsky, *Le monde grec et l'Orient*, vol. 2 (Paris: Presses Universitaires de France, 1975); C. Préaux, *Le monde hellénistique*, 2 vols. (Paris: Presses Universitaires de France, 1978); J. Seibert, *Das Zeitalter der Diadochen* (Darmstadt: Wissenschaftliche Buchgesellschaft, 1983); M. Grant, *From Alexander to Cleopatra* (New York: Scribner, 1982); F. Walbank, *The Hellenistic World* (Cambridge, Mass.: Harvard University Press, 1982); P. Green, ed., *Hellenistic History and Culture* (Berkeley: University of California Press, 1993) and *Alexander to Actium* (Berkeley: University of California Press, 1990); and Erich Gruen, *The Hellenistic World and the Coming of Rome*, 2 vols. (Berkeley: University of California Press, 1984). In addition to the bibliographies contained in these works, one may profit from S. Burstein, "Hellenistic Culture: Recent Resources (1960–1989)," *Choice* (June 1990): 1634–1643, and *The Hellenistic Period in World History* (Washington, D.C.: American Historical Association, 1996).

8. As noted in the *Suda* (a Byzantine lexicon) under the rubric "monarchy," the key to Hellenistic kingship was not simply descent or legitimacy but military and political competence. For an English translation, see M. M. Austin, ed., *The Hellenistic World from Alexander to the Roman Conquest* (Cambridge: Cambridge University Press, 1981), no. 37 (p. 67).

·

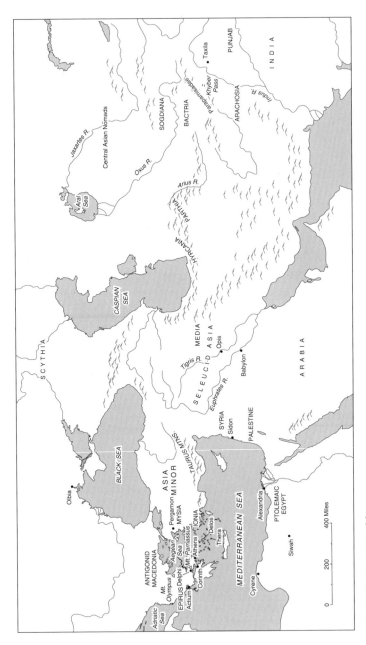

The Hellenistic World.

and naturally waged almost incessant war against one another. The turbulent world without Alexander guaranteed a trial of strength and eventually the triumph of audacity. Wealth and power awaited these wandering bold wherever they dared to go. Alexandrias, Antiochs, and other new cities as far east as India beckoned to warriors, writers, merchants, and adventurers of all ranks. The administrator Megasthenes could take the post of Seleucid envoy to Pataliputra on the Ganges River; the philosopher Klearchos could copy at Delphi and carry to the Oxus Valley the famous maxims of Apollo; the explorer Patrocles could trek to the Caspian Sea in search of new trade routes; the exiled writer and statesman Demetrius of Phalerum could win the job of Greek librarian in Alexandria. Opportunities and risks abounded in the Hellenistic world (map 1). After all, the "safest" career in this list—that of librarian—brought disgrace and death to the scholarly Demetrius in the pell-mell of Hellenistic politics.[9]

The Hellenistic Age forced the Greeks and Macedonians to give up all that Alexander's life and death had brought them or to gamble their winnings on an epic scale. That is why Hellenistic history reads so dramatically as a political and military narrative. But the confrontations and risks were cultural as well. Caught in the Hellenistic struggles for supremacy and survival were the peoples of many lands stretching from Italy to India. It is common today to criticize the Hellenistic Greeks for their reluctance to embrace readily all that these "barbarian" civilizations had to offer, but, to be fair, the Balkan peoples had been cultural elitists long before the life and death of Alexander put them in power amidst so many races. They could only bring to the Hellenistic Age their old deeprooted prejudices and fears; yet, to their credit, they included among the gambles of their times the occasional embrace of foreign ideas, peoples, and places. The extent to which Greek and non-Greek actually mingled depends, of course, upon where we look. Scholars have made this one of the key issues of Hellenistic historiography, ranging in their judgments from enthusiastic praise to bitter condemnation of Greek colonialism.[10]

9. On Megasthenes, See E. Olshausen, *Prosopographie der hellenistischen Königsgesandten*, vol. 1 (Louvain: Studia Hellenistica, 1974), pp. 172–174. Klearchos and Patrocles are discussed below (chap. 3). For Demetrius, consult the lively account in L. Canfora, *The Vanished Library* (Berkeley: University of California Press, 1990), translated from the original 1987 Italian edition by Martin Ryle.

10. On both sides of the cultural question in Hellenistic history, the arguments are often quite heated, especially when fired by issues in our contemporary history. These are among the most important assessments: Green, *Alexander to Actium*, pp. 312–335; A. E. Samuel, *The Shifting Sands of History: Interpretations of Ptolemaic Egypt* (Lanham, Md.:

Whatever its limitations, however, Hellenistic civilization was not only the road that carried Greek polis culture to Rome, the Middle Ages, and so the modern world but also the route by which Egyptian and Near Eastern cultures reached us through Alexandria and the Byzantine empire.[11]

The last breath of Alexander the Great inaugurated this extraordinary age because his true successors—man for man and sometimes woman for woman—had then to make their own decisions and run their own risks. The conqueror could no longer choose their dangers for them; obedience and advising gave way to ambition and action. As a result, there would never be more fertile ground for kingmaking and revolution than the area between the Adriatic and India from the death of Alexander to the rise of Augustus. Over a dozen new dynasties produced at least two hundred kings and queens as Alexander's successors divided the conquered lands. These sovereigns animated the lively social, religious, military, and political currents of the age; they embodied the Hellenistic ideals of aggressive, heroic, cultured, just, and generous leadership. In cult and at court, they wore these virtues openly in such titles as Nikator (Conqueror), Soter (Savior), Aniketos (Invincible), Euergetes (Benefactor), Dikaios (Just), Theos (God), and Philhellene (Greek-loving).[12]

The Hellenistic world, at least at its upper levels, revolved around its new royalty. Philosophers advised them, poets extolled them, artists portrayed them, priests adored them, and generals obeyed them. Surrounded by his *philoi* (friends), the personal retainers and privy council to the king, the ruler of Syria or Egypt embodied the state.[13] He was responsible for its total well-being, from the administration of justice to the conduct of

---

University Press of America, 1989); articles by Burstein, Holt, Samuel, Delia, Gruen, and Morgan in Green, *Hellenistic History and Culture;* E. Will, "Le monde hellénistique et nous," *Ancient Society* 10 (1979): 79–95; E. Will, "Pour une 'anthropologie coloniale' du monde hellénistique," pp. 273–301 in J. Eadie and J. Ober, eds., *The Craft of the Ancient Historian: Essays in Honor of Chester G. Starr* (Lanham, Md.: University Press of America, 1985); A. Kuhrt and S. Sherwin-White, eds., *Hellenism in the East* (Berkeley: University of California Press, 1987); S. Sherwin-White and A. Kuhrt, *From Samarkhand to Sardis* (Berkeley: University of California Press, 1993), esp. chap. 6; A. Momigliano, *Alien Wisdom* (Cambridge: Cambridge University Press, 1975); S. K. Eddy, *The King is Dead* (Lincoln: University of Nebraska Press, 1961); and V. Tcherikover, *Hellenistic Civilization and the Jews* (Philadelphia: Jewish Publication Society of America, 1959; rpt. New York: Atheneum, 1970).

11. A. Momigliano, "The Fault of the Greeks," in his *Essays in Ancient and Modern Historiography* (Middletown, Conn.: Wesleyan University Press, 1977), pp. 9–23.

12. Appian *Syr.* 65–70 runs through the king list of the Seleucid empire giving the epithets (and sometimes an explanation for them) of most of the rulers. For a Ptolemaic example, see appendix D, inscription 6.

13. F. Walbank, "Monarchies and Monarchic Ideas," pp. 62–100 in *CAH*[2] 7 (1984); G. Herman, "The 'Friends' of the Early Hellenistic Rulers: Servants or Officials?" *Talanta*

war. Conspicuous in his regalia, in particular the royal diadem tied about his head or helmet, the monarch was the very picture of wealth, courage, and wisdom. Great pains were taken to display these qualities through magnificent palaces, processions, banquets, gifts, monuments, and military campaigns.[14] The royal coinage was carefully designed to enhance this image, giving the public a chance to see the king's portrait, to read his name and titles, to identify the gods or heroes whose powers the king shared, and to enjoy spending part of the king's great personal wealth.[15]

Heavy were the burdens of rule in the Hellenistic world. Kings and queens had to live up to high and very public expectations or suffer the consequences. The modern image of ancient kings lounging upon pillows and eating peeled grapes must be balanced against the facts, most notably their high mortality rate at the hands of usurpers, assassins, and foreign enemies. Any king who failed his people in war, justice, wealth, or religion could expect a challenge; loss of face usually meant loss of life. The bloody competition for power never waned, and every weakness— real or imagined—was exploited by a rival. That is why only a handful of Hellenistic kings died peacefully in bed; most were assassinated or killed in battle.[16]

With their job security so seriously threatened, Hellenistic monarchs relied heavily upon family members to help run their states. Available sons, brothers, cousins, and so forth, were appointed to key positions of trust and power such as the office of satrap (regional governor). To establish some continuity in this hazardous environment, kings took great care to foster dynastic loyalty.[17] Chosen successors, usually sons, of course, were introduced early into public life and given appropriate tasks

---

(1981): 103–149; and chap. 1 of Inge Nielson, *Hellenistic Palaces: Tradition and Renewal* (Aarhus: Aarhus University Press, 1994).

14. As one example, see E. E. Rice, *The Grand Procession of Ptolemy Philadelphus* (Oxford: Oxford University Press, 1983). Note also the booty mentioned in appendix D, inscription 6.

15. Norman Davis and Colin Kraay, *The Hellenistic Kingdoms: Portrait Coins and History* (London: Thames and Hudson, 1973), provides a well-illustrated introduction. For the details, see Robert Fleischer, *Studien zur seleukidischen Kunst*, vol. 1, *Herrscherbildnisse* (Mainz am Rhein: Philipp von Zabern, 1991). Realistic portrait coinage probably allowed rustics to recognize their sovereign even without the trappings of office: Plutarch *Moralia* 508 D–E.

16. According to Elias Bickerman, *Institutions des Séleucides* (Paris: Paul Geuthner, 1938), p. 13, only two of the first fourteen Seleucid kings died at home in their palaces (and one of the two was murdered).

17. Sherwin-White and Kuhrt, *Samarkhand to Sardis*, pp. 114–140, esp. 125–140. Again, inscription 6, appendix D, provides a useful Ptolemaic example of strong dynastic sentiments.

to groom them for future rule. In some cases, an aging king would ele-
vate his royal heir to a vice-regal position, sharing image and power in
order to ensure a smooth transition in the face of possible challengers.
Naturally, special homage was also paid to a king's predecessor (especially his father) as part of this dynastic shield against usurpers. These
Hellenistic monarchs were, to give them their due, an ancient marvel of
adaptability in a fluid and risky world. In Egypt they governed largely
in Greek fashion but portrayed themselves in art as pharaohs, while in
India some took native titles and at least one ruled as a Buddhist. Reckoned among their ranks were kings and queens who emerged from many
backgrounds: Thracians, Celts, Greeks, Iranians, Arabs, Jews, Parthians,
Armenians, Indians, and others. Though Greeks and Macedonians clearly
dominated the politics of the period, they had to share with other groups
the opportunities for greatness that followed directly from Alexander's
death.[18]

All of these kings and queens merit the attentions of modern scholars, but our knowledge of them and their world is quite uneven. Unlike
the earlier Classical period of Greek civilization, the longer Hellenistic
Age has fewer narrative sources to guide us. Short periods or particular
reigns aroused the interest of such writers as Polybius, Appian, and
Plutarch, while Diodorus and others took a broader view, but nothing
better than Justin's condensed and confused Latin epitome of Pompeius
Trogus survives today as a larger historical treatment of the period. The
rest, a considerable miscellany of literary works, exists now only as fragmentary quotations in the texts of later Greek and Latin writers. Lacking the usual supply of written sources, Hellenistic scholars must rely
heavily upon a scatter of documentary inscriptions, papyri, archaeological data, and numismatic evidence. Approached with some ingenuity,
however, these records can be remarkably revealing.[19]

18. In addition to the general historical works already cited, which often contain discussions of Hellenistic kingship, there are numerous specialized treatments and now a grow-
ing number of biographies. As a representative sampling, see M. M. Austin, "Hellenistic
Kings, War, and Economy," *CQ* 36 (1986): 450–466; F. Adcock, "Greek and Macedonian
Kingship," *PBA* 39 (1953): 163–180; J. J. Farber, "The *Cyropaedia* and Hellenistic Kingship," *AJPh* 100 (1979): 497–514; H. Lund, *Lysimachus* (London: Routledge, 1992); and
R. Billows, *Antigonus the One-Eyed and the Creation of the Hellenistic State* (Berkeley:
University of California Press, 1990) and *Kings and Colonists: Aspects of Macedonian Im-
perialism* (Leiden: Brill, 1995). See chap. 2 for the Seleucids.

19. The written evidence is heavily Greek in both language and point of view; however, important steps are being taken to incorporate non-Greek sources into our latest reconstructions. See, e.g., the works by Kuhrt and Sherwin-White in n. 10 on the Seleucid
empire; Egyptian and Jewish history have been more balanced in the past because of a rel-

Given the extraordinary character of the Hellenistic Age and the poor quality of its literary sources, this period has posed a special challenge to modern historians. The importance of the age is undeniable, but how do we recover its many details without a Thucydides or Herodotus to guide us? In truth, Western scholars for many years have generally chosen to avoid the dilemma altogether. Many of their books about the ancient world simply skipped from Classical Greece to Republican Rome; many of their college courses about Greek civilization abruptly ended with the death of Alexander rather than venture into the Hellenistic Age. Curiously, scholarship itself acted out the crisis at Babylon: conservative pedants dared not cross the chasm but fell back upon the familiar ground of the Classical period and stopped time in its tracks. Some dreamed ahead from the "glory that was Greece" to the "grandeur that was Rome" without awakening to the awesome consequences of Alexander's death. But braver souls, the likes of Bury, Rostovtzeff, Will, Holleaux, Préaux, and Walbank, took their chances and faced the challenges of Hellenistic history. Like the kings and queens about whom they wrote, these scholars made what they could of the risky age after Alexander. Their work is one of the great wonders of the twentieth century.[20]

HELLENISTIC BACTRIA

Perhaps the most famous paradigm for the many prospects and pitfalls of Hellenistic research may be found in the history of the remote kingdom of Bactria. Uncovering it has been called the ultimate test of modern historical, archaeological, and numismatic science. In Bactria, the heirs of Alexander created a unique civilization that touched upon the diverse cultures of Greece, Iran, India, and China. Theirs became a story celebrated far and wide in the ancient world, and threads of that tale run right through the Renaissance—through Boccaccio and Chaucer—to reach us still as one of mystery and romance.[21]

---

ative abundance of non-Greek sources for those areas. Handy translations of Hellenistic sources may be found in Austin, *The Hellenistic World*, and S. Burstein, ed., *The Hellenistic Age from the Battle of Ipsos to the Death of Kleopatra VII* (Cambridge: Cambridge University Press, 1985). See chaps. 2 and 3 and appendix D.

20. See Chester G. Starr, *Past and Future in Ancient History* (Lanham, Md.: University Press of America, 1987), pp. 19–32.

21. For surveys of the Bactrian source problem, historiography, and fresh discoveries, consult F. Holt, "Discovering the Lost History of Ancient Afghanistan," *AncW* 9 (1984): 3–11, 13–28, "Hellenistic Bactria: Beyond the Mirage," *AncW* 15 (1987): 3–15, and "A History in Silver and Gold," *Aramco World* 45 (1994): 2–13. Popular treatments include

The romance arises from the exotic setting of a Hellenistic kingdom in Central Asia, some three thousand miles east of Athens. Stretching over mountain and desert where even today the tribesmen boast of their descent from Alexander and his soldiers, Bactria occupied much of modern Afghanistan; its northern region, called Sogdiana, covered parts of today's Uzbekistan and Tadjikistan. It was then, as now, a remarkably rugged and remote land.[22] The Hindu Kush, separating Bactria from ancient India, soars to seventeen thousand feet; the Pamirs in Sogdiana reach as high as twenty-five thousand feet. These peaks enclose the large territory of Bactria except to the west-northwest, where the Turkestan desert opens out toward the Aral Sea. Cutting through these mountains and desert is the Oxus River (modern Amu Darya), whose upper and middle course forms the heartland of historical Bactria. Along this major river and its tributaries, most notably the Kochba and Kunduz Rivers in Bactria, it is possible to sustain large populations only by irrigating the surrounding desert. The same is true of the Bactrus River to the west and the large Jaxartes River (modern Syr Darya) to the north. Traces of ancient canals can still be seen along many of these precious rivers.

This environment was totally alien to the Greeks and Macedonians who ventured there to run the risks of the Hellenistic Age. Though Greece was mountainous, its highest peak (Mt. Olympus, at less than ten thousand feet) would be dwarfed by those of Bactria and Sogdiana. The moderate climate of Greece contrasted starkly with the arid conditions and extreme temperatures of Bactria. In Greece the sea was never farther than a few miles away, while Bactria was landlocked. And the rivers of Greece, mostly just trickles of little consequence, could not compare with the large, life-giving torrents of Central Asia. When these Greek settlers left the Mediterranean world behind, they faced a difficult adjustment to the hot "oasis" culture of distant Bactria.

Yet this state came to rival in size and significance all others of its day, including Antigonid Macedonia, Ptolemaic Egypt, and Attalid Pergamon; the one exception was the mammoth Seleucid empire, of which Bactria had been a frontier province (satrapy) before the middle of the third century B.C. The thought of great Greek cities in those sandy wastes boggles the modern mind, but in antiquity this diverse land yielded through

---

M. Wheeler, *Flames Over Persepolis: Turning Points in History* (New York: Reynal, 1968), and G. Woodcock, *The Greeks in India* (London: Faber and Faber, 1966).

22. For the geographic background of Bactrian history, see Holt, *Alexander and Bactria*, pp. 11–32.

irrigation a myriad of grains, grapes, pistachios, and other products.[23] Grasslands and mountain pastures supported herds of cattle and horses, along with the famous Bactrian camel.[24] Through bitter winters and blazing summers, generations of adventurous Greeks won their living from this land. They had come boldly to a place once fabled in Greek literature as a never-never land untouched by civilization, where savages ate their own parents and the frontier teemed with ghastly creatures. Before them, only gods and heroes the likes of Herakles, Prometheus, and Dionysus had dared to walk this ground.[25] But here the Greeks came and made their new homes in the Hellenistic Age. They eventually grew wealthy on trade and turned out some of the most beautiful examples of Greek numismatic art ever to be found. Bactria therefore exemplifies fully the character and achievement of the Hellenistic Age, that remarkable but risky legacy of Alexander's last breath at Babylon.

For some, the romance runs much deeper. Believers in Alexander's "dream of world brotherhood" have often pointed to Bactria as the place where that dream actually came true. Calling it "a lesson for our weary world" in the aftermath of World War II, one professor borrowed the language of a fairy-tale to write of Bactria in a scholarly journal: "Once upon a time, and as a direct result of the inspiration of Alexander, there was a highly successful adventure in the field of international cooperation."[26] The later Greek kings of Bactria and India allegedly did what Alexander nobly dreamt—they created a true partnership with the native population, the peaceful union of Greek and barbarian that Alexander had intended. Thus, in our modern age, which generally frowns upon Alexander's achievements beyond the field of battle, Bactria has become the touchstone for his nobler legacy.

Over the course of the past century, Bactria has been in the middle of this debate.[27] What role *did* the Greek minority allow others to play in the administration and social life of such places as Bactria? Was there

23. Theophrastus *History of Plants* 4.4.7; Quintus Curtius 7.4.26.
24. Aelian *On Animals* 4.55; Athenaeus 5.219A; Aristotle *History of Animals* 498 b8 and 499 a14; Arrian *Anabasis* 3.30.6. See also F. Holt, "Spitamenes Against Alexander," *Historikogeographika* 4 (1994): 51–58 on the importance of Central Asian livestock.
25. Holt, *Alexander and Bactria*, pp. 25–34; J. Sedlar, *India and the Greek World: A Study in the Transmission of Culture* (Totowa, N. J.: Rowman and Littlefield, 1980), pp. 9–15.
26. C. A. Robinson Jr., "The Greeks in the Far East," *CJ* 44 (1949): 406. Behind this image of Alexander and Bactria lies the influential work of W. W. Tarn, a pioneering scholar who is discussed further in the following chapter.
27. See nn. 7 and 10, esp. Walbank, *Hellenistic World*, pp. 60–64, and Green, *Alexander to Actium*, pp. 312–335.

meaningful interaction between cultures, a true melting pot in the modern sense, or did an arrogant chauvinism keep ethnic groups segregated? Scholars who were themselves products of nineteenth-century European empires saw in Bactria the best of all ancient worlds, a place where the "Greek Man's burden" converted the Asian savages into useful political and social partners. These scholars viewed Hellenistic culture as a synthesis of Greek and non-Greek traditions, a harmonious and creative mixture that (in some cases, at least) prepared the world for Christianity.[28] Since World War II, however, this generous appraisal of Hellenistic civilization has been challenged by a generation of scholars disillusioned by the same record of European colonialism and imperialism that had inspired their forebears. Historians have been quick to identify in Hellenistic Egypt, Syria, Palestine, and Babylon the tragic legacy of imperialism that afflicts the modern Third World: a large, impoverished, exploited underclass of native peoples whose languages, arts, and religions were deemed of little value by colonialist superpowers. Living not so much together as parasitically in enclaves of cultural and ethnic isolation, the Greeks and non-Greeks of Hellenistic Alexandria and Antioch suddenly reminded modern scholars of our own ghettos and barrios. Was Bactria no better as a melting pot, or could scholars still find there some trace of that noble experiment for which Alexander and his successors had once been so admired?

Thus, after World War II, some experts began to question the Greeks' real interest in the foreign peoples over which Alexander had made them master.[29] Others minimized the ability of these wayward Greeks to influence the older cultures around them. Bactria became the center of this debate when, in response to William W. Tarn's epochal work *The Greeks in Bactria and India* (1938 and 1951), A. K. Narain published *The Indo-Greeks* (1957).[30] These two great books reached opposite conclusions by examining Bactrian history from opposite perspectives, one insisting that "in the history of India the episode of Greek rule has no meaning, it is really part of the history of Hellenism, and that is where its meaning resides"; whereas, the other countered, "Their history is part

28. Thus the famous formulation by the nineteenth-century German scholar who coined the term "Hellenistic"; see A. Momigliano, "J. G. Droysen Between Greeks and Jews," pp. 307–323 in his *Essays*.

29. See Holt, "Response," in Green, *Hellenistic History and Culture*, pp. 54–64.

30. Discussed by Holt in W. W. Tarn, *The Greeks in Bactria and India*, 3d ed., edited by Frank Holt (Chicago: Ares Press, 1984), pp. iii–xvi, and in *Alexander and Bactria*, pp. 3–6.

of the history of India and not of the Hellenistic states: they came, they saw, but India conquered."[31] Where does Bactria really fit into world history? Clearly, the answer is that the complex story of the ancient Bactrians must be seen in all of its relevant contexts: Persian history, Greek history, Central Asian history, Indian history.[32]

Only recently have historians begun to explore the non-Greek side of Hellenistic civilization, finding it to be more complex than previously imagined. Studies of Egyptian, Jewish, and Mesopotamian peoples have uncovered an intricate network of social and political subgroups. Some of these native elements did indeed remain aloof and unassimilated into the Greek dominant culture, but certain subgroups (e.g., Egyptian priests and village leaders, Syrian bureaucrats) became important and relatively powerful intermediaries between the Greek and non-Greek worlds. Such groups crossed over the cultural divide and sometimes gained status as Greek citizens. Though they met very little traffic moving in the opposite direction, these examples show that some meaningful interaction occurred, even if it was not quite so widespread as originally believed.[33]

In the field of economics, too, Bactria has been singled out as a test case for the entire Hellenistic Age. Since the nineteenth century scholars have seen Bactria as a prime example of Alexander's benevolent economic policies. This view links the plunder of Persia with the thriving economy of the Hellenistic East. Historians, moralists, economists, and poets long argued that Alexander used the idle wealth of the Persian kings to monetize with Greek currency the stagnant economy of Bactria and neighboring regions. Just as Alexander united two worlds divided by ideology, so he united two contrasting economic systems into a single wonder of productivity.[34] Although revisionist history has taken steady aim against the first half of this formula, the economic corollary has survived unscathed as one of the most enduring and optimistic of all judgments of Alexander. The paradigm for his benign economic transformation is still sought in Bactria, where the Alexander miracle allegedly touched men's purses as profoundly as their hearts. This Shangri-La of modern

31. *GBI*, p. xx, and A. K. Narain, *The Indo-Greeks* (Oxford: Clarendon Press, 1957), p. 11, respectively.
32. Consider the latest reflections on these issues by A. K. Narain, "Approaches and Perspectives," *Yavanika* 2 (1992): 5–34, and the various papers in Per Bilde et al., eds., *Centre and Periphery in the Hellenistic World* (Aarhus: Aarhus University Press, 1993).
33. Sherwin-White and Kuhrt, *Samarkhand to Sardis*, esp. pp. 141–187.
34. As one example, see Wilcken, *Alexander the Great*, pp. 283–284, 291. See chap. 2 for further discussion.

scholarship is another important vision that merits a fair testing of the evidence, such as it is, for Bactria.

And therein lies the mystery, because so little survives to guide the modern researcher in our quest for Bactrian history. In all of the surviving literary works of the ancient world, we can find today the names of only seven of the kings who ruled Hellenistic Bactria and, later, India: Diodotus I, Diodotus II, Euthydemus I, Demetrius I, Eucratides the Great, Apollodotus I, and Menander I.[35] Little more than a thousand words directly about these kings can still be read in the ancient languages of Europe and Asia, compared with the "meager" seventy-five thousand folios remaining in the Library of Congress from the administration of the first U.S. president. Thus, whenever Mikhail Rostovtzeff mentioned Bactria in his monumental *Social and Economic History of the Hellenistic World*, he fell back upon such phrases as "a matter of guesswork," "very little is known," "miserably defective evidence," "completely unknown," "scanty," "of course tentative and hypothetical," and "more or less hypothetical."[36] The lack of reliable evidence has rendered Bactria an enigma.

More recently, John Grainger notes in his work on the Seleucids that Bactria is famous and still studied today "for its mystery and its coins."[37] In fact, the lack of written sources has forced the modern researcher to take a closer look at these coins because they provide many clues about the shadowy kings who minted them and the invisible masses who used them. Here again, Bactria has become a well-known paradigm for the application of numismatic methods to the study of Hellenistic civilization. Quite unlike our own currency, most ancient coins were carefully designed to convey as much contemporary news and propaganda as was possible. Coins offered the handiest means of ancient mass communication as they traveled from person to person and city to city. Reading them today like texts, experts can often recover vast stretches of social, economic, political, religious, and military history from the coins of little-known—and even unknown—kings. This remarkable detective work adds, of course, to the mystery that it solves.[38]

35. Justin 41.4–6; *Periplus Maris Erythraei* 47; Polybius 10.49, 11.39; Strabo 11.9.2–3, 11.11.1–2, 15.1.3; Aelian *On Animals* 15.8. These sources are discussed in chap. 3 and translated in appendix D.

36. M. Rostovtzeff, *The Social and Economic History of the Hellenistic World*, 2d ed., vol. 1 (Oxford: Clarendon Press, 1953), pp. 542, 543, 547–549.

37. J. Grainger, *The Cities of Seleukid Syria* (Oxford: Clarendon Press, 1990), p. v.

38. On Bactrian coinage, consult these basic catalogs: A. N. Lahiri, *Corpus of Indo-Greek Coins* (Calcutta: Poddar Publications, 1965); M. Mitchiner, *Indo-Greek and Indo-*

The Bactrians excelled in the art of making money that pleases the eye and touches the mind. They stamped out complex stories in bronze and the precious metals and produced the world's first cupronickel coinage. They issued the largest silver and gold coins of the ancient world, struck posthumous coinages in honor of earlier kings, merged Greek and non-Greek designs, and even produced bilingual currencies. The volume of this mintage alone sets Bactria far above most other kingdoms of the Hellenistic world. In the opinion of the numismatist Philip Grierson, Hellenistic Bactria managed "the finest sustained artistic achievement in the whole history of coinage."[39] More than just masterpieces, much of this currency played a steady role in the day-to-day life of those who served the kings. Bronze coins, in particular, reveal the patterns of economic life for the underclasses. Here we may test the truth about eastern monetization in the wake of the Macedonian wars, probing in lumps of metal the imperial legacies of Alexander the Great.

The enduring mystery of Bactria has been compounded by the explorations of modern archaeology. The discovery of so many beautiful Bactrian coins has inspired a monumental search for the ancient peoples who mined the ores, minted the money, and spent their earnings in the marketplaces of Central Asia. Braving the harsh environment of Afghanistan, explorers from many nations set out to find the material remains of the famed "thousand cities of Bactria."[40] In March 1838 a British traveler happened upon an interesting site at the remote confluence of the Oxus and Kochba Rivers. Guides informed Captain John Wood that an ancient city had once stood upon this ground near the present village of Ai Khanoum. The captain could see the old walls outlining the dead city, in which only an Uzbek encampment then stirred. But when he inquired of them "about coins and other relics," he was laughed

---

Scythian Coinage, 9 vols. (London: Hawkins, 1975); and O. Bopearachchi, Monnaies gréco-bactriennes et indo-grecques: Catalogue raisonné (Paris: Bibliothèque Nationale, 1991). Also important is O. Guillaume, ed., Graeco-Bactrian and Indian Coins from Afghanistan (Delhi/Oxford/New York: Oxford University Press, 1991), a compilation translated by O. Bopearachchi of French articles on coin finds in Afghanistan. A general introduction may be found in Holt, "A History in Silver and Gold."

39. P. Grierson, Numismatics (Oxford: Oxford University Press, 1975), p. 16. Robinson, "The Greeks in the Far East," even attributes to the Bactrian coins "a spiritual quality" (p. 407).

40. Bactria was famous as "the land of a thousand cities" during the Hellenistic period, when Apollodorus of Artemita probably coined the phrase in his (now lost) history of the East. The sobriquet then found its way into the works of Strabo (15.1.3) and then Justin (41.4.6), who naturally read it in the history by Trogus (see chap. 3). It is still popular today; see Vadim M. Masson, Das Land der tausend Städte (Munich: Udo Pfriemer, 1982).

away by the locals—and thus narrowly missed one of the great archaeological discoveries of our time.[41]

The recovery of more than coins from the modern soil of ancient Bactria proved to be a test of will and, finally, of good fortune. Even the most promising site, the ruin of Bactria's capital city (Bactra, modern Balkh), seemed mysteriously barren. Alfred Foucher, a founder of the Délégation Archéologique Française en Afghanistan (DAFA), labored over this site with little success. He finally concluded that what he was seeking, the lost glories of Graeco-Bactrian art, was no more than a mirage.[42] His successors in the DAFA finally triumphed, however, and the mirage was lifted at Begram (ancient Alexandria-sub-Caucaso) and Ai Khanoum (perhaps ancient Alexandria-Oxiana).[43] The latter city, of course, was the ruined fortress from which Captain Wood had ridden away in 1838.

It was no less a personage than King Muhammad Zahir Shah of Afghanistan who recognized in 1961 what Wood and others had missed. While resting from a royal hunt on the very borders of his realm, the king noted the visible traces of an entire city laid out on the dusty ground. In the courtyard of a nearby house he was shown a Corinthian capital and other Greek objects. This evidence convinced him that at Ai Khanoum one of the "thousand cities" for which scholars had been patiently searching awaited only the trowel and brush of trained archaeologists. The work was handed over to the DAFA, which cleared this extraordinary ground for many years under the assiduous direction of Paul Bernard (see plates 1 and 2). By the time their efforts were ended by the Soviet invasion of Afghanistan late in 1979, Bernard and his colleagues had revolutionized not only Bactrian studies but our understanding of the Hellenistic world as a whole.[44]

41. Captain John Wood, *A Journey to the Source of the River Oxus* (London: John Murray, 1872; rpt. Karachi: Oxford University Press, 1976), pp. 259–260.

42. Holt, "Hellenistic Bactria."

43. On archaeological sites in Afghanistan, consult W. Ball, *Archaeological Gazetteer of Afghanistan*, 2 vols. (Paris: Editions Recherche sur les Civilisations, 1982). On the ancient name, see P. Bernard, "Diodore XVII, 83, 1: Alexandrie du Caucase ou Alexandrie de l'Oxus," *JS* (1982): 217–242, challenged in P. M. Fraser's *Cities of Alexander the Great* (Oxford: Clarendon Press, 1996), pp. 154–156. A dated but still useful survey of Central Asian history and archaeology may be found in Edgar Knobloch, *Beyond the Oxus: Archaeology, Art, and Architecture of Central Asia* (London: Ernest Benn, 1972).

44. On Ai Khanoum, consult Ball, *Gazetteer*, and especially the numerous works of excavation director Paul Bernard (listed in the bibliography below). On the widespread impact of this great discovery, see M. Grant, *The Visible Past* (New York: Scribner, 1990), pp. 54–57, the recent work listed in n. 7 above, and the works by Kuhrt and Sherwin-White listed in n. 10. Of course, excavating cities is not the only aim of modern archaeology. For an interesting review of current directions, see Susan Alcock, "Breaking Up the

The discoveries at Ai Khanoum have become justly famous, but impressive finds elsewhere deserve similar attention after years of painstaking exploration. Early work at Takht-i Sangin ("The Throne of Stone") on the right bank of the Oxus River produced little of note. Even though a fabulous treasure had been found near this site in 1877, excavators despaired during explorations in 1928 and 1956.[45] Then, twenty years later, this ground finally yielded its secrets to the South Tadjikistan Archaeological Expedition led by Boris Litvinsky and his collaborator, Igor Pichikyan. A walled citadel dominated by an impressive temple now shows a surprisingly rich mixture of eastern and western traditions along the banks of the ancient Oxus.[46]

At Ai Khanoum and Takht-i Sangin, the Greek heirs of Alexander lived out the drama of the Hellenistic Age. They were travelers and tradesmen who settled in an alien environment and sought their fortunes far from home. They dared to take new risks in a land totally unlike their native Greece and Macedonia, where the Aegean Sea and a temperate climate had played so vital a role in shaping Hellenic civilization. Here in Bactria they huddled in oases and depended upon irrigation. They obeyed kings who, like themselves, were ambitious gamblers in the high-stakes game created by Alexander's demise. First, they were ruled by the dynasty of one of the conqueror's generals, the Macedonian Seleucus I. In time, the huge Seleucid empire began to break apart into smaller kingdoms as the competition for power reached farther and farther down the ranks and across the realm. Along with Parthia and other provinces, Bactria established its own independence less than a century after the Hellenistic Age was born at Babylon.

The Greeks and non-Greeks at Ai Khanoum seemed to prosper under this new Bactrian dynasty, called the Diodotids. Yet, as an exemplar of the period, the people of Bactria endured the two-edged sword of am-

---

Hellenistic World: Survey and Society," pp. 171–190 in Ian Morris, ed., *Classical Greece: Ancient Histories and Modern Archaeologies* (Cambridge: Cambridge University Press, 1994).

45. On the Oxus treasure, part of which is displayed in the British Museum, see O. M. Dalton, *The Treasure of the Oxus,* 3d ed. (London: British Museum, 1964); and A. R. Bellinger, "The Coins from the Treasure of the Oxus," *ANSMN* 10 (1962): 51–67. A lost portion of this treasure is now said to be in a Japanese museum: I. Pichikyan, "Rebirth of the Oxus Treasure: Second Part of the Oxus Treasure from the Miho Museum Collection," *Ancient Civilizations* 4 (1997): 306–383.

46. B. A. Litvinsky and I. R. Pichikyan, "Monuments of Art from the Sanctuary of Oxus (North Bactria)," *AAASH* 28 (1980): 25–83, "From the Throne of Stone: A Treasure Trove of Graeco-Bactrian Art," *UNESCO Courier* (July 1985): 28–31, and "The Temple of the Oxus," *JRAS* (1981): 133–167.

bitious kingmaking. Not one generation passed in Hellenistic Bactria without a struggle for the throne. Down to the final destruction of Ai Khanoum in about 150 B.C., every king from the first Diodotus to the ill-fated Eucratides either seized the monarchy through civil war or defended it from rebels. Some of these dire struggles we know from the scant literary sources; others have been uncovered from the archaeological and numismatic record.[47] Polybius, for example, has left us the longest single passage about these wars. He describes the Herculean effort made by the Seleucid ruler Antiochus the Great to regain control of Bactria by defeating its upstart king Euthydemus I.[48] The Bactrians held out under a two-year siege until Antiochus finally settled for a nominal "victory." Euthydemus kept his throne, still insisting that he was no rebel against the Seleucids but rather the usurper of a throne already usurped by the earlier Diodotids. No statement could better express the unending struggles that characterized the Hellenistic Age.[49]

"To understand Alexander," C. A. Robinson Jr., once said, "we need not go beyond Bactria," because "the genesis of every one of Alexander's extraordinary ideas is to be discovered by the time he left Bactria."[50] To understand the world after Alexander, both as it was and as we have sometimes chosen to imagine it, we need only to look in the same place. Hellenistic history, that of Bactria in particular, is a story of romance and mystery, of tumultuous events that shaped successive civilizations, and of complex social interactions. It is a story that can only be told after centuries of searching and scholarship and yet one still unfolding as we

47. The literary sources outline for us the struggles of the Diodotids first against the Seleucids and then against Euthydemus, of Euthydemus later against the Seleucids, of Demetrius against Eucratides, and of Eucratides against his own (unnamed) son: Justin 41.4–6; Strabo 11.9.2, 15.1.3; Polybius 10.49, 11.39. The material record, primarily numismatic, adds the reigns of Euthydemus II, Agathocles, Pantaleon, Antimachus, Apollodorus, Menander, Heliocles, and Plato to the royal wars stretching down to the end of Greek rule in the Oxus Valley.

48. Polybius 10.49, 11.39, with commentary by F. Walbank, *A Historical Commentary on Polybius*, vol. 2 (Oxford: Clarendon Press, 1967), pp. 264–265, 312–316. See discussion below in chap. 7 and translation in appendix D.

49. In the numismatic record, Billows has pointed out the frequent use of the spearthrower type on Bactrian coins to show that kings such as Eucratides and Menander ruled by virtue of military conquest: *Kings and Colonists*, p. 27. While his reference to the concept of "spear-won territory" (*doriktetos chora*) in Bactria and India is certainly correct, his inclusion of Diodotus in this list of kings who used the coin-type is wrong. Either Billows has mistaken Zeus and his thunderbolt for the king and his spear or he has confused Diodotus with the later king Diomedes, who did employ the spear-thrower type: see, e.g., Bopearachchi, *Monnaies*, p. 297, for these coins.

50. Robinson, "The Extraordinary Ideas of Alexander the Great," *AHR* 62 (1956/57): 326–344, esp. 343–344.

challenge old assumptions, find new sources, and ask harder questions of the elusive evidence.

In this book, we shall take these steps in order to explain for the first time the origins of Bactria as an independent Hellenistic state. The focus must be on Diodotus I and II, the father and son who dared to break free of the Seleucid empire beginning around 250 B.C. Through the examination of ancient texts, archaeological sites, and, most important, the Bactrian coins, the Diodotids emerge from the shadows of Hellenistic history as true heirs of Alexander. An ambitious and opportunistic gambler who made good on his chances for greatness, the elder Diodotus became less a loyal satrap of the Seleucid ruler and more an autocratic dynast. He revised the Bactrian coinage and eventually, in about 246 B.C., elevated his son to a powerful position as co-ruler within the province. This Diodotus II established a second major mint in Bactria and, like his father, graced the coinage with his own portrait. Still, these men hedged their bets in their high-stakes game by keeping the name of the Seleucid king, Antiochus II, on the coin of the realm.

In about 240 B.C. the fortunes of father and son took a turn for the better when their military forces drove from Bactria a renegade named Arsaces, later the founder of the Parthian empire. This victory was celebrated on the coinage and allowed Diodotus I to take the cult title Soter for saving the Greeks of Bactria from a barbarian invader. All of the elements of an independent Hellenistic monarchy were then in place, but the death of the father passed that honor to his son in about 235 B.C. Diodotus II finally put his own name on the coinage and declared Bactria the newest Hellenistic kingdom; the evolution from a Seleucid satrapy to a sovereign state was at last complete.

The nature of that newborn state can also be revealed by close scrutiny of the scattered evidence. Important matters regarding Bactrian economic development, cultural interaction, and dynastic politics come to life here for the first time. In these pages, Bactria remains a paradigm for the Hellenistic Age but with a depth and detail never before possible. The most mundane coins open our eyes to the way in which Greeks and non-Greeks lived on this frontier. In the end, we find all of the qualities—good and bad—that distinguish the Hellenistic period, among them the paradox for which Bactria is the model: the motive forces behind the building of the Hellenistic world were essentially the same forces that destroyed it. The ambition, aggression, opportunism, and chauvinism let loose at Babylon in 323 B.C. made and unmade the Bactrian monarchy, the envious example of each new dynasty quickening the pace of destructive revolution. The Romans would later build their own powerful empire on the principle of "divide and rule," but, beginning at Babylon and ending far away in Bactria, the Greeks reversed the phrase and so their own fortunes.[51] The competition for personal power led them to "rule and divide" until no strong states remained to gamble for the relics of Alexander's greatness.

51. For the advance of Rome into the fragmented world of Hellenistic states, see A. N. Sherwin-White, *Roman Foreign Policy in the East 168 B.C. to A.D. 1* (Norman: University of Oklahoma Press, 1983); Richard Sullivan, *Near Eastern Royalty and Rome* (Toronto: University of Toronto Press, 1989); and Gruen, *The Hellenistic World and the Coming of Rome.*

CHAPTER 2

Across the Chasm

THE SELEUCIDS AND CENTRAL ASIA

Imagining Bactria to be the realization of all that Alexander dreamed, William Woodthorpe Tarn (1869–1957) set the tone for much of twentieth-century scholarship. In his monumental work *The Greeks in Bactria and India*,[1] Tarn achieved many extraordinary things with the meager evidence at hand, bringing to life the first full treatment of the subject with such aplomb that "it became impossible for even those who refused to accept it to see the Greek East of the second century B.C. except through his eyes."[2] That inescapable vision bridged the chasm of Alexander's demise by linking Bactria to a "brotherhood of mankind" that might otherwise have perished, too, at Babylon. King Euthydemus and his son Demetrius, alone of all the Hellenistic successors, attempted in the pages of Tarn that political experiment of which death cheated Alexander. This Bactria was a civilized enclave, a "march state" fighting for survival against a sea of nomadic barbarians. It was a land first brought into the

---

1. First published in 1938, Tarn's *GBI* was later revised in a second edition (1951) and reprinted by Cambridge University Press in 1966. An updated version, with preface, notes, and new bibliography, edited by F. Holt, was published in 1984 by Ares Publishers (Chicago). According to Robinson, in "The Greeks in the Far East," *GBI* "may well represent the greatest triumph of historical scholarship in our day" (p. 406).

2. Richard Todd, "W. W. Tarn and the Alexander Ideal," *The Historian* 37 (1964): 51; see also chap. 4, n. 9. Hampered by ill health, Tarn relied more heavily upon others than he would have liked for knowledge of the eastern evidence: see the obituary written by Frank Adcock for *PBA* 44 (1958): 261, as well as Tarn's own "Preface to the Second Edition," written in 1950. His stoic lament appears also in a letter published by Julian P. Romane, "W. W. Tarn and the Art of History," *AncW* 15 (1987): 21–24.

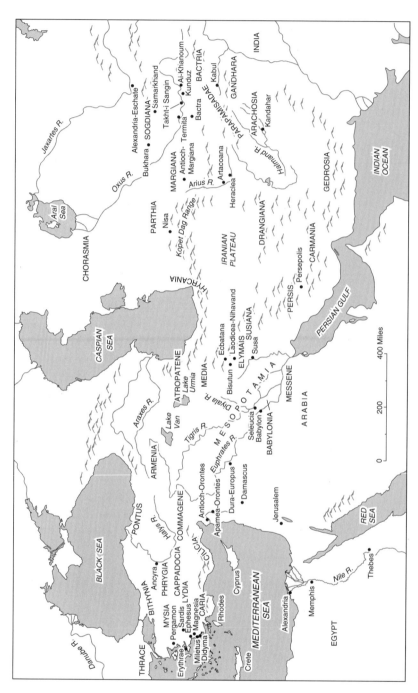

The Seleucid Empire.

light of history by Alexander's benevolent conquest, a backward and savage nation finally made safe for Hellenism.[3] Its native people were taught to live in towns and cities, to be farmers rather than brigands, to cultivate the fine arts, to be the loyal and enlightened partners of the superior Greeks. Had the West not intervened in the guise of Seleucid nationalism (map 2), the East might well have perfected Alexander's ideal of human brotherhood. For Tarn, the Hellenistic imperative to repeat Alexander's deeds eventually killed its only chance to realize Alexander's dreams.[4]

Much has been written in recent decades to refute Tarn's famous portrayal of Alexander the dreamer; in particular, the works of Ernst Badian and A. B. Bosworth have pricked the bubble of Alexander's alleged brotherhood of mankind.[5] Considerable research has also been devoted to Alexander's actual achievements in Bactria, which were not after all so conducive to goodwill. On the early side of the great divide, in all the days leading up to Babylon, there exists little evidence that *any* leader dreamed of so lofty a goal as universal peace and brotherhood. But thoughts are impossible to trace with any precision, especially after twenty-three centuries, and the dreams of extraordinary individuals (no one would deny Alexander that) may yet have existed and energized others without being reflected in our troublesome sources. What, then, of the nearer side of the chasm? Does Bactria in the second century B.C. really suggest to us that something about Alexander inspired there a tangible world along the lines that Tarn made famous?

The truth must be sought patiently, using the tools and accepting the limits of sober history. Tarn and his followers not only made a leap of faith across the chasm of 323 B.C. in order to carry forward Alexander's alleged dream but did so with such fervor that the jump landed them deep in the Hellenistic Age. They did not touch solid narrative ground until the time of the Euthydemid kings—over a century after Alexander's death. Part of the fourth and most of the third century B.C. pass quickly in such treatments of the problem. As a result, the early Seleucid and Bactrian kings have not been given their due. Whatever Alexander's legacy across the di-

---

3. *GBI,* pp. 409–410, echoed by N. G. L. Hammond, *Alexander the Great: King, Commander, and Statesman* (Park Ridge, N.J.: Noyes Press, 1980), p. 196.

4. *GBI,* pp. 411–413; W. W. Tarn, *Alexander the Great,* vol. 2 (Cambridge: Cambridge University Press, 1948), p. 449.

5. As examples, see E. Badian, "Alexander the Great and the Unity of Mankind," *Historia* 7 (1958): 425–444, and A. B. Bosworth, "Alexander and the Iranians," *JHS* 100 (1980): 1–21.

vide, it was carried on the shoulders of such men as Seleucus and Diodotus.

To be fair, Alexander alone did not transform Bactria so dramatically as Tarn and others have believed. Alexander certainly brought to the region many Greek mercenaries, and he made them stay, but they created no brotherhood of man in Bactria. Their assigned task and natural temperament were to impose a severe, age-old antithesis between Greeks and barbarians, civilization and savagery, urbanization and tribalism, farming and nomadism. A militarized barrier across Sogdiana reflected this one-dimensional dynamic for eastern history—the (Greek) struggle for "progress" (represented by cities, laws, monumental art, coinage) against "obstinate barbarism" (represented by poverty, anarchy, nomadic raiding). The latest research has shown the immediate consequences of Alexander's policies in Central Asia.[6] This work stresses the *longue durée*, the diversity of Central Asian populations, and the extent to which pastoral nomadism and farming could be complementary rather than competing lifestyles. We find a Bactria where Alexander created turmoil, not peace, by imposing a stern and disruptive military settlement upon the region. The task of understanding and improving the situation in Central Asia required long years of commitment, more years certainly than Alexander (or even Seleucus) could at first afford to give it.

Thus, from the moment Alexander died at Babylon, his work in Bactria lay in serious jeopardy. The large and restless Greek army of occupation quartered there had been the only one in the East to rebel during the king's lifetime and was the first to try to leave its post after Alexander died. Some years later, after a bitter civil war, Bactria had to be invaded again. Between 308 and 305 B.C. Seleucus I campaigned over much of the same ground as had Alexander; he no doubt wrestled with the very problems that mere battle had not yet resolved in the region.[7] As the fourth century ended, Bactria was still in a state of flux, awaiting the attentions of men still too busy burying Alexander to build their brave new world.

For Seleucus I, that opportunity came in about 295 B.C., a decade after he had last campaigned in the area and three decades after the demise

6. Holt, *Alexander and Bactria*, and the seminal work of Pierre Briant, e.g., *L'Asie centrale et les royaumes proche-orientaux du premier millénaire (c. VIIIe–IVe siècles avant notre ère)* (Paris: Editions Recherche sur les Civilisations, 1984).

7. For the Asian aftermath of Alexander's campaigns, consult Holt, *Alexander and Bactria*, pp. 87–103, and "Alexander's Settlements in Central Asia," *Ancient Macedonia* 4 (1986): 315–323; J. D. Grainger, *Seleukos Nikator: Constructing a Hellenistic Kingdom* (London: Routledge, 1990); A. Mehl, *Seleukos Nikator und sein Reich* (Louvain: Studia Hellenistica, 1986); and L. Schober, *Untersuchungen zur Geschichte Babyloniens und der oberen Satrapien von 323–303 v. Chr.* (Frankfurt, 1981).

FIGURE I: KINGS AND CHRONOLOGY

		BACTRIA
323: Death of Alexander	308 ————	
		BACTRIA
ca. 295: Co-regency of Antiochus I	SELEUCUS I	
	281 ————	
ca. 275: Bactrian satrap sends		Unknown satraps
elephants	ANTIOCHUS I	
	261 ————	
ca. 260: Second Syrian War begins		
ca. 258: Asoka edict at Kandahar	ANTIOCHUS II	
		-----------------------
ca. 246: Third Syrian War begins	246 ————	
Co-regency of Diodotus II		DIODOTUS I
ca. 240: War of the Brothers begins	SELEUCUS II	

		DIODOTUS II
ca. 228: Seleucus II vs. Parthia		
	225 ————	-----------------------
	SELEUCUS III	
	223 ————	
208: Siege of Bactra begins		EUTHYDEMUS I
	ANTIOCHUS III	
188: Peace of Apamea		-----------------------
	187 ————	
	SELEUCUS IV	DEMETRIUS I
	175 ————	-----------------------
	ANTIOCHUS IV	EUTHYDEMUS II
		PANTALEON
	164 ————	AGATHOCLES
	ANTIOCHUS V	ANTIMACHUS
	162 ————	vs.
	DEMETRIUS I	EUCRATIDES I
ca. 146: Fall of Ai Khanoum	150 ————	

of Alexander (see fig. 1). Everything achieved in Bactria by the Greeks owed its origin first to the wandering spirit of Alexander but foremost to the steadfast work of the early Seleucids. Current research has proven that these kings, Seleucus I and his son Antiochus I, were far more interested in the East than Tarn and others believed.[8] Earlier generations

8. Older views of Seleucid policy in the East have been effectively challenged by Sherwin-White and Kuhrt, *Samarkhand to Sardis*, esp. pp. 7–113. I agree strongly with their revisionist approach, as noted in my review for *JIH* 25 (1995): 664. Some cautions are sounded by P. Bernard, "L'Asie centrale et l'empire séleucide," *Topoi* 4 (1994): 473–511.

of scholars expressed little appreciation for a Seleucid empire that eventually shrank so considerably, as if this dissolution were a rapid disease brought on by inherent weakness. Thus, according to Tarn, "The Seleucid empire was nothing organic" but a "crustacean" held together by a weak outer shell of king, soldiers, and bureaucrats.[9] In the light of better evidence, however, the early Seleucid empire should not be dismissed as a fragile and fragmentary state. The Seleucids did not entirely ignore the native peoples in their administration of the empire but instead built a somewhat "vertebrate" state with some living tissue of a non-Greek nature. This we know from the newly uncovered archaeological record, information unknown to Tarn, who lamented that "the first half of the third century is still almost a blank."[10]

That blank has been filled in part by the discovery of nearly forty Seleucid sites in Afghanistan and important settlements in Turkmenistan and across the Oxus in ancient Sogdiana.[11] From about 295 B.C. onward, Seleucid activity in these areas intensified. Antiochus I, son of Seleucus I Nikator and grandson of the Sogdian warrior Spitamenes, supervised this work as viceroy in the East.[12] As joint king with his father, Antiochus issued royal coinage, established or refounded cities, controlled the eastern satraps, and managed the overall effort to bring order and stability to an important and integral part of the empire.[13]

9. *GBI*, p. 4.

10. He speaks, essentially, of the years 312–262 B.C.: *GBI*, p. 5.

11. Consult F. R. Allchin and N. Hammond, eds., *The Archaeology of Afghanistan from the Earliest Times to the Timurid Period* (London: Academic Press, 1978), pp. 187–299; and Ball, *Gazetteer*, vol. 2, index (p. 374), and map 61. For Erk Qala see Z. I. Usmanova, "New Material on Ancient Merv," *Iran* 30 (1992): 55–63; for Sogdiana see Sherwin-White and Kuhrt, *Samarkhand to Sardis*, pp. 106–107, and discussion below.

12. Will, *Monde grec*, vol. 2, pp. 359–362, 368–379, 376–381. The beginning of Antiochus's co-rule has been dated as late as March–December 291 B.C.: R. Parker and W. Dubberstein, *Babylonian Chronology 626 B.C.–A.D. 76* (Providence, 1950), p. 21, and A. J. Sachs and H. Hunger, *Astronomical Diaries and Related Texts from Babylonia*, vol. 1 (Vienna: DAW, 1988), no. 291. Other evidence suggests that the co-regency was established by late 294 B.C.: Joachim Oelsner, *Materialien zur babylonischen Gesellschaft und Kultur in hellenistischer Zeit* (Budapest, 1986), pp. 505–506. On Spitamenes, whose daughter Apama was married to Seleucus I, see F. Holt, "Spitamenes Against Alexander," *Historikogeographika* 4 (1994): 51–58. The sharing of royal power is chronicled in Appian *Syr.* 59–62 and Plutarch *Demetrius* 38.10.

13. The position held by Antiochus I as joint king and heir apparent may have had Achaemenid antecedents, but it also established a Hellenistic model that the Bactrian kings would perpetuate on a smaller scale. See Elias Bickerman, "The Seleucids and the Achaemenids," in *Atti del Convegno sul Tema: La Persia e il mondo greco-romano* (Rome: Accademia Nazionale dei Lincei, 1966), p. 90; P. Briant, "The Seleucid Kingdom, the Achaemenid Empire, and the History of the Near East in the First Millennium B.C.," pp. 40–65 in Bilde

We glimpse all of this in the literary, archaeological, and numismatic record. Pliny tells us that the Seleucid general Demodamus of Miletus campaigned across the Jaxartes River during this period.[14] As part of this commission, Demodamus set up altars to Didymaean Apollo near those already established by Cyrus, Semiramis, and Alexander the Great at the Jaxartes frontier. In the official propaganda of Seleucus I, the oracle of Apollo at Didyma had special significance—not unlike that of Zeus-Ammon at Siwah for Alexander.[15] Probably at this same time, Demodamus refounded Alexandria-Eschate under the auspices of Seleucus I. Similar work was probably done at Maracanda and Ai Khanoum, while in neighboring Aria the cities of Artacoana and Heraclea were refounded by Antiochus. The city of Alexandria-Margiana (Merv) had been overrun after Alexander's day, so Antiochus rebuilt it as an Antioch.[16]

et al., *Religion and Religious Practice in the Seleucid Kingdom* (Aarhus: Aarhus University Press, 1990), esp. pp. 48–51 (cautionary).

14. Pliny *HN* 6.18(49); Marianus Capella 692. For modern bibliography, see Goukowsky, *Mythe d'Alexandre*, p. 351 n. 116.

15. Besides the iconography of Seleucid coinage, there is inscriptional evidence to this effect: W. Dittenberger, *Orientis Graeci Inscriptiones Selectae*, vol. 1 (Leipzig, 1903), 227. Appian *Syr.* 56 records the oracle's advice to Seleucus that he seek his fortune in Asia rather than Europe. On Seleucus's propaganda and the prophecies of Asian conquest, see R. A. Hadley, "Hieronymus of Cardia and Early Seleucid Mythology," *Historia* 18 (1969): 142–152, and "Seleucus, Dionysus, or Alexander?" *NC* (1974): 9–13.

16. On the basic literary sources for Greek city foundations in Central Asia, see G. A. Koshelenko, *Grecheskij Polis na ellinisticheskom Vostoke* [The Greek Polis in the Hellenistic East] (Moscow: Nauka, 1979), pp. 122–180, and P. M. Fraser, *Cities of Alexander the Great* (Oxford: Clarendon Press, 1996). Appian *Syr.* 57 notes that Seleucus named some cities to honor Alexander's memory and asserts that the city's name Alexandria-Eschate was so maintained. The fame of this city made it all the more symbolic; the original foundation was commemorated in the Parian Marble as late as 265–263: Jacoby, *FGrH* 239 B,7. On this site, see N. Negmatov, "Ancient Khojent-Alexandria Eschata," *Journal of Central Asia* 9 (1986): 41–48. On Maracanda, see Galina Chichkina, "Les remparts de Samarcande à l'époque hellénistique," pp. 71–78 in P. Leriche and H. Tréziny, eds., *La fortification dans l'histoire du monde grec* (Paris: CNRS, 1986); P. Bernard et al., "Fouilles de la mission franco-soviétique à l'ancienne Samarkand (Afrasiab): Première campagne, 1989," *CRAI* (1990): 356–380, and "Fouilles de la mission franco-ouzbèque à l'ancienne Samarkand: Deuxième et Troisième campagnes (1990–1991)," *CRAI* (1992): 275–311; and P. Bernard, "Maracanda-Afrasiab Colonie Grecque," pp. 331–365 in *La Persia e l'Asia Centrale da Alessandro al X Secolo* (Rome: Accademia Nationale dei Lincei, 1996). For the recent (mainly Russian) literature on Sogdian and Bactrian archaeological sites, consult P. Bernard, "Alexandre et l'Asie centrale: Réflexions à propos d'un ouvrage de F. L. Holt," *Studia Iranica* 19 (1990): 21–35. The operation of a Seleucid mint at Ai Khanoum after the arrival of Antiochus as viceroy proves that this city was made an important administrative center in this period: P. Bernard, *Fouilles d'Ai Khanoum*, vol. 4 (Paris: Boccard, 1985), pp. 35–41. Similar efforts were apparently made to strengthen the city of Bactra during this early Seleucid period: B. Dagens, M. LeBerre, and D. Schlumberger, *Monuments préislamiques d'Afghanistan* (Paris: Klincksieck, 1964), pp. 61–104. On Merv, see Pliny *HN* 6.47; Strabo

In the same period, we catch sight of the famous Seleucid general Patrocles at work on the eastern frontier.[17] He carried out explorations of the lower Oxus and the Caspian Sea as part of a larger Seleucid plan to develop and exploit these regions for the future. This effort later created much geographical confusion, but it nevertheless went far beyond the limited reconnaissance made by Alexander's envoys to the Scythian tribes of that area.

Without exaggeration, we may detect in this period of Seleucus's reign a new resolve to settle the problems of Central Asia on a more permanent basis. His was an approach that went beyond the limited, ad hoc military and political aims of Alexander. The latter was at times a visionary, but in Bactria he sought *immediate* ends: capture and punish Bessus, seal off the Sogdian frontier, suppress the resistance of Spitamenes and the nomads, capture or co-opt the local aristocracy, quarter a very large army in the region to protect his further advance into India, and then move on. Seleucus, in contrast, ceded northwestern India and Arachosia to Chandragupta Maurya in ca. 305 B.C. and thereafter concentrated upon Bactria itself as the proper frontier of his empire. The early years of the Hellenistic Age had taught him a valuable lesson about the East. India could not be held against the long tradition of local rule under native rajahs; the best solution was a diplomatic agreement that gave the Greeks access to India's resources without making heavy military demands. Thus, a formal treaty (renewed a century later by Antiochus the Great) settled the matter, and Seleucid ambassadors duly took up their posts at the Mauryan capital.[18] This made Bactria the key to Seleucid military and economic interests in the East. Now this great satrapy was to be more than a military road to India, and Sogdiana was to be more than a flank guard against Scythian nomads who might threaten that highway. The new frontier was permanent and literally an end in itself.

What Alexander had begun Seleucus and his son Antiochus brought to a logical (Greek) conclusion. Without the Indian ambitions of Alexan-

---

11.10.2 (describing a wall of 1,500 stades), and Isidorus, *FGrH* 781 F2 (14). See Usmanova, "New Material on Ancient Merv," for evidence of this refounding. On Aria, see Pliny *HN* 6.48, 6.93. Achai, the new name for Heraclea, may reflect the Seleucid name Achaios, known from an Asia Minor inscription (267 B.C.); for a convenient translation see Burstein, *Hellenistic Age*, pp. 24–25, or Austin, *Hellenistic World*, pp. 241–242.

17. For the sources: Pliny *HN* 6.36; Strabo 11.6.1, 7.3, 11.5.

18. Holt, *Alexander and Bactria*, p. 100, and "Response" in P. Green, ed. *Hellenistic History and Culture* (Berkeley: University of California Press, 1993), pp. 54–64.

der, the Seleucids could concentrate on building up Bactria. They did so, in many ways, along the general lines that Alexander had himself laid down. The essential difference is that the Seleucids intensified the effort with an eye toward permanent development, economically as well as militarily. There is no good evidence that the Seleucids here were merely responding to a sudden incursion of nomads into Central Asia, a view held by Tarn and Josef Wolski.[19] Wolski dates this invasion to ca. 282 B.C., a decade *after* Antiochus's appointment to the East, and if this was the case, then surely the nomads were reacting to the Seleucid initiative and not vice versa. As in Bactria during the reign of Alexander, Greek military colonization tended to spur the Scythians and Sogdians to action. Blocking the frontier to the normal movements of nomadic peoples encouraged banditry and may well account for the troubles identified by Wolski. In other words, state building in Bactria on the Greek model meant that nomads were likely to respond with raiding or outright invasion. It was not Greek weakness in Bactria but Greek strength that prompted military attack by outsiders.

This interpretation of the evidence suggests that Seleucus I Nikator patiently committed himself to a strong policy in the East, one that demanded long-term investments such as his son's attentions as viceroy, the efforts of some of his best generals and administrators, fresh reserves of colonists, refounded cities, and something else quite certain and significant—the first royal mints in the Farther East. Alexander often gets full credit for work he left unfinished in the area, and consequently the Seleucids generally fall short of the recognition they deserve for finally integrating these satrapies into the mainstream of Hellenistic civilization. In the economic development of Bactria we have a perfect example of this problem and another paradigm for Hellenistic studies.

MONETIZING THE EAST

Drawing upon the latest research tools, namely, numismatics and hoard statistics, scholars still argue that Alexander used the plundered wealth of the Persian kings to monetize with Greek currency the moribund

---

19. Wolski takes a standard approach in his numerous studies of the Hellenistic East. He sees everything in terms of massive invasions of barbarians, as had W. W. Tarn. For their views, see *GBI*, pp. 116–118; J. Wolski, "L'éffondrement de la domination des Séleucides en Iran au IIIe siècle av. J.-C.," *Bulletin Internationale de l'Académie Polonaise des Sciences et Lettres* 5 (1947): 13–70, "Le problème de la fondation de l'état gréco-bactrien," *Iranica Antiqua* 17 (1982): 131–146, and his other works listed in the bibliography.

economy of Bactria and other eastern satrapies. This notion, without its
modern mathematical justifications, goes back at least nineteen centuries
to the time of Plutarch. This Greek moralist claimed that Alexander "enriched his enemies by conquering them," acting for the good of all by
putting to proper use the barbarians' idle wealth.[20] The full effect of
Alexander's pillage does raise interesting economic and moral questions.
After all, in only a few months of plundering unprecedented in ancient
(if not all) history, the Macedonian king captured some 170,000 talents
of Persian treasure at Susa and Persepolis alone.[21] The magnitude of this
one haul of precious metals has often been compared to the massive economic exploitation of the New World by the major powers of early modern Europe.[22] Put in the best light possible, Alexander seized this useless
bullion, immediately coined it, circulated it, and thus stimulated economic growth in the East. This generous viewpoint has been shared by
innumerable biographers, historians, and political economists over the
course of centuries.[23]

No one can deny the great volume of coinage minted in Alexander's
name both during and after his lifetime.[24] But in most cases the degree

20. Plutarch *Moralia* 1.5 (328E); 1.8 (330D); 2.11 (342A); 2.12(343D), and *Alexander* 5.5–6.
21. This sum equals about 4,835 tons of silver, nearly nineteen times the total monetary reserves of the wealthiest Classical Greek city (Athens): Thucydides 11.13.3, citing
9,000 talents of silver at the outset of the Peloponnesian War. Ancient sources record only
116.2 tons of silver plundered in all the wars of the Aegean world between 490 and 336
B.C.: W. K. Pritchett, *Ancient Greek Military Practices*, pt. 1 (Berkeley: University of California Press, 1971), pp. 53–84, esp. 75–76.
22. John Mahaffy, *Alexander's Empire* (London: T. F. Unwin, 1887), p. 27; Pierre
Jouget, *Macedonian Imperialism and the Hellenization of the East* (London: Kegan Paul,
1928), p. 173; Ulrich Wilcken, "Alexander der Grosse und die Hellenistische Wirtschaft,"
*Schmollers Jahrbuch für Gesetzgebung, Verwaltung und Volkswirtschaft im deutschen Re-
ich* 45 (1921): 350; M. Rostovtzeff, *The Social and Economic History of the Hellenistic
World*, 2d ed. (Oxford: Clarendon Press, 1953), vol. 1, pp. 127–129, and vol. 3, p. 1338
n. 3; and W. L. Adams, "In the Wake of Alexander the Great: The Impact of Conquest on
the Aegean World," *AncW* 27 (1996): 29–37, esp. 34. A. B. Bosworth, *Conquest and Empire* (Cambridge: Cambridge University Press, 1988), p. 88, calls the resultant outpouring
of Alexander's new wealth "unique in history."
23. For examples, see C. Rollin, *The Life of Alexander the Great, King of Macedon*
(Providence: B. Wheeler, 1796), p. 142; Rostovtzeff, *SEHHW*, vol. 1, pp. 134–135,
142–143, 147, 152; G. Glotz, *Ancient Greece at Work* (Paris, 1920; rpt. New York: Norton, 1967), pp. 325–331; Agnes Savill, *Alexander the Great and his Times* (London, 1955;
3d ed., New York: Dorset, 1990), p. 56; John Maynard Keynes, *A Treatise on Money*, vol.
2 (New York: Harcourt Brace, 1930), pp. 150–152, 291 n. 1. For the strangest manifes-
tation of this view see Michael Meyers, *The Alexander Complex* (New York: Times Books,
1989), p. 4. This business writer makes Alexander the corporate model for such modern
entrepreneurs as Ted Turner, Steven Jobs, and Ross Perot.
24. Documented partially by Price, *Alexander*, vol. 1. See F. Holt, "Alexander the Great
and the Spoils of War," *Ancient Macedonia* 6 (forthcoming) for greater detail.

to which this transformed the eastern economy has been exaggerated by both numismatists and historians. We may not assume that the Persian kings were slothful or their empire stagnant until Alexander conquered them. After all, economic exchange without the use of coinage answered all public and private needs for the first 2,500 years of recorded history. Mesopotamia, Egypt, China, and even Greece long managed quite well with other forms of money (cattle, ingots, cowrie shells) to facilitate exchange, to render taxes or rents, and to enhance social standing. Barter can be conducted with or without money; an ox may be traded for oil, grain, and cloth of equal value, whether or not that value is further reckoned as so much copper in monetary terms. Some regions, beginning with Lydia in the sixth century B.C., developed the use of uniformly weighted metals (electrum, silver, gold) bearing a stamp of authority to guarantee value. Thus was coinage invented as one form of money whose advantages were seized upon by some and ignored by others. The Greeks seem to have preferred this new medium of exchange and carried its use to the regions that they colonized or conquered.[25] In some cases, the employment of Greeks as mercenaries compelled foreign rulers in Egypt or Persia to mint coinage even though most of their own subjects might have little interest in or opportunity to use it; in other cases, as in northwestern India, coinage developed independently of the Greek tradition.[26]

Ancient economies could therefore flourish on the basis of barter, even without money. Furthermore, money did not need to be in the form of coinage, much less *Greek* coinage, to facilitate trade. Thus, shedding some of the biases inherited from our ancient Greek sources, we may see the Achaemenid empire as a complex collection of successful economies. Some areas, especially along the Mediterranean coast, issued and

25. Plato, Aristotle, and others wrote extensively on the origins, advantages, and spread of coinage. These commentaries have been conveniently assembled and translated in John Melville Jones, *Testimonia Numaria*, vol. 1 (London: Spink, 1993).

26. On wealth and coinage in Persia, see Illya Gershevitch, ed., *The Cambridge History of Iran*, vol. 2, *The Median and Achaemenian Periods* (Cambridge: Cambridge University Press, 1985), pp. 502–528 (Memphis), 588–609 (Persepolis), 610–639 (Achaemenid currency). The extravagance of the Persian kings was a Greek topos: Herodotus 7.190, 9.80; Strabo 15.3.21; Plutarch *Alex.* 20.10–13. It was common, as in Plutarch's time, to contrast Darius's extreme wealth and Alexander's extreme but virtuous poverty. And yet the Macedonian kings (especially Philip and Alexander) were hardly models of effective money management: Hugo Montgomery, "The Economic Revolution of Philip II—Myth or Reality?" *Symbolae Osloenses* 60 (1985): 37–47; Bosworth, *Conquest and Empire*, pp. 9–10; R. D. Milns, "Army Pay and the Military Budget of Alexander the Great," pp. 233–256 in W. Will and J. Heinrichs, eds., *Zu Alexander der Grosse*, vol. 1 (Amsterdam: Hakkert, 1987). On India, see B. N. Mukherjee, "Emergence of Coinage in the Indian Subcontinent," *JNSI* 51 (1989): 38–47; A. K. Banerjee, "Role of Coin in Agrarian Economy of Northern India during Pre-Mauryan and Mauryan Age," *JNSI* 52 (1990): 112–115.

used coinage but, given the high value of precious metals, not necessarily below a certain socioeconomic level. Simple barter and other traditional forms of money might still be used, effectively, in large parts of the empire. On the eastern frontier, coinage from a different tradition predominated.[27]

In Bactria, that great crossroads of ancient cultures, all of these economies operated at once: exchanges were based variously upon barter, bullion as money, imported Greek coinage, Achaemenid coinage, and Indian coinage. What impact did Alexander have here? Is it true, as some of our leading scholars have contended, that a moribund Achaemenid economy was suddenly transformed by the conversion of idle Persian wealth into Greek coinage? J. K. Davies reports in the latest edition of the venerable *Cambridge Ancient History* the "dramatic" results of Alexander's plunder of Persia:[28]

> In consequence the early Hellenistic period saw a major qualitative shift towards the use of coined metal as a medium for exchange or transfer of revenues: that no fewer than 1,900, or 79.6% of the 2,387 Greek coin hoards known in 1973 were buried in the three centuries from 330 to 31 B.C. is a rough but fair reflection of the change in this respect from the classical period.

This statistical "fact" has enjoyed wide circulation and even shows up in Peter Green's magisterial *Alexander to Actium:* "It was Alexander and his successors who in effect converted the East to a Greek-style money economy. . . . It is no accident that 79.6% of all known Greek coin hoards are datable to the Hellenistic period."[29]

The idea here is to vindicate a long-held economic view by counting the number of buried Greek coin deposits (each containing anywhere from two to thousands of pieces) and comparing the results for the period before Alexander (Classical) to the period after him (Hellenistic). These scholars find a sharp increase from one era to the next and thus make a cause-and-effect connection ("It is no accident") for the conversion of the East to a Greek moneyed economy in the time of Alexander.

---

27. See e.g., E. S. G. Robinson, "The Beginnings of Achaemenid Coinage," *NC* 18 (1958): 187–193; A. D. H. Bivar, "Bent Bars and Straight Bars: An Appendix to the Mir Zakah Hoard," *Studia Iranica* 11 (1982): 49–60; Julian Reade, "A Hoard of Silver Currency from Achaemenid Babylon," *Iran* 24 (1986): 79–87; Daniel Schlumberger, "L'argent grec dans l'empire achéménide," pp. 3–64 in Raoul Curiel and D. Schlumberger, *Trésors monétaires d'Afghanistan* (Paris: Klincksieck, 1953), and the papers entitled collectively "L'or perse et l'histoire grecque," edited by R. Descat in *REA* 91 (1989).

28. *CAH* 7.1, p. 277.

29. Green, *Alexander to Actium*, p. 362, citing Davies (among others) in the notes.

This influential argument, measured out so precisely to the nearest tenth of a percent, implies a mathematical certainty. It offers us the chance to test old assumptions and new kinds of evidence for the writing of Hellenistic history.

First, we must be aware that most of the numbers given by Davies and passed on to Green are, in fact, wrong.[30] He should report, as of 1973, a total of fewer Hellenistic hoards (1,830). The dramatic comparison with the number of Classical hoards also misleads us, since the Hellenistic period, as defined by Davies's source (331–330 B.C.), is twice as long as the Classical (480–330 B.C.). Clearly, the raw data have not been compared fairly over time and space, and therefore we are given nothing like a "fair reflection of the change" in the numbers of hoard finds.[31]

In other ways, too, the degree and rate of change have been exaggerated. For instance, the way in which numismatists assign hoards to specific time periods favors attributions to the Hellenistic as opposed to the Classical period. Among the "Hellenistic" hoards from Greece are seven dated 350–325 B.C., eleven dated simply "fourth century," and six dated "late fourth century." The tendency, then, is to slide these hoards from the Classical to the Hellenistic category, thereby skewing the crucial numerical comparisons.[32] In every way possible, the evidence and its analysis overrepresent the early Hellenistic period at the expense of the Classical, giving a falsely precise measure of the Greek monetization of

30. The unstated source of his numbers for coin hoards is M. Thompson, O. Mørkholm, and C. Kraay, eds., *An Inventory of Greek Coin Hoards* (New York: American Numismatic Society, 1973). Under the guidance of the International Numismatic Commission, *IGCH* revised and updated the earlier work of Sydney Noe, *Bibliography of Greek Coin Hoards*, published in 1937. See also Tony Hackens, "L'apport de la numismatique à l'histoire économique," pp. 151–169 in T. Hackens and P. Marchetti, eds., *Histoire économique de l'antiquité* (Louvain-la-Neuve: Seminaire de Numismatique Marcel Hoc, 1987), and the review by M. J. Price in *AJA* 78 (1974): 308–309.

31. Davies uses data from the *entire* Hellenistic period to validate his claim of "a major qualitative shift" in the *early* Hellenistic period. The geographically larger Hellenistic world must also be taken into account, especially if only *Greek* hoards are to be counted. Are Persian, Parthian, and Indian hoards to be counted or not?

32. Are we to count only recovered hoards or also all those reported in ancient sources? As one instructive example, among the Hellenistic hoards listed in *IGCH* is no. 1731 (p. 242). Described by the authors as "a curiosity" and admittedly (like no. 1732) dated *after* the Hellenistic period (p. 227), hoard 1731 is known only from a complaint of robbery lodged in A.D. 28–29, as recorded in an extant papyrus. At the same time, *not* listed in *IGCH* is a similar savings hoard, clearly from the Classical period, known from Lysias's speech *Against Eratosthenes* (22.12.1). This should reduce the number of Hellenistic hoards by two and increase by one the total for the Classical period. The change may seem small, but who can tell us how many Hellenistic "literary hoards" should be counted (cf. PTeb. 46) or what to make statistically of the hoarding evident in Appian *BCiv* 4.73, Philostratus *VA* 2.39, 6.39, or Plutarch *Alex.* 12?

the old Persian empire arising from Alexander's invasion. If further broken down and analyzed, these same data give a totally different (but still imprecise) picture of recovered hoards, showing (1) a steady (not incrementally sharp) rise in hoard numbers on an annualized parts-per-thousand basis from the Archaic to the Classical to the Hellenistic period and (2) a similar rate of change for the East as for Greece over these same time periods. In other words, the evidence at hand does not prove that something economically extraordinary occurred in the East because of the Greek pillage of Achaemenid treasuries. Over the *longue durée*, we find no new direction for Greek hoard patterns. If Alexander meant to stimulate the old Achaemenid economy, if the wealth stored at Persepolis became the new coinage specifically of the eastern empire, then we must seek the proof elsewhere.

The hoard evidence simply cannot bear the interpretive load placed upon it by Davies and, later, Green. We must be more cautious in our assumptions. In fact, many experts would dispute the relevance of hoard finds to the question of monetization. Our numbers, such as they are, indicate not how much hoarding actually occurred but rather how many hoards were never recovered by their owners. They tell us more about situations of crisis than about booming economies: soldiers summoned away to war who never returned home, the ravages of rival armies, civil disturbances, dislocation, disease, disaster, death. If there was in fact a sudden increase in unrecovered Greek hoards during the early Hellenistic Age, the reason might be the widespread warfare and political turmoil occasioned by Alexander's death rather than the fruits of his enlightened spending of Persia's idle wealth. The miscalculated statistic of Davies, if corrected, would still be an index of misery rather than of monetization. If it is the economic life of the East that truly interests us, we should be looking for random coin losses as revealed in archaeological contexts. We should not, of course, limit our attention to Greek coins only. If we seek the masses as well as the elites, we should be mapping the distribution of low-denomination, bronze fiduciary money in addition to dazzling treasures of silver and gold. To appreciate what happened in the early years of the Hellenistic Age, historians must not be misled either by the praises and apologies of Plutarch or by the unreliable use of modern statistics.[33]

Yet numismatists also make this fundamental mistake. Relying heav-

---

33. See chap. 6 for further discussion of the economic, social, and religious impact of the eventual introduction of low-denomination bronze coinage in Bactria.

ily upon the old scholarship of B. V. Head and others, David MacDowall has published several times a study of Alexander's monetary impact upon Afghanistan and northwestern India that neglects the real source of economic initiative.[34] Using hoard evidence once again, MacDowall traces the conversion of these regions from a barter economy to a coinage economy (based on Attic-standard silver) and attributes this major change directly to Alexander:[35]

> In these kingdoms and provinces coins of the period prior to Alexander are hardly ever found in the numerous hoards of Hellenistic date. Alexander's radical reform triumphed and the medium of exchange in the eastern provinces became the silver coinage of the political ruler bearing his name, instead of cut silver and old Greek silver coinage imported from the Mediterranean and used as bullion.

But this case is based upon another misleading representation of the hoard evidence, which again hides the truth behind a massive generalization. First, the "numerous hoards of Hellenistic date" amount only to nine (*IGCH* 1821–1829) for Bactria-Sogdiana and forty-one (*IGCH* 1831–1871) for Parapamisadae and India.[36] One hoard in this small sample (*IGCH* 1821) actually comes from China (or Olbia!) rather than from the area in question. Of the remaining forty-nine, only *two* are earlier than the second century B.C. (none fourth-century, two third-century). Of these two, both from Bhir Mound (Taxila), the first (*IGCH* 1831) contains 3 coins of Alexander III/Philip III, 1 Persian siglos, and 1,163 Indian punch-marked silver coins; the second (*IGCH* 1832) contains 1 Bactrian gold stater (of Diodotus) and 166 Indian punch-marked silver coins. Thus, the "radical reform" of the local economy has been traced by way of but two hoards over a period of more than 125 years following Alexander's invasion of these territories. Furthermore, each of these hoards was overwhelmingly composed of native Indian (not Greek) currency.

---

34. D. W. MacDowall, "Der Einfluss Alexanders des Grossen auf das Munzwesen Afghanistans und Nordwest-Indiens," pp. 66–73 in Jakob Ozols and Volker Thewalt, eds., *Aus dem Osten des Alexanderreiches* (Cologne: Du Mont, 1984). The subsequent English version in *NumDigest* 11 (1987) is a corrupted text; elsewhere, the gist of this argument may be found in MacDowall's contribution to Allchin and Hammond, *The Archaeology of Afghanistan*.

35. The translator in "Der Einfluss Alexanders des Grossen," p. 69, speaks of "Alexanders durchgreifende Reform" (Alexander's "decisive" or "thorough" reform).

36. Note that *IGCH* lists *only* those hoards containing Greek coins. The ongoing publication *Coin Hoards*, in contrast, lists all hoards and therefore includes (so far) nineteen purely Indian hoards: three Archaic, three Classical, and thirteen Hellenistic.

What does this evidence really suggest? If we use the hoards at all, we find that any apparent conversion to a *Greek* coin-based economy was a longer and later process far removed from the reign of Alexander himself. Some may argue that without Alexander those who eventually did establish a Greek-style currency in the East would not have been there to do so, but this is not to say that Alexander himself had a grand and successful policy of supplying Bactria or India with enough Greek coinage to transform the native economy. Seleucus I Nikator was the first king to open a royal mint in the region, a full thirty years after the death of Alexander. He and his son deserve credit for taking decisive measures to provide Bactria with something more than imported currency.

Since Alexander himself never established a royal mint east of Babylon, until the reforms of Seleucus I all monetary needs in Bactria had to be met by imported western currency or periodic emissions of a local "unofficial" character.[37] This pre-Seleucid and early Seleucid money has nothing to do with Alexander's imperial currency. Some of these Bactrian emissions were not on the Attic standard but rather on a local (Indianized) standard or an earlier Macedonian (pre-Alexander) one. The coin-types also derive from sources other than Alexander's imperial currency (pseudo-Athenian and perhaps earlier Macedonian). Clearly, after the death of Alexander, the Greeks still stationed in Bactria were not living in a region newly monetized by the conqueror's massive production of coinage. The nearest such mint was Babylon, and its output tended to circulate westward. The Greeks in the Farther East had to find other sources of money. Mercenary captains and local dynasts such as Sophytes struck a few coins to meet the needs of their troops largely because Alexander had *not* introduced a radical reform in Bactria.

Then, after more than a generation, the Greek monetization of Bactria expanded significantly, no doubt in conjunction with the Seleucid policy of recolonization, commercial growth, and exploration on a scale demanding ready supplies of coin. During the last decade of Seleucus's life, gold, silver, and bronze coins were minted in Bactria first in the king's own name and later jointly in his name and that of his son Antiochus I. During the sole reign of Antiochus I Soter (280–261 B.C.), Bactria produced a full range of gold, silver, and bronze coinages. In fact, the lion's share of bronze stray finds from the Ai Khanoum excavations belong to Antiochus I (sixty-two coins, or 34 percent); overall, the first two Se-

---

37. On Alexander's eastern mints, see Price, *Alexander,* vol. 1, pp. 451–453. On local issues, see Holt, *Alexander and Bactria,* pp. 96–98, and P. Bernard, *AK* 4, pp. 20–32.

leucids account for nearly 37 percent of the total stray bronze finds at the site. These facts are significant because small bronze coins, the low-value "pocket change" of everyday transactions, reveal the true depth of monetization for a given area. At Ai Khanoum, only nine *possibly* pre-Seleucid bronzes (they may in fact be Seleucid) were recovered from the whole site, whereas the twelve-year period from 293 to 281 produced at least sixty-six of the stray bronze finds. The evidence confronting us suggests that we should look to the Seleucids for the radical reform attributed by others to Alexander.[38]

Alongside local barter, Bactria acquired a fully functioning Hellenistic coin-based economy no earlier than the reigns of Seleucus I and Antiochus I, when mints there provided a steady output of coinage for the first time. This money fueled the engines of Seleucid policy in the East by circulating among soldiers, settlers, builders, administrators, explorers, and artists. Bactria took on the look of a typical Hellenistic province, fully integrated into the larger scheme of Seleucid colonial development. What Seleucus I Nikator was doing in the West he committed himself to do through his son in the East. This was one key to Bactria's sustained growth as a Hellenistic state.

A TRAVELER'S TALE

To get some sense of what was being accomplished in Bactria during this period, we may follow in the footsteps of a Greek visitor named Klearchos, who traveled from the Aegean to the Oxus sometime in the first half of the third century B.C. His mission was to carry a copy of the famous Delphic maxims to Bactria, as attested in a remarkable Greek inscription unearthed at Ai Khanoum in 1966.[39] Like a beacon "blazing from afar," these "wise sayings of earlier men" were meant to guide the Greeks who settled in the alien world of Afghanistan. His getting them there was certainly one of the most intriguing episodes in ancient history.

Our traveler may have been the philosopher Klearchos of Soli (ca. 340–250 B.C.), an Aristotelian with interests in the varied precepts of

38. The relevant numismatic data may be found in P. Bernard, *AK* 4, esp. 5–54 (with addenda and appendices). Also significant is Arthur Houghton and Wayne Moore, "Some Early Far North-Eastern Seleucid Mints," *ANSMN* 29 (1984): 1–9; B. Kritt, *Seleucid Coins of Bactria* (Lancaster: CNG, 1996); and E. V. Zejmal, "Problèmes de circulation monétaire dans la Bactriane hellénistique," pp. 273–279 in J.-C. Gardin, ed., *L'archéologie de la Bactriane ancienne* (Paris: CNRS, 1985).

39. Louis Robert, "De Delphes à l'Oxus," *CRAI* (1968): 416–457. See appendix D, inscription 4.

Greece, Persia, and India. Whether he undertook this journey on his own initiative or on a royal commission we cannot say, but someone clearly considered it an important step to give the settlers at Ai Khanoum the benefit of the most Greek of all teachings. This was not an unprecedented idea—similar copies of the Delphic maxims were set up in the gymnasia of places such as Mysia and Thera.[40] In a Greek sanctuary for Kineas, presumably the founder of Ai Khanoum, this practice was continued during the era of Seleucid patronage, "a stunning testimony to the fidelity of these Greek settlers of remote Bactria to the most authentic and venerable traditions of Hellenism."[41] Although Delphi and Ai Khanoum were separated by three thousand miles of land and sea, the intellectual and cultural divide between them was shrinking dramatically.

Delphi stood at what the Greeks considered the center (*omphalos*) of the world. The Hellenistic city there, like its Classical predecessor, stretched up the steep slopes of Mt. Parnassus. Enriched by kings and protected by the Aetolian League, Delphi boasted the famous Apollo temple and fine treasuries filled with the religious dedications of Greeks and foreigners. In 279 B.C. these were saved from an invading force of barbarian Gauls, an event later celebrated with a pan-Hellenic Soteria (Savior) festival. Klearchos could see, as tourists still do, the theater and stadium on the upper terraces of the city and the gymnasium on the lower southeast side.[42] These constituted the defining institutions of Greek civic life, as essential as the olive and the grape to the sustenance of Hellenic civilization. When he had finished his work at the center of the Greek world and turned eastward toward its edge, Klearchos passed through many places that lacked these essentials of Greek culture. Still, the heavy colonization associated with the reign of Seleucus I provided a fairly urbanized and comfortable passage from the Mediterranean shores upland to Bactria. As sketched so vividly for us by Susan Sherwin-White and Amélie Kuhrt, care had been taken by Seleucus I Nikator to maintain if not improve the road system linking the Aegean and the Oxus frontiers with cities and stopping points "like service-stations on motorways."[43]

40. See the brief discussion in F. Walbank, *The Hellenistic World* (Cambridge, Mass.: Harvard University Press, 1982), pp. 60–61.

41. P. Bernard, "Ai Khanoum on the Oxus: A Hellenistic City in Central Asia," *PBA* 53 (1967): 89. Oliver Taplin begins and ends his book *Greek Fire: The Influence of Ancient Greece on the Modern World* (New York: Athenaeum, 1990) with the mission of Klearchos.

42. The notable tourist and travel writer Pausanias (second century A.D.) produced a vivid description of Delphi in his *Guide to Greece* 10.5.3–10.32.1.

43. Sherwin-White and Kuhrt, *Samarkhand to Sardis*, pp. 62, 72–73.

Some of these places were true poleis, such as Antioch in Syria or Laodicea (Nihavend) in Media, with a mixture of locals and Greek settlers, eclectic architecture, art, and varied languages. Not all, however, could claim such things as a Greek theater or gymnasium; only one of each has been found anywhere east of Babylon, and both were built at Ai Khanoum.[44] Passing beyond Mesopotamia and Media, Klearchos probably stopped at Antiochia in Margiana, where Antiochus I had enclosed an area of 1,500 stades to found a polis there. The old Achaemenid citadel (modern Erk Qala) became the acropolis of the new Seleucid city (known today as Gyar Kala).[45]

Farther on, Klearchos crossed into Bactria and witnessed a Seleucid miracle in progress—cities and fortified towns dotted the oases and were rising along each major confluence of the Oxus River (map 3). Against the Bactrian backdrop of soaring mountains that formed "The roof of the world" (the Pamirs and the Hindu Kush), Greek columns were sprouting from the irrigated soil of Central Asia. Bactra, perhaps still the satrapal capital, stood near the Bactrus River where its waters emerged from the mountains to snake northward until the last life-giving drop was swallowed by the desert. At the end of that century, the formidable walls of Bactra would defy the army of Antiochus the Great, but modern eyes have yet to behold the city as it was seen by Klearchos. It was already an old city in his day, known in local (and later Islamic tradition) as the oldest on earth: Umm-al bilad, the "Mother of all Metropolises." It sustained a large population and served as the hub of communications to all parts of Bactria-Sogdiana. Having arrived here from the Mediterranean, Klearchos could have gone southeast to India by way of the Bamian Valley and the Khyber Pass. He might also have headed north across the desert to the Oxus crossing at Termita (Termez) and thence to Maracanda, Bukhara, or the Jaxartes frontier. Heading east instead toward Ai Khanoum, our traveler might well have stopped at Takht-i Sangin. [46] This walled site on the right bank of the Oxus River would surely

44. On the heartland of the Seleucid state, see John Grainger, *The Cities of Seleukid Syria* (Oxford: Clarendon Press, 1990), pp. 85–86: "It has not been possible to find a single example of a Hellenistic theatre in Syria. . . . The only stadium known in Syria is at the Phoenician city of Marathos." Not all was purely Greek, of course; see S. Downey, *Mesopotamian Religious Architecture: Alexander Through the Parthians* (Princeton: Princeton University Press, 1988), and L. Hannestad and D. Potts, "Temple Architecture in the Seleucid Kingdom," pp. 91–124 in Bilde et al., *Religion and Religious Practice in the Seleucid Kingdom*, stressing local influences.

45. See nn. 11 and 16 for the cities in Margiana, Bactria, and Sogdiana.

46. To the works cited in chap. 1, n. 46, one should add Igor Pichikyan, "The Oxus Temple Composition in the Context of Architectural Comparison" and "The Graeco-

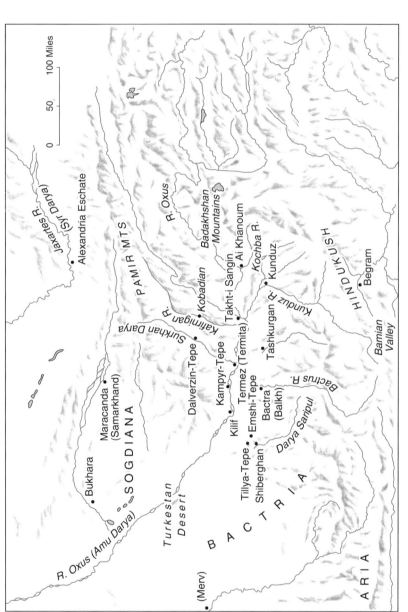

Diodotid Bactria.

have interested a philosopher of Klearchos's bent; dominating the citadel was a monumental Iranian temple.

Guarding an ancient caravan route, the heights at Takht-i Sangin had been inhabited since the Achaemenid era. In the early third century B.C., the temple itself was built according to eastern design but with Greek architectural features and strong Asia Minor influences. Modern scholars have associated its development with the Seleucids. The excavated temple includes storerooms filled with votive offerings, many of which were buried in pits. Among the most important finds to date are a "Seleucid School" clay portrait bust of "a ruling dynast" (strongly resembling, in my view, the young Euthydemus I), a "Graeco-Bactrian School" alabaster portrait of a local (non-Greek) aristocrat, an ivory sheath decorated with a miniature portrait of Alexander the Great/Herakles, the so-called Apollo of Takht-i Sangin, an altar inscribed in Greek by a native descendant (Atrosokes), and the largest assemblage of Hellenistic weapons found anywhere in the ancient world. These offerings therefore took many forms and were manufactured over many years.[47]

Alongside Greek and Iranian deities, the Oxus River itself was worshipped at Takht-i Sangin. Tumbling across barren lands, the Oxus carried silt and snowmelt down from "The roof of the world" with enormous force and volume. Seleucus I was perhaps anxious to pay homage to this great waterway. At every strategic confluence the Greeks built cities, shrines, and citadels. At the end of this long urban chain traveled by Klearchos stood Ai Khanoum, rising on terraces up the steep banks between the Oxus and the Kochba. It was perhaps the most Hellenized place Klearchos had seen since leaving the Mediterranean, and his mission was to make it even more so.

Bactrian Altars in the Temple of the Oxus (Northern Bactria)," *IASCCAInfB* 12 (1987): 42–55,56–65. A note of caution has been sounded by P. Bernard, "Le temple du dieu Oxus à Takht-i Sangin en Bactriane: Temple du feu ou pas?" *Studia Iranica* 23 (1994): 81–121. For Uzbekistan, see G. A. Pugachenkova, "The Antiquities of TransOxiana in the Light of Investigations in Uzbekistan (1985–1990)," *Ancient Civilizations* 2 (1995): 1–38. For Kobadian, see A. V. Sedov, *Kobadian: Facing the Dark Ages* (in Russian) (Moscow: Nauka, 1987).

47. This temple was not destroyed like those at Ai Khanoum when Bactria was later overrun by the Yueh-Chi, and it certainly flourished under the rule of the Kushana. On the chronology and coins, see E. V. Zejmal, "Coins from the Excavations of Takht-i Sangin (1976–1991)," pp. 89–110 in K. Tanabe et al., eds., *Studies in Silk Road Coins and Culture: Papers in Honour of Professor Ikuo Hirayama* (Kamakura: Institute of Silk Road Studies, 1997). For photographs, see I. Pichikyan, *Bactrian Culture: Achaemenid and Hellenistic Periods* (in Russian) (Moscow: Nauka, 1991). See also R. Fleischer, *Studien zur seleukidischen Kunst* (Mainz am Rhein: Philipp von Zabern, 1991), pp. 102, 142. For the inscription, see appendix D, inscription 10.

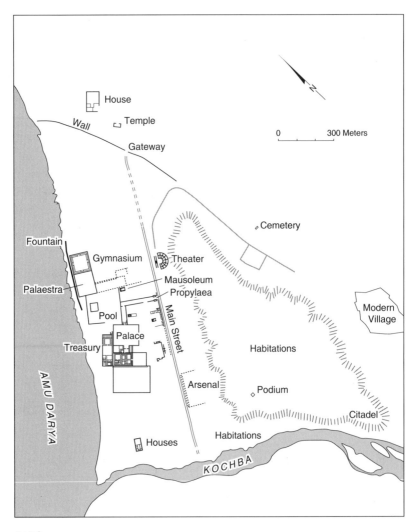

House

Wall Temple

Gateway

0   300 Meters

Cemetery

Fountain

Gymnasium   Theater

Mausoleum

Palaestra   Propylaea

Pool   Modern
                          Village

Palace

Treasury   Habitations

Arsenal   Podium

AMU DARYA   Citadel

Houses   Habitations

Main Street

KOCHBA

Ai Khanoum.

The first major building phase at Ai Khanoum took place between ca.
280 and 250 B.C. (map 4).[48] Already, houses were rising on the level ground
inside and outside the impressive walls of the site; some of these dwellings
have been described by archaeologists as the mansions of wealthy Greek
squires.[49] A monumental propylaeum, not unlike the grand entryway to
the Athenian acropolis, eventually controlled access to such major public
areas as the precinct of Kineas, the gymnasium, and a sprawling palace.[50]
If not already, the city's storehouses would eventually hold jars of precious
olive oil imported from the West to maintain a Greek lifestyle in Central
Asia. A limestone wine press has also been found. A palace library would
hold Greek philosophical texts of the very school from which Klearchos
had come. The people of the city bore such Greek names as Strato, Cosmas, Philoxenos, Philiskos, Theophrastus, Zeno, Hermaios, Isidora, Lysanias, Hippias, and Callisthenes; others had indigenous names such as Oxyboakes and Oxybazos, reflecting the local importance of the Oxus River.
These people would later hold typical Hellenistic positions in the city's bu-
reaucracy such as *agoranomos* (market supervisor) and *dokimastes* (as-
sayer).[51] Their public and private business benefited greatly from the presence, already mentioned, of a Seleucid royal mint in the city.

Builders would cut into the steep slopes of the city a Greek theater
like that of Delphi and larger than the one at Babylon. The citizens worshipped the patron deities of the Greek *paideia* (educational system), Hermes and Herakles, and paid homage to other gods at the several Persian-

---

48. Olivier Guillaume, *Fouilles d'Ai Khanoum*, vol. 2, *Les propylées de la Rue principale* (Paris: Boccard, 1983), p. 29; Pierre Leriche, *Fouilles d'Ai Khanoum*, vol. 5, *Les
remparts et les monuments associés* (Paris: Boccard, 1986), pp. 67–70, 79–84. Leriche suggests that the provisional defenses of the fourth century B.C. were replaced by strong permanent Seleucid structures between 300 and 250 B.C. Burning along the Oxus wall does
not denote a major attack on the city ca. 275 but some local event after which that wall
was reconstructed and an elaborate fountain begun. There *was* a major attack on the city's
defenses ca. 225 B.C.
    49. P. Bernard, "Fouilles d'Ai Khanoum (Afghanistan), campagnes de 1972 et 1973,"
CRAI (1974): 280–308, esp. 281–287. The fine mausolea of such Greek colonists awaited
the dead of passing generations outside the city walls where one has been excavated. See
Bernard, "Campagne de fouilles 1976–1977 à Ai Khanoum (Afghanistan)," *CRAI* (1978):
439–441, and appendix D, inscription 3.
    50. P. Bernard et al., "Campagne de fouille 1978 à Ai Khanoum (Afghanistan)," *BE-
FEO* 68 (1980): 1–104, esp. 7; for details see O. Guillaume, *AK* 2 and S. Veuve, *Fouilles
d'Ai Khanoum*, vol. 6 (Paris: Boccard, 1987).
    51. Claude Rapin, *Fouilles d'Ai Khanoum*, vol. 8, *La trésorerie du palais hellénistique
d'Ai Khanoum* (Paris: Boccard, 1992), and "Les inscriptions économiques de la trésorerie
d'Ai Khanoum (Afghanistan)," *BCH* 107 (1983): 315–372; C. Rapin et al., "Les textes
littéraires grecs de la trésorerie d'Ai Khanoum," *BCH* 111 (1987): 225–266. See appendix D, inscription 11, and, for regions beyond Ai Khanoum, inscription 7.

style temples inside and outside the city walls. In the heart of the city, Klearchos faced the imposing mausoleum of Kineas, where the well-traveled maxims of Apollo would be engraved. Outside the city walls were other graves with Greek inscriptions, some for children born into this brave new world but unable to live out the five stages of Apollo's creed as Klearchos had recorded it.[52] Those who did survive these challenges could indeed be confident of dying Greek, without sorrow. Everything that could be done to nurture the traditions of Greek life in an alien environment the Seleucids deliberately sponsored for them at Ai Khanoum. The kings took great pains to placate the Greeks settled in this region, wishing for no repetition of the seditions of Alexander's day. What the Greeks craved was their Greekness, plain and simple, from cradle to grave. In the words of Diodorus (18.7.1), describing the earlier rebellion of Alexander's settlers, "they longed for a Greek upbringing and way of life."

The Greek colonist of Seleucus was thus a happier man than the mercenary of Alexander. Granted, the Seleucids could not bring the sea to Central Asia or quarry Pentelic marble from the foothills of the Hindu Kush. Nevertheless, these kings and their architects could adapt the construction methods of the East to raise a polis with mud bricks and soft limestone. They imported architectural styles from the Aegean and Asia Minor, blending with local elements the courtyards and Corinthian capitals of the Hellenistic canon. Unlike anything in the area when Alexander had invaded fifty years earlier, Ai Khanoum emerged from the dust of Seleucid builders as a monumental Greek city. What Klearchos saw there was the familiar features of his Greek world far to the West: a Macedonian palace, Rhodian porticoes, Coan funerary monuments, Athenian propylaea, Delian houses, Megarian bowls, Corinthian tiles, and Mediterranean amphorae. Traditionally Greek but cosmopolitan and eclectic, this city provided a fitting home for the easternmost copy of the Delphic maxims.[53]

The steps taken by the first Seleucids to Hellenize Bactria are no less impressive than those taken by Klearchos to bring there the essence of

52. Texts are given in appendix D, inscriptions 3 and 4.

53. For the best-illustrated accounts in English of these finds, see P. Bernard, "An Ancient Greek City in Central Asia," *Scientific American* 246 (1982): 148–159, and "Ai Khanoum on the Oxus." The evolution of the Ai Khanoum palace from that of a Seleucid governor to that of later Bactrian kings may be followed in Nielson, *Hellenistic Palaces: Tradition and Renewal* (Aarhus: Aarhus University Press, 1994), pp. 124–129, stressing Oriental (Babylonian/Mesopotamian) functions. Note also the generalized treatment by Walter Posch, *Baktrien zwischen Griechen und Kuschan* (Wiesbaden: Harrassowitz, 1995).

Greek wisdom. But Ai Khanoum was an island surrounded by a sea of Central Asian peoples still largely immune to the coming of the Greeks. When Klearchos stepped out of these new cities he traveled a true frontier of the ancient world. Its mountains, desert steppes, fertile plains, and wooded piedmont worked together to form a vast meeting place of diverse folk and folkways.

Around the cities stretched irrigated fields worked by local farmers as they had been since the centuries of the Achaemenids. These were probably the ancestors of the Tadjiks, speakers today of a Persian language. In their world of water and mud, sedentary peoples broadened their oases by extending their canals deeper into the desert fringe. They fed themselves, traded goods with passing nomads, and served the growing population of Greek immigrants in the area. Most spoke non-Greek languages, even those who later took up residence on the upper terraces of Ai Khanoum. Huddled in single-room houses looking down upon the tiled roofs of Greek "mansions" in the elite lower section of the city, these people may have acquired some measure of Greekness but not an equality with Seleucus's settlers.[54] It seems unlikely that Klearchos made his journey on their behalf.

Pastoral nomads in unknown numbers moved in and out of this settled land, leaving behind little that would allow us to know them archaeologically. No cities, walls, mints, roads, or temples—theirs was a world in motion, of consumable wealth, of herds and lightweight possessions made of perishable wood and leather.[55] Their caravans and camps, all but invisible to us today, could surely be seen by Klearchos as he passed from city to city. We can scarcely doubt that these nomads were carefully watched by Greek authorities and their caravans closely controlled by Seleucid forces and fortresses. Though perhaps less dogmatic about the matter, the Seleucids followed Alexander's lead in the handling of nomadic peoples. This was, of course, Greek prejudice but also the genuine fear that nomadic tribes might again join forces with native Sogdians and Bactrians. Just as Delphi had had to be saved from the ma-

54. P. Bernard, "Campagne de fouilles 1978 à Ai Khanoum (Afghanistan)," *CRAI* (1980): 451–459. Perhaps a useful comparison may be found in the Arab conquest of the same region, where garrisoning, ethnic separation, and efforts to preserve a strong cultural identity have also been identified: Giorgio Vercellin, "Bactria: Past, Present, and Future," pp. 25–38 in Giancarlo Ligabue and Sandro Salvatori, eds., *Bactria: An Ancient Oasis Civilisation from the Sands of Afghanistan* (Venice: Erizzo, 1989).

55. Henri-Paul Francfort, ed., *Nomades et sédentaires en Asie centrale: Apports de l'archéologie et de l'ethnologie* (Paris: CNRS, 1990); Anatoli M. Khazanov, *Nomads and the Outside World,* trans. Julia Crookenden (Cambridge: Cambridge University Press, 1984).

rauding Gauls, so Ai Khanoum had to be protected from desert Scythians. This was the Greeks' conception of their expanding world.[56] They
generally advocated a closed society that exploited other people but
walled them off. Accentuating the "otherness" of indigenous peoples
helped to assuage the phobia of the Greeks about "going native" like the
infamous "wretches" found by Alexander years before—Greeks in
Mesopotamia and Central Asia who had lost some of their culture to the
barbarians.[57] At Ai Khanoum this had not needed to happen. Every
essence of Hellenism had been offered them by the Seleucids. Most nomads were kept at bay by the renewal of a military exclusion zone in Sogdiana, and Greeks and "others" were largely segregated in the city.

    Without thinking less of the Seleucid achievement or its Alexandrian
antecedents, we must see this brave new world in Bactria as a limited social and cultural experiment. The East continued to be diversely popu-
lated, with many groups living economically integrated but socially iso-
lated lives. Alexander brought here no visible traces of universal peace
and brotherhood, no equal partnership of Greeks and barbarians. Nor
did the Seleucids, who fostered a strong military and economic presence
alongside a favored culture of Hellenism. Given the evidence, it is hard
to see Bactria now as Tarn imagined it only a few decades ago. He believed firmly in the benevolence of Alexander and in the rekindling of
that liberal spirit after the long hiatus of Seleucid and Diodotid rule in
Bactria. Today, Tarn's vision—correct in so many particulars—must be
modified to reflect the larger reality of the late fourth and third centuries
B.C. Whatever Alexander dreamt, the aspirations and deeds of his successors were the by-products of the new dynamics let loose at Babylon.
More than the policies of Alexander's life, the predicament of his death
shaped the Hellenistic Age. Bactria exemplifies this fact; the region never
reached back across the chasm of 323 B.C. to revive some dream of
Alexander's youth. Instead, it developed along the typical path of Hellenistic state building, consciously favoring Hellenism while conforming
to local conditions as a necessary expedient. Most of that work was the
achievement, whether political, economic, or military, of the Seleucids,

---

56. On the ancient view of barbarians, see J. DeRomilly, "Les barbares dans la pensée de la Grèce classique," *Phoenix* 47 (1993): 283–292. For Bactria and Sogdiana in particular, see Pierre Leriche, "Structures politiques et sociales dans la Bactriane et la Sogdiane hellénistiques," pp. 65–79 in Heinz Kreissig and Friedman Kühnert, eds., *Antike
Abhängigkeitsformen in den griechischen Gebieten ohne Polisstruktur und den romischen
Provinzen* (Berlin: Akademie Verlag, 1985).
57. For example, the Branchidae, who had "betrayed" both Greece and their own
Greekness: Holt, *Alexander and Bactria*, pp. 73–75.

and none of their Bactrian successors broke free of this heritage in pursuit of some lost Alexander ideal.

We can see this evolving world much better than ever before, and yet the myriad sights and sounds of that Bactria traveled by Klearchos cannot all be known to us. Much remains out of focus—for now. We do know that here, at some uncertain place and time, a Greek named Diodotus (meaning "Zeus-given") entered upon Seleucid service on this frontier. Building upon the monumental efforts of his kings, this Diodotus would lead Bactria into its next phase of Hellenistic development. Together with his son, he dared (like Seleucus and the other successors of Alexander) to declare political independence and found a new dynasty. Although in our meager sources the Diodotid kings of Bactria emerge from nowhere, we must never forget the powerful Seleucid context from which they most certainly sprang.

CHAPTER 3

An Elusive Dynasty

DOCUMENTS AND DEBRIS

Few dynasties of the ancient world have so eluded the modern researcher as the Diodotids of Bactria. Though celebrated in their own day and for centuries thereafter, these kings have now slipped into the twilight that obscures so much of Hellenistic history. We know only that these two Greeks, father and son, transformed a Seleucid satrapy into a powerful sovereign state and that their revolution was later remembered by western writers as one of the defining events of the age.[1] This was also a decisive episode for the history of the Farther East, referred to repeatedly today as "an event fraught with momentous consequences for India's immediate future."[2]

To have lost such men and events may seem impossible in our age of massive documentation, multimedia, and information overload. Yet, the problem afflicts much of ancient history (representing *over half* of "recorded" history) and remains especially acute for the Hellenistic period. When addressing this general issue we must remember that our loss of Bactria's history really has little to do with the remoteness of the region or with any lack of interest among the well-known writers of Greece and Rome. It has been argued, for example, that Plutarch's failure to com-

---

1. See, e.g., Justin 41.4–6.
2. Narain, *IG*, p. 12, taking the sentiments—and very phrases—from the earlier work of George MacDonald, "The Hellenistic Kingdoms of Syria, Bactria, and Parthia," in vol. 1 of E. J. Rapson, ed., *The Cambridge History of India* (Cambridge, 1922; rpt. Delhi, 1962), p. 391.

pose a biography of any Bactrian king must reflect the marginality of Bactria to western, Mediterranean interests.[3] But though he was a prolific writer and did know about at least one Bactrian king, Plutarch never intended to chronicle all of the important people of his past, and he insisted that he was not a historian obligated to cover what was most significant. As a Greek moralist living under Roman rule, he chose his subjects and sources in terms of other criteria. Thus, Plutarch actually passed over *most* of the great rulers of the Hellenistic Age, including the Seleucids and Ptolemies. Surely this does not mean that the major powers of the eastern Mediterranean were somehow marginal to Mediterranean interests!

The survival of evidence cannot be used to measure the real importance of anything ancient. There are paupers of the Hellenistic Age about whom we know the deepest secrets, and yet there are kings about whom our sources are silent. The papyrus scribblings of a religious recluse in Egypt tell us about his dreams and how he interpreted them, his sexual fantasies, his begging and bleating, his family and (few) friends.[4] This man may be interesting to us by the sheer accident of discovery, but he ventured nowhere and did nothing of consequence. In Bactria, meanwhile, not one king of the entire Hellenistic period can be known so intimately. The current historical movement to probe deeper into the social mix in order to find what some have called "the people without history" has been turned on its head for Hellenistic studies.[5] Because of our fickle sources, we are likely to know as much or more about a commoner as about a king of that elusive ancient world.

How did this come to pass? Human nature conspires to destroy the best and most important while often saving the mundane. Our wars, for example, seldom strike lesser places with the same frequency or ferocity as they do our leading cities and states. Cultural centers inspire envy and invite attack. Temples and tombs lure plunderers in proportion to the fame and riches of those buried and/or worshipped there.

---

3. Claude Rapin, "La trésorerie hellénistique d'Ai Khanoum," *Revue Archéologique* (1987): 70, repeated in *AK* 8, p. 299. Plutarch certainly knew about Menander: see appendix D.

4. These texts are discussed in detail by N. Lewis, *Greeks in Ptolemaic Egypt* (Oxford: Clarendon Press, 1986), pp. 69–87, and D. Thompson, *Memphis Under the Ptolemies* (Princeton: Princeton University Press, 1988), pp. 212–265.

5. This large-scale historical movement manifests itself across several related disciplines, from the *Annales* school and "New Social History" to the "New Archaeology"; see, e.g., E. R. Wolf, *Europe and the People Without History* (Berkeley: University of California Press, 1982).

The human animal does not prey upon the weak; it greedily seeks out the most impressive and passes by the innocuous. As historians and archaeologists, we therefore suffer from a sort of unnatural selection that leads to "reverse Darwinism"; for us, the least significant is most likely to escape the ravages of man and thus survive to propagate the future of our past. This phenomenon confronts us at all points of ancient society. Of all the great pharaohs of Egypt, why is little Tutankhamun the most widely known today? The best-preserved temple in Athens is not, alas, the Parthenon. The remains of Alexander the Great, displayed for centuries, have disappeared, but the hanged corpse of anonymous Tollund Man survives in remarkable condition. Nearly all of the seven wonders of the ancient world fell into ruin and were lost, but the Roman bars and brothels on the Bay of Naples have emerged virtually unscathed from the ash of Vesuvius. Nature may save, but humans *must* destroy.

Our search for the first of Bactria's kings suffers from the harmful effects of this very human malady. As we have noted, the ancient accounts of this kingdom did not escape the devastation of human neglect and war. The central Bactrian city, ancient Bactra, is today a mute ruin; the impressive Bactrian city at Ai Khanoum was looted and left all but empty by invaders of the second century B.C. What chanced to survive there has recently been targeted again by vandals using trucks and metal detectors. Royal coins endure, but even these must somehow elude the melting pot, the making of cannon, the private hoarding of unpublished collections, and the looting of modern museums.[6]

So far, then, not a single word ever written or uttered by the Diodotids has been recovered. No contemporary documents bear their name except for the coins minted under their authority.[7] Sometimes, however, we seem to get close. In 1969, a broken ostracon was discovered at Emshi-Tepe, the site of a large Hellenistic town four kilometers northeast of Shiberghan.[8] The pottery fragment bears an incomplete word in Greek: ΔΙΟΔ . . . , which could be the beginning of the name ΔΙΟΔΟΤΟΣ (Dio-

---

6. These important matters are discussed further in the next chapter.

7. This may not always be the case, however, since new evidence still emerges from Central Asia. The reign of Antimachus Theos was attested solely by his coinage until the very recent discovery of a parchment tax receipt dated to the fourth year of his rule: see appendix D, inscription 7. Similar documentation may yet be found for the Diodotids.

8. Irina Kruglikova and Shahibye Mustamandi, "Résultats préliminaires des travaux de l'expédition archéologique afghano-soviétique en 1969," *Afghanistan* 23 (1970): 84–97, includes the material from Emshi-Tepe, pp. 90–97. On this site in general, see Ball, *Gazetteer,* vol. 1, p. 96 (site no. 314).

dotus). The word might also, however, be *ΔΙΟΔΟΣ* (thoroughfare, passport) or the start of the common Greek name *ΔΙΟΔΩΡΟΣ* (Diodorus).[9] Even if we could read the whole name "Diodotus," would we have found a trace of the famous satrap and king? The name was not particularly rare, and therefore the ostracon might simply refer to a nonroyal Bactrian with that appellation.[10] The *possible* link between this stray sherd and one of the rulers named Diodotus thrills the desperate researcher, but the conjecture merely underscores how thoroughly history has erased the contemporary evidence of their reigns.

There exists in the British Museum another interesting document, a cuneiform fragment of a Babylonian astronomical text that refers to a Seleucid satrap of Bactria, though not by name.[11] Dated 276–274 B.C., during the reign of the Seleucid king Antiochus I Soter, the text mentions the dispatch of twenty war elephants from the governor of Bactria to his counterpart in Babylonia, who then forwarded the beasts to the king in Syria, where a military campaign was under way. The pioneering scholar George MacDonald was tempted to see in this "Chaldaean" document a reference to Diodotus I, who allegedly was appointed satrap of Bactria early in the reign of Antiochus I (i.e., in about 280 B.C.) and held that post for three or more decades.[12] This bold surmise has little to support it beyond our desire to find *some* documentary evidence for Diodotus and the fact that a monogram on several early Seleucid coins from Bactria (and now on a brick from Ai Khanoum) looks a little like the first letters in the name Diodotus.[13] But resolving this monogram (⊘) into *ΔΙΟ* and thence *ΔΙΟ[ΔΟΤΟΥ]* carries no greater conviction than reading this same name on the ostracon from Emshi-Tepe. In fact, A. K. Narain has effectively demolished the idea that this monogram represented the name of the satrap Diodotus; however, Narain now believes

9. A Diodorus, "overseer of revenues," now appears in the tax receipt mentioned above (n. 7).

10. Among others, we know of the famous Diodotus of Athens, who debated Cleon, a moneyer/judge at Erythrae, a Ptolemaic *strategos*, the Seleucid officer who rebelled in Syria, a Sidonian philosopher, the teacher of Metellus Nepos, the teacher of Cicero, and a court secretary in the entourage of Alexander. See, e.g., Price, *Alexander*, vol. 1, p. 262; Strabo 145.2, 16.2.24; and Plutarch *Moralia* 205.6.

11. For recent discussion, see Sherwin-White and Kuhrt, *Samarkhand to Sardis*, pp. 46–47. See appendix D, inscription 1.

12. MacDonald, "Hellenistic Kingdoms," p. 393.

13. For discussions of this monogram, consult MacDonald, "Hellenistic Kingdoms," pp. 390–393; *GBI*, p. 73; E. T. Newell, *The Coinage of the Eastern Seleucid Mints* (New York: American Numismatic Society, 1938; rpt. 1978), pp. 228–246; Bernard, *AK* 4, pp. 35–52; Narain, *IG*, pp. 14–15.

that it does represent the lost name of the city at Ai Khanoum, suppos-
edly Diodotopolis, Dionysopolis, or Diodoteia.[14] Such speculation about
city names, a very old practice in Bactrian studies, adds nothing but another undocumented "sighting" of Bactria's first independent ruler. No
royal city named Diodotopolis or Diodoteia is mentioned anywhere in
our ancient sources, and there is no reason to invent one just to fit two
or three scrambled letters in a Greek monogram.[15] In any case, it will
become clear in subsequent chapters that what these monograms stand
for is not cities at all but magistrates—as one would expect on Seleucid
coins.

The origins of Diodotus I therefore remain obscure. Lacking inscriptions and other documents that refer to his career, we must rely instead
upon three other kinds of evidence: the general situation in Hellenistic
Bactria as revealed in the archaeological record, a few Greek and Latin
texts that are extracts from lost original works, and the all-important
coins, which have yet to be studied and properly sorted.

Let us begin with the archaeological picture. First and foremost, the
material evidence shows that, whatever the local political situation, Bactria remained fully integrated into the cultural milieu of the larger Hellenistic world. The remains at Ai Khanoum prove that trade goods and
artistic/architectural trends flowed from the West without interruption
in the third century B.C. Contrary to the popular notion that the rise of
Parthia ca. 250 B.C. had walled off the East from the West, Bactria
showed no signs of isolation from the Mediterranean seaboard during this
period.[16] At the same time, eastern products passed from India and Bactria to the West. We have already seen that an unnamed Bactrian satrap
forwarded elephants to Antiochus I in ca. 275 B.C. From India, the Mau-

14. A. K. Narain, "The Greek Monogram ⊕ and Ai Khanoum—the Bactrian Greek
City," *NumDigest* 10 (1986): 4–15, and *CAH²* 8, p. 396.

15. For example, Alexander Cunningham thought that he could read the word "Zariaspa," an alternative name for Bactra, in the monogram "found on most of the coins of
Diodotus II"; on other Bactrian coins he "found" many of the known place-names of the
region. See his *Coins of Alexander's Successors in the East* (1884; rpt. Chicago: Argonaut,
1969), pp. 45–77, esp. 50. It should be a warning to us that the earliest attempts to find a
"Diodotopolis" or "Diodoteia" in the Bactrian monograms actually involved a different
monogram altogether, as Narain himself notes (*CAH²* 8, p. 396). This game, then, is well
over a century old and has yet to bear fruit: see below, chap. 4, n. 41.

16. In particular, note the strong ceramic evidence analyzed by Jean-Claude Gardin,
"Les relations entre la Méditerranée et la Bactriane dans l'antiquité, d'après des données
céramologiques inédites," pp. 447–460 in *De l'Indus aux Balkans: Recueil Jean Deshayes*
(Paris: Editions Recherche sur les Civilisations, 1985), and "La céramique hellénistique en
Asie centrale: Problèmes d'interpretation," pp. 187–193 in *Akten des XIII Internationalen
Kongresses für klassische Archäologie* (Berlin, 1988).

ryan king Bindusura (ca. 297–272 B.C.) asked Antiochus I (281–261 B.C.) for Greek wine, figs, and a philosopher; the Seleucid king obliged his fancy for consumables but replied that philosophers were not for sale or trade.[17] The great Indian king Asoka (ca. 272–237 B.C.), son of Bindusura, sent Buddhist missionaries westward to the Hellenistic rulers Antiochus II of Syria, Ptolemy II of Egypt (282–246), Magas of Cyrene (274–253), Antigonus Gonatus of Macedonia (276–239), and Alexander of Epirus (272–240).[18] Thus, at some time soon after Asoka's conversion to Buddhism (ca. 260 B.C.), Indian missionaries made their way to the Mediterranean kingdoms.[19] No Greek king of Bactria is mentioned, of course, because that area was still a loyal Seleucid satrapy and not yet an independent kingdom under the Diodotids (ca. 260–253 B.C.).[20]

The Mauryas had won control of northwestern India and Arachosia from Seleucus Nikator, but clearly a number of Greek colonists were still settled in these regions. The use of Greek on Asoka's various inscriptions in this area attests to the importance of these foreigners.[21] There can be no doubt, then, of the unbroken presence of Greeks throughout the East in spite of new political and cultural developments. The Mauryan kings were not trying to contact unknown cultures but merely following their Greek subjects' lead in the solicitation of Greek products. How else would the Indians have known what to request? Conversion might be a slow and unlikely process, but commerce was another matter.

---

17. Athenaeus, *Deipnosophistae* 14.652–53; see appendix D. Bindusura was the son of Chandragupta, who had established peace and diplomatic relations with Seleucus I. For earlier gift exchanges between Seleucids and Mauryas, see Athenaeus, *Deipn.* 1.18e, 13.590 a–f.

18. Rock edict 13 of Asoka, for which see F. R. Allchin and K. R. Norman, "Guide to the Ashokan Inscriptions," *South Asian Studies* 1 (1985): 43–50, and David A. Scott, "Ashokan Missionary Expansion of Buddhism Among the Greeks," *Religion* 15 (1985): 131–141; cf. appendix D.

19. We may be skeptical of the results, of course, though Ptolemy II did send an ambassador to India: E. Olshausen, *Prosopographie der hellenistischen Königsgesandten* (Louvain: Studia Hellenistica, 1974), vol. 1, pp. 33–34 (Dionysios). See also Giovanni Pugliese-Carratelli, "Asoka e i re ellenistici," *La Parola del Passato* 33 (1953): 449–454, and A. J. Festugière, *Etudes de religion grecque et héllenistique* (Paris: J. Vrin, 1972), pp. 210–225.

20. Scott suggests in "Ashokan Missionary Expansion" that later, when Diodotus assumed independence, Asoka did send missionaries to Bactria: pp. 135–137. By reading (boldly) between the lines, he argues that this mission had some success among the native Bactrians and that years later (ca. 232 B.C.) Asoka donated gold to "Thogar" (Bactria).

21. For more on these inscriptions, see R. Thapar, *Asoka and the Decline of the Mauryas*, 2d ed. (Oxford: Oxford University Press, 1973); K. R. Norman, "Notes on the Greek Version of Asoka's Twelfth and Thirteenth Rock Edicts," *JRAS* (1972): 111–118; A. Christol, "Les édits grecs d'Asoka: Etude linguistique," *Journal of the Royal Asiatic Society* 27 (1983): 25–42; and appendix D. For discussion see Holt, "Response."

Although these scattered references are few, they do support the archaeological evidence for sustained contact between East and West during the first half of the third century B.C.[22] At Ai Khanoum, this picture extends smoothly through the rest of the century. The growth of the city, as witnessed by Klearchos, continued in peaceful fashion down to ca. 225 B.C. The excavators naturally found it difficult to mark off dramatic, eventful phases of evolution. The regional development associated with Seleucus I and Antiochus I had no serious interruption. Signs of some burning along the Oxus wall, dated ca. 275 B.C., denoted some local phenomenon but no large-scale attack on the city's defenses. This was, moreover, the same period during which a Bactrian satrap could send war elephants to Antiochus I; we can hardly imagine that Bactria was enduring some military crisis at this juncture. The Oxus wall was reconstructed, with an elaborate and expensive fountain, between ca. 275 and 250 B.C. Irrigation was improved as well in this period.

This evidence gives no sign of military concern or economic crisis. The same is true of the years between 250 and 225 B.C. In fact, the defensive ramparts were actually neglected and allowed to fall into disrepair along the Oxus and northern sides of the city. Even so, the ornamental fountain underwent more construction, and dwellings were built on the acropolis; it was the defensive system alone that was allowed to decline. In the opinion of the archaeologist Pierre Leriche, the establishment of Bactrian independence under Diodotus I during this period caused no major changes or troubles that might be detected archaeologically.[23] There was, if anything, a relaxation of defensive concern among the Greek inhabitants of Ai Khanoum and perhaps some loosening of the strictures on non-Greek residents of the city.

Then, in ca. 225 B.C., a serious attack did occur. Not only burning but sapping operations as well were carried out against the city's walls. The excavation team found no reason to associate this warfare with the Seleucid invasion of Antiochus III of 208–206 B.C.; the logical solution was to see in this evidence the rise of Euthydemus I and the overthrow

---

22. For the archaeological evidence, see n. 16 above and Rapin, *AK* 8, esp. pp. 95–130 on the treasury texts. On the chronology, see Henri-Paul Francfort, *AK* 3 (Paris: Boccard, 1984), p. 122; Pierre Leriche, *AK* 5 (Paris: Boccard, 1986), pp. 67–70; Veuve, *AK* 6, pp. 108–110.

23. Leriche, *AK* 5, p. 82: "Apparement, et c'est un fait à souligner, la proclamation de sa royauté par Diodote n'a pas provoqué à Ai Khanoum de troubles majeurs susceptibles de laisser des traces sur les remparts. L'argument n'est pas en soi décisif, mais il va dans le même sens que les textes (et le monnayage) qui laissent à penser que le passage de la Bactriane province séleucide en royaume indépendant s'est fait de manière progressive et sans heurt."

of Diodotus II. Then, during the last quarter of the third century B.C., Ai Khanoum enjoyed another phase of building activity along its walls and elsewhere, including the palaestra. Finally, around 200 B.C. and afterward, Leriche detects across Central Asia a fundamental change in the defensive urbanism of the region, including not only architectural innovations but also an expanded military force drawing perhaps on native recruits and mercenaries (as had already happened in places such as Ptolemaic Egypt).[24] By that time, of course, the Diodotid dynasty had long been extinguished.

Until its end, therefore, the rule of the Diodotids in Bactria left no traces of warfare or other cultural disruption at Ai Khanoum. The skilled elaboration of the city begun by the Seleucids continued unabated except for the upkeep of its defensive walls. The fact that, archaeologically, the Diodotid period at Ai Khanoum was uneventful stands in marked contrast to the views of it generated by the ancient literary texts. From these sources, modern scholars tend to create event-laden reconstructions that include fairly precise dates for each dramatic action. Are the material and the literary sources really at odds, or must we simply interpret them in a new way?

LITERARY SOURCES

Just as we take care to identify the human and natural forces that have shaped the archaeological record, we must also pay heed to the various influences that have molded the Greek and Latin texts used by historians. In the case of literature, we worry less about random natural destruction and humans' greedily targeting specific works for ruin and more about bias and selectivity. For Hellenistic Bactria in the time of the Diodotids, we have but two basic written accounts that probably derive, ultimately, from the same lost original work—Apollodorus of Artemita's *Parthika* (Parthian History), written in the first century B.C.[25] Strabo (64 B.C.–A.D. 21) used this source for the eastern sections of his *Geography*, in which Diodotus is mentioned several times.[26] It is quite possible that

24. Ibid., pp. 94–98, where the archaeological evidence is not limited to Ai Khanoum.
25. See above, chap. 1, n. 21. On Apollodorus and his milieu, see Arnaldo Momigliano, *Alien Wisdom: The Limits of Hellenization* (Cambridge: Cambridge University Press, 1975), pp. 123–150. These sources are discussed at length in Franz Altheim and Ruth Stiehl, *Geschichte Mittelasiens im Altertum* (Berlin: Walter de Gruyter, 1970), pp. 362–390.
26. For the circumstances shaping the work of Strabo (and Trogus, below), see Claude Nicolet, *Space, Geography, and Politics in the Early Roman Empire* (Ann Arbor: University of Michigan Press, 1991).

at about the same time Pompeius Trogus (a Romanized Gaul) consulted Apollodorus's work while composing a history of the civilized world.[27] We have Trogus's history only as it was condensed later in a Latin work by Marcus Junianus Justin (second/third century A.D.).

Each writer worked the basic information available to him into an account of his own choosing. Clearly, Strabo had no intention of writing narrative history; thus, we find his Bactrian references divided among different geographical sections, and most of the Diodotus story gets lost as a result. In book 11, for example, Strabo mentions in passing that "some sources" claim that Arsaces (a nomadic barbarian) fled from the growing power of Diodotus in Bactria and raised a rebellion in Parthia. Instead of explaining further, Strabo refers the reader to his other works (now lost), which might have given us the very information we need.[28] In another passage he seems to make a basic historical error in his juxtaposed geographical sketches: he writes "Euthydemus" instead of "Diodotus" as the name of the satrap who first caused a rebellion in Bactria.[29] To make use of Strabo, then, we must bear in mind his purposes, methods, and mistakes as a geographer rather than a narrative historian.

Trogus, who may have been Strabo's approximate contemporary, chose to write a detailed "world" history that included (in book 41) a narrative of Parthian and Bactrian affairs. It was natural, of course, to treat these two emergent kingdoms together (as Apollodorus had originally done), since the histories of Bactria and Parthia overlapped considerably. From the preserved prologue (or, rather, summary) to this part of Trogus's history we learn something of what his lost book 41 covered: the independence of Parthia under King Arsaces, the story of his major successors, and an excursus on Arabia; the emergence of independent Bactria under King Diodotus, the later fate of Bactria, and an excursus on India under Kings Apollodotus and Menander. Thus, the treatments

---

27. Tarn believed that Trogus used a Greek source similar to Apollodorus in most respects but still distinguishable from it on the basis of variant spellings used for some peoples: *GBI*, pp. 45–50. But Tarn's own methodology (p. 46) undermines his insistence upon a second (unknown) source. See the cogent remarks of Thérèse Liebmann-Frankfort, "L'histoire des Parthes dans le livre XLI de Trogue Pompée," *Latomus* 28 (1969): 894–922; Josef Wolski, "The Decay of the Iranian Empire of the Seleucids and the Chronology of the Parthian Beginnings," *Berytus* 12 (1956–57): 35–52; and the background article by Elias Bickerman, "Notes on Seleucid and Parthian Chronology," *Berytus* 8 (1944): 73–83.

28. Strabo 11.9.3; see appendix D for translation.

29. Strabo 11.9.2.

of Parthia and Bactria were perfectly balanced narratives right down to the appendices on Arabia and India respectively.[30]

For his part, Justin arranged Trogus's history to his own taste. The Latin writer took less notice of India and therefore dismissed that portion altogether. He decided instead to include a section paralleling the principal leaders of Parthia and Bactria.[31] He described the (roughly) simultaneous rise to power of Arsaces (Parthia) and Diodotus (Bactria) and then the roughly synchronous careers of the "great" kings of each state, Mithridates (Parthia) and Eucratides (Bactria). It may be seen, therefore, that Justin's conception of eastern history followed a different path from that of Trogus. Perhaps the long Roman experience with the military might of Parthia had swayed his judgment. The role of Bactria in *that* story hinged upon two key events: the creation of the Parthian and Bactrian kingdoms (Arsaces/Diodotus) and then the reversal of fortunes for Bactria under Eucratides, which opened the way for the simultaneous fateful expansion of Parthia under Mithridates. In the condensed fashion of Justin's work, these particular people and events most impacted the later history of Imperial Rome. After all, these events insured that the great empire of Alexander would be divided eventually between Parthia in the east and Rome in the west.

There are other filters through which Justin sifted the historical narrative he found in Trogus.[32] For example, the rhetorical Justin was less concerned to record all of the proper facts of chronology and cause/effect than he was to tell an exciting tale. He preferred in Trogus the marvelous and emotional, using this material to demonstrate dramatic changes of fortune or to present a sharp antithesis. This explains further his particular interest in the Bactrian kings Diodotus and Eucratides, since both rose to greatness only to be betrayed by their sons: Diodotus II reversed his father's policies regarding Parthia, while Eucratides's son killed him and defiled his corpse.[33]

---

30. The "Prologi Historiarum Philippicarum Pompeii Trogi" are printed in the Teubner edition of Justin's *Epitoma*, edited by O. Seel (Stuttgart, 1972).

31. Justin 41.1–6, esp. from 41.4.1.

32. This view now gains support from the interesting work of J. C. Yardley, whose study (so far) of Justin through book 23 indicates that Justin did more than simply condense Trogus's history. Contrary to the established appraisal of Justin, Yardley finds in him good evidence for an original mind that reshaped Trogus into an independent work: "The Literary Background to Justin/Trogus," *AHB* 8 (1994): 60–70; J. C. Yardley and W. Heckel, eds., *Justin, "Epitome of the Philippic History of Pompeius Trogus"* (Oxford: Clarendon Press, 1997), vol. 1, pp. 1–30.

33. This heartrending tale of Eucratides's death also caught the eye of Boccaccio, who included it as part of his *De Casibus Illustrium Virorum* ("On the Downfalls of Famous

Given the predispositions of their authors, the surviving accounts of Bactria focus on different things even though derived from the same source. In other instances, such as the great history written by Polybius (ca. 200–118 B.C.), it was suitable to stress the reigns of different kings altogether (Euthydemus and Demetrius) rather than the Diodotids, Eucratides, Apollodotus, or Menander.[34] Elsewhere, in a discussion of pearl gathering in the Indian Ocean, the third-century author Aelian mentions King Eucratides in passing, much as the anonymous *Periplus Maris Erythraei* (a first-century sailing guide) notes that old coins of Apollodotus and Menander were long in circulation in southern India.[35] Plutarch records an anecdote about the division of Menander's cremated remains among competing cities in India.[36] Such scattered notes are all that survive in Graeco-Roman literature. Nowhere do we find a complete, unified account; we have only a medley preserved in different keys.

Citing Justin and Strabo to support their positions (emending or selecting portions of the texts in each case), scholars advocate either a "high" or a "low" chronology for the revolts of Parthia and Bactria.[37] The "high" chronology places these events in the reign of Antiochus II, whereas the "low" dating brings them down to the time of his successor, Seleucus II. To support either reconstruction, scholars have also adduced sparse information from other sources such as Herodian, Ammianus Marcellinus, Arrian, and Appian (all sources are translated below in appendix D). These sources provide various contextual clues for the chronology of Bactria and Parthia, but without settling the con-

Men") in 1358. A facsimile reproduction of the Paris edition of 1520 has been published by Louis B. Hall (Gainesville, Fla.: Scholars' Facsimiles and Reprints, 1962).

34. Polybius 10.49, 11.39, together with Frank Walbank, *A Historical Commentary on Polybius* (Oxford: Clarendon Press, 1967), vol. 2, pp. 264–265, 312–316.

35. Aelian *On Animals* 15.8; *Periplus* 47. These texts may also be found in appendix D.

36. Plutarch *Moralia* 831D (see appendix D).

37. In general, the high chronology has been preferred by numismatists (e.g., Bartholomaei, Wilson, Cunningham, Lassen, Newell, Bellinger, Narain, Mitchiner, and Bopearachchi) and such historians as Altheim and Musti. The low chronology has been favored by Wolski, Burstein, Brodersen, and other historians, with a growing number unwilling to choose a lesser of two evils (e.g., Préaux, Kuhrt and Sherwin-White). For the basic arguments, see *CAH*² 7, pp. 219–220: "The Date of the Secession of Bactria and Parthia from the Seleucid Kingdom," by Domenico Musti, to which responses have come from Kai Brodersen, "The Date of the Secession of Parthia from the Seleucid Kingdom," *Historia* 35 (1986): 378–381; the review of *CAH* by Stanley Burstein in *CPh* 82 (1987): 165; and Josef Wiesehöfer, "Discordia et Defectio—Dynamis kai Pithanourgia: Die frühen Seleukiden und Iran," pp. 29–56 in Bernd Funck, ed., *Hellenismus: Beiträge zur Erforschung von Akkulturation und politischer Ordnung in den Staaten des hellenistischen Zeitalters* (Tübingen: Mohr, 1996).

ther. There are, of course, merits to each side
efore we must look into the texts with open

ilable to us comes from Justin 41.4.1–20. This
ffairs from 323 to ca. 235 B.C. shows that
l against the Seleucid empire at about the same
ce suggests a precise date of 256 B.C. (the year
us were consuls of Rome), most of this text as-
vith the reign of Seleucus II (246–226 B.C.).
es do not offer much chronological help, but
nts (except the mistaken reference to Euthy-
with Justin's account. In Herodian's account
, composed in the third century A.D., we find
) version.
; Marcellinus (fourth century A.D.) in his his-
23.6.2–3), the kingdom of Parthia flourished
as the obscure brigand Arsaces matured into a wise and successful leader.
This accords well with the general accounts of Justin, Strabo, and Herodian, although Ammianus Marcellinus mistakenly associates Arsaces's
rise with the reign of Seleucus I; he must mean either the dynasty of Seleucus I or the king Seleucus II. An elaborated story of Arsaces's career
may be found in the *Parthika* of Arrian of Nicomedia, a reputable historian of the second century A.D. We know this version only in two fragments preserved by Photius (ninth century A.D.) and Syncellus (twelfth
century A.D.). Photius indicates that Pherecles, appointed satrap of
Parthia by Antiochus II, was overthrown by Arsaces and his brother Tiridates. When this occurred is not stipulated; it could even be as late as
the reign of Antiochus's successor. Syncellus, in his chronicle for the year
284 B.C., makes a garbled reference to either Antiochus II or Seleucus
II and then elaborates the story of Arsaces and Tiridates as he found it
in Arrian. In contrast to Photius, Syncellus calls these brothers Persians
and governors in Bactria; he then refers to an *eparch* (administrator) of
Persia named Agathocles who was their victim in a sordid tale of ped-
erasty. Thus we add the name of Agathocles to those of Pherecles (in
Photius) and Andragoras (in Justin) as alleged governors overthrown by
Arsaces.

Finally, without reference to any of these individuals, the Alexandrian
writer Appian (roughly the contemporary of Arrian) puts the rebellion
of Parthia in another historical context. In his history of the Syrian Wars,
Appian says that when Laodice, the wife of Antiochus II, poisoned him

in 246 B.C. she also murdered her rival—the daughter of King Ptolemy (II) Philadelphus of Egypt. The son of Philadelphus, Ptolemy III, exacted revenge by invading Syria and killing the murderous queen. Ptolemy III allegedly reached as far as Babylon, allowing the Parthians to seize this moment of Seleucid weakness to break free. Indeed, the famous Adulis inscription of Ptolemy III makes the claim that the Egyptians crossed the Euphrates River and subjugated the Seleucid satrapies as far east as Bactria.[38] These boasts in the Adulis inscription, set up by Ptolemy III on the Red Sea coast of Ethiopia, probably exaggerate the actual successes of the Ptolemaic king. Yet the repercussions of his advance toward Babylonia may indeed have been felt in Bactria during the course of this Third Syrian War. Certainly this document, along with the passage from Appian's history, provides evidence for a Parthian and Bactrian secession during this period (246–241 B.C.).

There is little else in ancient literature that touches upon the problem of the Diodotid revolt, and it is quite obvious that most of what has come down to us really deals with Arsaces and the Parthians. This, in part, reflects the original source for most of this information, the *Parthika* of Apollodorus of Artemita. Whatever was cogently written soon after these events actually occurred, the telling and retelling over the centuries has left us a series of discordant whispers.

HISTORICAL PROCESSES

These various texts have been made eventful by their ancient authors and modern interpreters. The general condition of the eastern Seleucid empire during the third century B.C. has been selectively filtered and then reduced to one or more specific incidents. We see the East episodically and usually linked in some way to an event in the West: in the East *this happened* while, or because, in the West *that happened*. Our ancient writers were trying to explain, for the most part, which events precipitated other events. This was natural, of course, especially for writers such as Justin, who liked to organize historical accounts by pairing events and personalities and whose interests in the East were never independent of his interests in the West. This ancient habit of mind creates for us the dilemma of multiple (and contradictory) synchronisms. Major eastern

---

38. *OGIS* 54; see appendix D, inscription 6. Excavators found at Ai Khanoum a broken garnet intaglio, probably Ptolemaic and possibly depicting Queen Arsinoë II: Francfort, *AK* 3, p. 75. This suggests contact with Egypt but certainly not a conquest.

events (e.g., Parthia's revolt, the invasion of Arsaces) turn upon major western events (the Punic Wars, the Seleucid War of the Brothers, the Third Syrian War). In some cases there is no causal connection (the Punic Wars), but in others the writer may see a direct link. We should expect, therefore, some inexactness and disagreement among our sources. The further habit of linking eastern events to each other by such vague phrases as "at that same time period" or "afterward" should alert us again to the inherent vagueness of our chronology.

Behind these collections of paired events in our sources we should seek the larger historical processes at work in the East. Putting aside for the moment all concern about absolute chronologies and western events, the development of Parthia and Bactria becomes more comprehensible. We find that these eastern Seleucid satrapies clearly acquired a strong sense of regional independence and that their satraps gained more and more autonomy in the course of the third century B.C. The satrap in Parthia, whether named Pherecles, Agathocles, or Andragoras,[39] governed free of Seleucid restraint, but it was his counterparts in Bactria who eventually declared themselves secessionists and sovereigns. As was their satrapal/ regal responsibility, the Diodotids pursued the ongoing development of Bactria. Perpetuating the policies of Alexander and Seleucus, Diodotus I policed the frontier against nomads, among whom arose a leader in Arsaces. Described by Strabo and Justin in exactly the same terms as Alexander's Central Asian adversaries were characterized by Classical authors (i.e., a brute nomadic bandit and plunderer), this Arsaces was duly driven from Bactria by the power of Diodotus. Even those writers who do not

---

39. We shall see in chapter 4 that earlier scholars were tempted to find this Parthian satrap in some Bactrian coins bearing the name "Agathocles"; however, that connection had to be abandoned when it was proved that the Agathocles coins were actually struck much later in the second century B.C. There are, however, a few coins struck in the name of an Andragoras from some (uncertain) eastern mint sometime between ca. 320 and 240 B.C. The staters show a bearded portrait (probably of Zeus) on the obverse and a four-horse chariot with rider and driver on the reverse. The tetradrachms have a city goddess with mural crown on the obverse and a standing Athena with her owl and armor on the reverse. Both issues bear the name ΑΝΔΡΑΓΟΡΟΥ (Andragoras), without royal title. For their discovery, see Percy Gardner, "New Coins from Bactria," NC 19 (1879): 1–12, and "Coins from Central Asia," NC 1 (1881): 8–12; C. Allotte de la Füye, "Monnaies incertaines de la Sogdiane et des contrées voisines," RN (1910): 282–292. See also I. M. Diakonov and E. Zejmal, "The Parthian Dynast Andragoras and His Coins" (in Russian), VDI (1988): 4–19. A nearly mint-condition stater, only the fourth known (two earlier specimens are in the British Museum, one in Berlin), has recently appeared for auction in NFA 25 (Nov. 1990) no. 202. This specimen shows the chariot rider to be a bearded man in satrapal headgear, perhaps Andragoras himself. It remains uncertain, however, whether these coins were struck by the man who was the victim of Arsaces.

call Arsaces a Bactrian nevertheless associate his early career in some way with Bactria.[40]

Arsaces then moved from Bactrian to Parthian territory, where he enjoyed a fateful success against the Seleucid satrap there.[41] For some time, Arsaces and his followers fought for control of Parthia against the Greek settlers and then gathered strength to expand into neighboring regions. The threatening power of Arsaces prompted Diodotus to respond, either in pure self-defense or out of the old Greek sense of warding off the enemies of Hellenism. The point made in Justin is that Arsaces himself feared Diodotus on the one side of Parthia and the Seleucids on the other, but whether this meant a *joint* action by the Graeco-Macedonians against him, the new Spitamenes, we cannot say. It was enough for Diodotus, of course, that Arsaces had earlier harassed Bactria and killed a neighboring satrap. It would be enough for the Seleucids that part of their empire had been stolen.

The imminent war between Arsaces and Diodotus never occurred because of the sudden death of the latter.[42] The new ruler of Bactria, Diodotus II, then chose to ally himself with Arsaces. War with the Seleucids did transpire a little later, but Arsaces prevailed. The role of Bactria in this conflict remains unknown. Of course, later in the century, Diodotus II fell at the hands of Euthydemus I, bringing an end to the Diodotid dynasty.

There is nothing in this general account that appears contradictory or inherently unlikely in the larger context of eastern history. Nor does it clash, as a patchwork narrative, with the archaeological record. Bactria under Diodotus I remained prosperous. Building continued at Ai Khanoum, irrigation expanded, and the frontiers were protected.[43] There is no sign that Diodotus attained independence except gradually and peacefully. In time, the eastern Bactrian frontier at Ai Khanoum even relaxed

40. Because of a confused interpretation of a fifth-century text (Moses of Charene), it was once believed that this Arsaces was a native of Bactra itself: J. Prinsep, *Historical Results from Bactrian Coins and Other Discoveries in Afghanistan*, edited by H. T. Prinsep (London, 1844; rpt. Chicago: Ares, 1974), pp. 24–25.

41. J. Wolski, "Le problème d'Andragoras," *Ephemeridis Instituti Archaeologici Bulgarici* 16 (1950): 111–114, and "Andragoras, était-il iranien ou grec?" *Studia Iranica* 4 (1975): 159–169.

42. There is no indication of foul play in the sudden death of Diodotus I. Given the predilections of Justin as discussed above, he would scarcely have passed up an opportunity to mention such intrigue if he had found it in Trogus's work (cf. the Eucratides story). Diodotus probably died of old age.

43. Strabo 11.11.1 echoes the achievement of Diodotus, and Ammianus Marcellinus 23.6.55 says that Bactria was ruled by kings who seemed formidable even to Arsaces.

its military defenses; we cannot yet know why. Perhaps Diodotus I was shifting attention westward against Arsaces or Diodotus II felt confident in his new peace with the Parthians. Later, around 225 B.C., Ai Khanoum underwent strong attack and apparently witnessed the end of the Diodotids and the emergence of Euthydemus.

The long-standing debate between adherents of the "high" and "low" chronologies should not distract us from the significance of what we have found in these sources: a coherent vision of eastern affairs that shows a general trend of development. The desire of historians to put *exact* dates on each event cannot be indulged, since we cannot trust so completely the synchronisms adduced by the various texts. Let us look into the first event of most chronological reconstructions, namely, the independence of Parthia. What would suggest to us that this was a specific, datable occurrence? Our sources offer a number of variations on the name of the satrap responsible for it (Pherecles, Agathocles, Andragoras) and even the circumstances surrounding his character and demise. No source really suggests that this satrap, whatever his name, took the royal title, and even the coins of Andragoras lack such a title. Everything, in fact, urges us to see a gradual political process and not an event; the only exception is the extraordinary Roman consular date given by Justin. This represents Justin's one attempt in the forty-four books of his history to give an exact synchronization between East and West, and yet it fails us.[44] The specific year, 256 B.C., does not fall into the period Justin otherwise gives us for Parthia's first independence (the reign of Seleucus II, 246–226 B.C.). By emending the first initial of one of the consuls (C. Atilius Regulus instead of M. Atilius Regulus) it is possible to obtain a later date, 250 B.C., but this is still outside the period of Seleucus II's reign.[45] Many scholars will nonetheless insist upon one of these particular years (256 or 250 B.C.) as the date of Parthian independence under (say) Andragoras or Arsaces, in spite of the obvious textual problems and internal inconsistencies.

As previously noted, Justin's work habits suggest that he was not a fastidious chronologist. He chose to link two great events relevant to Roman history, the first invasion of Carthaginian Africa (256 B.C.) and the first independence of Parthia, and fudging the facts or assigning exact dates to inexact processes did not trouble him. We must not lose sight

---

44. Wolski, "The Decay of the Iranian Empire," pp. 51–52.
45. Similarly, Eusebius's *Chronicle* gives two dates, 248–244 B.C. (1.207) and 250 B.C. (2.120), for the rise of Arsacid Parthia. Conversion errors and conflations were common mistakes in ancient manuscripts.

of the way he reorganized the presentation of otherwise reliable information in Trogus. The consular date obviously tells us more about the situation in the West during the second century A.D. than about the situation in the East during the third century B.C.

There is no specific date for the satrapal revolt in Parthia that any modern authority should yet trust. Clearly, the last Seleucid satrap of Parthia was appointed by Antiochus II (261–246 B.C.), but that does not tell us when this governor reached for nominal independence.[46] The critical period fell mostly during the reign of Seleucus II, whose ongoing crises (the invasion by Ptolemy, his war against his brother, the battle with the Gauls) provided our sources with useful synchronisms and sometimes explanations for what was happening in the East. All that can be safely alleged about the chronology is that the process of growing independence among the eastern satraps was *completed* during the years of Seleucus II's troubled reign; that this process (long under way) may also have been accelerated by those problems; that it was probably during the early 230s B.C. that Arsaces was driven from Bactrian territories and invaded Parthia and Hyrcania; that before the end of that decade Diodotus II succeeded his father in Bactria and made common cause with Parthia, perhaps even against the punitive invasion of Seleucus II in ca. 228 B.C.; and, finally, that in the 220s B.C. the Diodotid line ended with the rise of Euthydemus to power in Bactria. Even this chronology may be too exact for the texts as we have them, but the general historical process must be along these lines and within the broader limits of the period 250–225 B.C.

For Diodotus I, satrap and would-be king, this means a long tenure as head of the emerging state of Bactria. We cannot find him in the slim documentary evidence of the period and may never know the precise dates and circumstances of his early career. We know him from the literary sources as a Greek who was made satrap of Bactria as early as the reign of Antiochus II.[47] As satrap Diodotus was the chief royal agent in Bactria. He commanded regional military forces, hence the Greek term *strategos* (general) for his office. He managed the local economy, collected taxes, oversaw the construction of cities and shrines, and responded to

46. Brodersen, "The Date of the Secession," p. 379, citing Wolski, "The Decay of the Iranian Empire."

47. Our sources stress the "Macedonianness" of the Seleucids and the "Greekness" of the defectors Diodotus and, later, Euthydemus; the ethnicity of Arsaces was clearly uncertain but variously reported as Scythian, Bactrian, Parthian, and Persian. Ethnic background clearly mattered to the ancients and may have played a part in the way in which loyalties were divided on the eastern frontier.

the needs of his distant sovereign whenever eastern resources (troops, wealth, elephants) were required in the West.[48] As the king's representative, the satrap acted royally within his own province; he wielded a king's power and enjoyed a king's lifestyle. This was the inherent danger of ancient empire, whether Achaemenid, Hellenistic, or even Roman. Distances were vast, and communications slow. Kings (or emperors) could do no better than trust regional governors to act decisively on their behalf and yet hope that these men would remain loyal in the face of temptation. Care had to be exercised whenever satrapal appointments were made, and kings sought to create personal bonds of loyalty through special favors, land grants, and other luxuries to offset rival ambitions. It was a risky business for all concerned. The consequences may be seen in the numerous satrapal revolts in Achaemenid and Seleucid history, and not just on the frontiers.[49]

Under these conditions, the situation in the East gradually elevated able satraps to a higher status. Along with his counterpart to the west in Parthia, Diodotus assumed more and more autonomy until reaching a de facto position of independence from the Seleucid empire. Unlike the Parthian governor, however, Diodotus I (or perhaps Diodotus II in this compressed narrative) seems (from Justin) to have formally proclaimed himself king (*basileus*) at the end of this long process.

This political *evolution* was not a *revolution* that could leave traces in the archaeological record at Ai Khanoum. Bactria was not torn by visible strife or factional fighting; the region did not fall into cultural isolation from the rest of the Hellenistic world. No event or special condition compelled the eastern satraps to revolt. They apparently exercised growing autonomy because they were expected to and could; the whole character of that era encouraged risk taking and dynasty building. Thus the Diodotids took their place as true heirs of Alexander, alongside Ptolemy, Seleucus, Antigonus, and all the others of that ambitious age who rose from satrap to sovereign.

By dividing this new realm into satrapies, the Diodotids followed the established path of Hellenistic state building.[50] The number and names of these satrapies remain unknown, except for the two nearest Parthia

---

48. In fact, the (pre-Diodotid) cuneiform text mentioned above (n. 11) provides some of our best evidence for the duties of Seleucid satraps.

49. For example, Molon, the satrap of Media, and his brother Alexander, the satrap of Persis: Polybius 5.40–54. Molon took the royal title and issued his own coins: *ESM*, pp. 85–86.

50. Strabo 11.11.2.

to the west, Aspionus and Turiva (Tapuria?).[51] It seems possible that Bactria proper, south of the Oxus and west of Ai Khanoum, was subdivided into satrapies on the basis of habitation zones (e.g., Darya Saripul, with perhaps an administrative center at Emshi-Tepe). Sogdiana, too, might have been organized in this way. The major tributaries to the Middle Oxus formed natural valley enclaves that Alexander's army had invaded in separate missions and subsequently colonized.[52] In two of these valleys archaeologists have identified what appear to be regional administrative centers of the third century B.C.: Dalverzin Tepe in the heart of the Surkhan Darya Valley and Kobadian alongside the Kafirnigan River. They resemble Ai Khanoum but on a smaller scale, with walls, a citadel, temples, palace, aristocratic quarters, and so forth.[53] Here might be the satrapies and their local capitals in the time of Diodotus I and II.

We would expect (though the written sources do not say so) that among the satraps of Diodotus I would be his son and successor. On the Seleucid model, that son would become viceroy on a frontier of the new state. He would establish a subsidiary administrative center, probably including another royal mint, in order to share his father's work. We know that the emerging dynasty did all that the Hellenistic imperative required, continuing to build in the cities, to patronize Hellenic institutions, art, and architecture, to defend its territory against outsiders, and to promote trade between East and West. Its prosperity may be measured in the ongoing monetization of Bactria by Diodotus and his son. In that wealth, too, has been written another version of the story revealed to us in the archaeological and literary records.

---

51. Number: Seleucus I is said to have tripled the number of satrapies in his realm (Appian *Syr.* 62). For recent discussion, see Sherwin-White and Kuhrt, *Samarkhand to Sardis*, pp. 44–45. Names: The usual emendation of Strabo gives Tapuria, an area somewhere between Hyrcania and Aria, in a mountainous region once part of Media: Strabo 11.8.8; 11.9.1; 11.11.8; 11.13.3. This, however, is very far to the west of Bactria. In another case, Polybius 10.49.1 has been emended to read Tapuria (instead of Ta Gourana) for the locale of Euthydemus's battle to forestall the punitive invasion of Antiochus the Great. The exact geography escapes us.

52. Holt, *Alexander and Bactria*, pp. 60–62.

53. P. Leriche, "Structures politiques et sociales dans la Bactriane et la Sogdiane hellénistes," in Heinz Kreissig and Friedman Kühnert, eds., *Antike Abhängigkeitsformen in den griechischen Gebieten ohne Polisstruktur und den romischen Provinzen* (Berlin: Akademie Verlag, 1985), pp. 65–79, esp. 75–76.

CHAPTER 4

How Money Talks

EVERYTHING, AND NOTHING

Ancient coins have contributed greatly to the study of Hellenistic civilization, illuminating much that might otherwise be lost with our vanishing written records. In fact, numismatics has lately been hailed as "the frontier of ancient studies," and not just for the study of ancient frontiers such as Bactria.[1] The obvious connection between kings and their coins helps us to understand the elusive leaders of the Hellenistic period. From these carefully designed disks of information technology we can learn important new facts about royal personalities, propaganda, portraiture, religion, art, and the particulars of war and peace. Lack of caution in such studies can, however, generate more nonsense than knowledge. We have met this problem already, especially in terms of Hellenistic hoard statistics, but in Bactria the beautiful coins of individual reigns tend to inspire even greater flights of the imagination. As a result, we have come to know everything, and nothing, about the first two leaders of this new Hellenistic state.

When Tarn more or less leaped over the third century B.C. in his effort to link Alexander to the Euthydemids, he merely glanced at the pivotal work of Diodotus I and II in Bactria. Indeed, he noticed little more than one convenient numismatic "fact": the later Euthydemids used spe-

1. Chester G. Starr, *Past and Future in Ancient History* (Lanham, Md.: University Press of America, 1987), p. 60. Starr rightly observes of numismatics that "without doubt its potential future utility is of major order."

cial commemorative coins to trace a fictitious pedigree connecting themselves to Alexander the Great.[2] These unusual coins were minted by two
kings, Agathocles and Antimachus, sometime in the second quarter of
the second century B.C.[3] In each case, the reigning monarch identified
himself as the issuing authority, but the coin otherwise imitated the
mintage of an earlier king of Bactria. For example, Agathocles would produce some coins bearing the portrait and name of Alexander, complete
with Alexander's famous coin-type of Zeus enthroned, but with the additional inscription "[minted] during the reign of Agathocles Dikaios"
to clarify this as a commemorative issue in honor of Alexander. Included
in this special series of coins were such "honorees" as Antiochus Nikator, Diodotus Soter, Diodotus Theos, Euthydemus Theos, Demetrius
Aniketos, and Pantaleon Soter (see plates 3–6).

Tarn saw in this practice a unique attempt by Agathocles and Antimachus to advertise their royal pedigree, tracing their bloodline back
through the Euthydemids, Diodotids, and Seleucids all the way to Alexander himself. As far back as the Seleucids, Tarn considered this a genuine
pedigree based on actual blood ties; Alexander alone, he argued, had been
fictitiously patched into this genealogy. Thus the first dynasties of Hellenistic Bactria (Seleucids, Diodotids, Euthydemids) were allegedly all
related. From that premise Tarn deduced the "quite certain fact" that
Diodotus I had married the sister of the Seleucid king Seleucus II Callinicus in about 246 B.C. This union had been arranged, Tarn suggested,
to secure the loyalty of Diodotus I during the tumultuous years following the death of Antiochus II Theos, from whom Diodotus had slowly
been gaining his independence. When Diodotus I allegedly died some sixteen years later, his son by a *previous* marriage ascended to the Bactrian
throne as Diodotus II. Unlike his father, the son could not be reconciled
to Seleucid authority and quickly allied himself with the rival kingdom
of Parthia. According to Tarn, this move naturally upset Diodotus's Seleucid stepmother, who took matters into her own hands. She supported
a Seleucid loyalist named Euthydemus in his bid to overthrow Diodotus
II; this pact was sealed by the marriage of Euthydemus to her daughter
by Diodotus I. Euthydemus, his new Seleucid/Diodotid bride (Diodotus
II's half-sister), and the widow of Diodotus I (Diodotus II's evil step-

2. *GBI*, pp. 72–74, 446–451.
3. On this whole issue, see F. Holt, "The So-Called 'Pedigree Coins' of the Bactrian
Greeks," pp. 69–91 in W. Heckel and R. Sullivan, eds., *Ancient Coins of the Graeco-Roman
World: The Nickle Numismatic Papers* (Waterloo, Ontario: Wilfrid Laurier University
Press, 1984).

FIGURE 2: THE DIODOTID DYNASTY
ACCORDING TO TARN

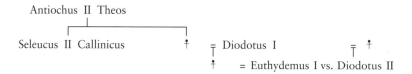

Antiochus II Theos

Seleucus II Callinicus   †   Diodotus I   †

†   = Euthydemus I vs. Diodotus II

mother) then killed Diodotus II and seized the throne in ca. 226 B.C. According to Tarn, therefore, we can see in certain Bactrian coins a remarkable record of the Diodotid family tree (see fig. 2). Throughout this brief exposition on the Diodotid family Tarn relied heavily upon a battery of interlocking surmises that stand or fall together. For example, once he supposed that the Euthydemids *must* be related to the Diodotids, then Euthydemus I *must* be married to a daughter of Diodotus I. That marriage is then dated to ca. 227 B.C. because Demetrius, Euthydemus's son, was about twenty years old in 206 B.C. This allegedly gives us also the age of Demetrius's presumed mother (Diodotus's daughter) and therefore a few years earlier the date of Diodotus's presumed wedding to the daughter of Antiochus II. That date, ca. 246, will then explain the marriage alliance between the Seleucids and Diodotids. These dates make it "almost certain" that Diodotus II was not the son of Diodotus's Seleucid wife but rather the offspring of some earlier union. Given Tarn's training as a barrister, the case may seem well argued and secure, but any one mistaken assumption condemns the whole chain of reasoning. If, for example, Demetrius was the product of an earlier marriage of Euthydemus, then the whole chronological system crumbles. Demetrius, by his possible marriage to a daughter of Antiochus the Great, need not be the son of a Diodotid/Seleucid princess to fit into Tarn's pedigree series.[4]

In spite of its shaky foundation, Tarn's extraordinary vision seemed to be independently vindicated by the work of the leading Hellenistic numismatist of his day, Edward Theodore Newell (1886–1941).[5] In pre-

4. On Demetrius's possible Seleucid marriage, see Polybius 11.34.9. This is the *only* union referred to in our sources, yet Tarn must deny it (*GBI*, p. 201 n. 1) in order to preserve his string of *imagined* marriages.

5. For Newell's considerable achievements in the field, consult P. Lederer's obituary notice and bibliography in *Revue Suisse de Numismatique* 29 (1942): 81–86; note also A. Paul Clement, "A Bibliography of the Writings of Edward T. Newell," *AJP* 68 (1947): 427–432, and the remarks in Elvira Clain-Stefanelli, *Numismatics—An Ancient Science* (Washington, D.C.: U.S. Government Printing Office, 1965), pp. 65–66.

cisely the same year (1938) that Tarn first published *The Greeks in Bactria and India,* Newell published a masterpiece of his own. Using a series of die-linked coins in this groundbreaking study, *Coinage of the Eastern Seleucid Mints,* Newell carefully documented the steps that marked the emerging independence of Diodotus I from the Seleucid empire of Antiochus II.[6] This numismatic evidence clearly nailed down the process by which Bactria became a separate kingdom under the Diodotids: the Bactrian mint issued the standard coinages of the early Seleucid kings until, in the reign of Antiochus II, the governor (satrap Diodotus I) gently took steps to make these issues his own. He struck the usual Seleucid coin-type (seated Apollo) with the name and portrait of Antiochus II but soon replaced the Apollo type with his own dynastic badge, thundering Zeus. In the next stage he put his own portrait in the place of Antiochus II's, and finally he introduced his own name onto the coinage to complete his numismatic evolution from subject to sovereign. While this evidence changed a few points in Tarn's reconstruction of events,[7] the overall picture drawn by these two scholars seemed to mesh beautifully and found its way quickly into the standard books about Hellenistic history and coinage.

As it turns out, however, there is little truth in the tale spun out by Tarn and reinforced by Newell. The die linkage traced by Newell tells us everything about the emerging independence of Bactria and yet nothing of certainty: the coins he used have proved to be modern fakes.[8] As for Tarn's work, we may share the reaction of the historian Charles Edson, who wrote in an early review, "Tarn's book is one of the most significant contributions to the study of classical ancient history. . . . But after the initial sensations of excitement and, be it said, of aesthetic pleasure had subsided, the reader began to ask the question: Is it all true?"[9]

The answer is negative, at least on the Diodotus problem. Tarn's reconstruction reads all too much like a steamy chapter from the Julio-

---

6. *ESM,* first published in 1938 as Numismatic Studies no. 1 of the American Numismatic Society, was republished in 1978 with "A Summary of Recent Scholarship, Additions and Corrections" by Otto Mørkholm. On the Bactrian coins, see pp. 228–249.

7. Tarn had believed in 1938 that all the coins bearing the name "Diodotus" belonged to the second Diodotus, not the elder who rebelled against Antiochus II; the second edition of *GBI* (1951) acknowledged on p. 523 that Newell's work suggested otherwise and thus removed "an old difficulty." Tarn had been following in 1938 the numismatic judgments of MacDonald, discussed later in this chapter.

8. G. K. Jenkins, "A Group of Bactrian Forgeries," *RN* 7 (1965): 51–57, a dramatic piece of detective work too often overlooked by later scholars.

9. In his review of *GBI,* published in *CPh* 49 (1954): 112–118, esp. 112.

Claudian period of imperial Rome. His history of the Diodotid family
hinges upon the wives and widows of the dynasty, Agrippinas of another
era who steered Bactria behind the scenes. According to Tarn, "these
Macedonian girls were often anything but nonentities, and the pawns
sometimes queened with surprising results."[10] Unfortunately, he was
playing this elaborate chess game with imaginary pieces. In Bactria, these
"Macedonian girls" are indeed "nonentities" whose politics and personalities Tarn invented; they are nowhere mentioned in any ancient text.
Tarn's mistake was his assumption that the later Euthydemid coins were
pedigree issues giving a bloodline (partly real, partly fictitious) that entitled him to fabricate all of these female members of the Diodotid family and give them various loyalties. That erroneous assumption about the
coins, now exposed like the forgeries that misled Newell, leaves us back
in the dark about the elusive Diodotid dynasty.[11]

Many, however, still believe in the Bactria conjured by these scholars
in 1938. Some authorities continue to use as evidence the demonstrably
fake coins cited by Newell.[12] Others continue to play the family guessing game popularized by Tarn. Two noted numismatists, for example,
have recently arranged a slightly different family tree for the Diodotids,[13]
this time marrying off the elder Diodotus to the sister (rather than the
daughter) of Antiochus II (see fig. 3). Strangely, there is no Diodotus II
in this story. Instead, Euthydemus marries the daughter of the Seleucid
queen and Diodotus I and ascends the throne in about 235 B.C. at the
death of his father-in-law. This account, then, rests upon a lineage that
replaces a person we know (the son of Diodotus I) with persons we do
not know even existed (a sister of Antiochus II and a daughter of Diodotus I). Furthermore, as in Tarn's fanciful version, this latest one takes
us without evidence into the minds of the persons involved. Here the numismatists tell us that Antiochus II welcomed the independence of

10. *GBI*, p. 74.
11. Holt, "Pedigree Coins."
12. For example, Mitchiner, *IGISC*, vol. 1, pp. 40 and 42; Raoul Curiel and Gerard
Fussman, *Le trésor monétaire de Qunduz* (Paris: Klincksieck, 1965), p. 74 n. 8 (published
in the same year as Jenkins's "Group of Bactrian Forgeries"); the die link referred to by
E. V. Zejmal seems to be the (false) example in *ESM*, p. 248 no. 712, a work that Zejmal
cites in the preceding sentence: "Problèmes de circulation monétaire dans la Bactriane hellénistique," in J.-C. Gardin, ed., *L'archéologie de la Bactriane ancienne* (Paris: CNRS,
1985), p. 274.
13. Ian Carradice and Martin Price, *Coinage in the Greek World* (London: Seaby,
1988), p. 124. Though unstated, this reconstruction rests in part upon the commemorative series of coins used by Tarn (*GBI*, pp. 446–451). The series is incorrectly listed (p.
125). For another notorious example, see chap. 7.

FIGURE 3:   THE DIODOTID DYNASTY
ACCORDING TO CARRADICE AND PRICE

Antiochus II Theos   † ⊤ Diodotus I

† = Euthydemus I

Diodotus and Bactria "as a buffer with the Indian Empire beyond."
There is simply no basis for believing that this was the case, except for
the further belief that Antiochus gave his sister as a bride to his "ally"
Diodotus, and there is no proof that she even existed.

These examples are not meant to place any particular blame on some
of this century's greatest scholars. Because of the arduous nature of Bactrian studies, the margin for error is generally large enough to lure us all
into danger with false evidence or daring surmises.[14] The real danger is
not knowing that one has fallen or been dragged into the snare. Only a
solid grasp of the facts, meager though they are, can keep us out of trouble. Unfortunately, the facts of one generation may be the downfall of
the next.

MISSING KINGS

False coins, false hopes, and false history have been the bane of Bactrian
studies. Exactly two hundred years before Tarn and Newell published
their influential works, the modern search for the Diodotids began in error. In his pioneering treatise *Historia Regni Graecorum Bactriani*,
Theophilus Bayer illustrated two ancient coins and offered the world's
first scholarly analysis of the available numismatic and literary evidence
for ancient Bactrian history.[15] One coin he identified properly—a silver
tetradrachm of Eucratides, the first Bactrian king to have his mintage correctly attributed by modern research. The other coin Bayer mistakenly

14. Many other cases could as easily be cited, such as that of the numismatist/histo-
rian Michael Grant's inferring what Diodotus I *believed* as the satrap contemplated rebellion: *From Alexander to Cleopatra: The Hellenistic World* (New York: Scribner, 1982),
p. 85. Some writers have even claimed to read in the ancient sources things that are patently
not there, as when we are told that "Justin states that Diodotus was slain by his own son
soon after his successful revolt": T. L. Comparette, *A Descriptive Catalogue of Greek Coins
Selected from the Cabinet of Clarence S. Bement, Esq.* (New York: American Numismatic
Society, 1921), p. 92. This is apparently a strange mix-up with Justin's later account of
Eucratides's demise: see appendix D.
15. Published in Latin by the Academy of Sciences in St. Petersburg, 1738. A rare copy
is kept in the Bibliothèque Nationale in Paris.

believed to be a bronze issue of Diodotus, an error eventually caught by the careful scholars of the next century.[16] Thus, the first "discovery" of a Diodotus coin proved to be a false lead.

Meanwhile, research into the extraordinary past of Bactria illuminated the lives of other kings as new coins came to light.[17] After Eucratides, the next correct identification was that of a gold coin of King Euthydemus, followed in 1799 by the attribution of a coin to Heliocles, the first Bactrian king attested solely by numismatic evidence.[18] The pace accelerated in the early nineteenth century as the result of extensive explorations and avid collecting inspired as much by the celebrated "great game" then taking place in Central Asia as by the pursuit of pure knowledge.[19] It was reported that some generals melted down for cannon the excess coinage they recovered from ancient sites; one find alone yielded more than thirty thousand coins.[20] Charles Masson, a notorious player of the "great game," estimated that thirty thousand ancient coins *per year* were found in the vicinity of Kabul alone.[21] Culled from these vast numbers of coins were the invaluable pieces that illustrated the reigns of the lost Bactrian kings.

By 1838, the centennial of modern Bactrian studies, scholars and soldiers had succeeded brilliantly in the task begun by Bayer. Almost all of the seven kings mentioned in ancient Greek or Latin texts could be accounted for in the numismatic record. Scholars could at last see the portraits and study the coin-types of Euthydemus, Demetrius, Eucratides, Apollodotus, and Menander. Kings otherwise unattested included Anti-

16. Horace H. Wilson, *Ariana Antiqua: A Descriptive Account of the Antiquities and Coins of Afghanistan* (1841; rpt. Delhi: Oriental Publishers, 1971), pp. 3, 218; cf. *Revue Belge de Numismatique* 1 (1845): 150.

17. For the first century of Bactrian discoveries, H. H. Wilson, *Ariana Antiqua*, pp. 1–50, offers a fascinating and detailed account. It has been largely copied into the expanded report of J. N. Tiwari, "A Survey of Indian Numismatography (Pre-Muhammadan Coinage), 1738–1950," *Numismatic Notes and Monographs* (Numismatic Society of India) 10 (1964): 1–28. A similar survey may be found in Lahiri, *Corpus*, pp. 3–10.

18. A coin of Heliocles was earlier listed among the "rois inconnus" (unknown kings) in the *Catalogue des médailles antiques et modernes, du Cabinet de M. D'Ennery* (Paris: de Monsieur, 1788), p. 40 no. 253.

19. For a readable account of this international competition for control of Afghanistan and its environs, see Peter Hopkirk, *The Great Game: The Struggle for Empire in Central Asia* (New York: Kodansha, 1992). See also Holt, "The Autobiography of an Ancient Coin," *Aramco World* 48 (1997): 10–15.

20. A. de Longpérier, "Collection numismatique du Géneral Court," *RN* (1839): 83; Ernst Babelon, *Traité des monnaies grecques et romaines*, vol. 1 (Paris: Ernest Leroux, 1901), pp. 22–23.

21. Wilson, *AA*, pp. 10–13. See also Gordon Whitteridge, *Charles Masson of Afghanistan* (Warminster: Aris and Phillips, 1986).

machus, Heliocles, Agathocles, Pantaleon, Antalcidas, and others. In
fact, the only men missing from the recorded king list of Hellenistic Bactria were the elusive founders of the state, Diodotus I and II, for whom
not a single coin could be identified among the tens of thousands turning up annually in Central and South Asia.[22] The adventurous savant
James Prinsep, linguist, numismatist, and founding member of the Asiatic Society of Bengal, marveled in print that "the coins of the first
princes of Bactria, by name Theodotus I and II, are yet unknown; perhaps they never struck money. . . ."[23]

Where were the coins of Bactria's first kings? In his own review of the
state of Bactrian studies in 1834, Raoul Rochette met this nagging question with an ingenious theory: he associated the rebellion of the Diodotids
mentioned in some sources (notably Justin and Strabo) with the reference to a Seleucid governor named Agathocles (or, alternatively, Pherecles) in other texts (Syncellus and Photius).[24] The existence of Bactrian
coins in the name of a King Agathocles could in this way be used to fill
the glaring numismatic gap at the very beginning of Bactrian independence. For his part, Prinsep worried that the design of the Agathocles
coins seemed later than the third century B.C. and that their occasional
bilingual inscriptions suggested that they should be attributed to a realm
south of Bactria proper, but he conceded that "the non-discovery of
Theodotus' medals is certainly in favor of M. Raoul Rochette's argument. . . ."[25] The Diodotus mystery was still playing havoc with these intellectuals after a century of hard research, for Prinsep himself had un-
wittingly published an ancient coin of Diodotus I.

This coin reached the eyes of European scholars through the work

---

22. No Diodotus specimen was known to Christian Lassen in his important work *Zur
Geschichte der griechischen und indo-skythischen Könige in Baktrien, Kabul und Indien*
(Bonn, 1838), which surveyed the state of Bactrian studies on the centennial of Bayer's first
book; see esp. p. 147.

23. J. Prinsep, "Further Notes and Drawings of Bactrian and Indo-Scythic Coins," *JASB*
4 (1835), republished in Prinsep, *Essays on Indian Antiquities*, ed. Edward Thomas (1858;
rpt. Varanasi: Indological Book House, 1971), p. 179. Note again that "Theodotus" is simply a variant spelling of "Diodotus"; compare, for example, Trogus's use of the form
"Diodotus" ("Prologus Libri XLI") and Justin's use of the form "Theodotus" in his abridg-
ment of that work (41.4.1–10).

24. R. Rochette, *Notice sur quelques médailles grecques inédites, appartenant à des
rois inconnus de la Bactriane et de l'Inde* (Paris: L'Imprimerie Royale, 1834), pp. 3–19; he
also set forth these views in contemporary issues of the *Journal des Savants*.

25. J. Prinsep, "Application of the Early Bhilsa Alphabet to the Buddhist Group of
Coins," *JASB* (1837), republished in Prinsep, *Essays*, vol. 1, p. 7. For the background of
Prinsep's many contributions to knowledge, see O. P. Kejariwal, *The Asiatic Society of Ben-
gal and the Discovery of India's Past, 1784–1838* (Delhi: Oxford University Press, 1988).

of Alexander "Bokhara" Burnes, a young British lieutenant and intelligence agent who traveled widely through the treacherous lands between czarist Russia and British India, living among the notorious emirs, maharajahs, slavers, and sultans immortalized by Rudyard Kipling and others. Like the later Lawrence of Arabia, Burnes gathered a great reputation as the result of his daring exploits, and he also gathered coins. These relics were avidly studied and published by Prinsep and H. H. Wilson.[26] Among them was a tetradrachm showing on the obverse the profile of a king wearing a diadem; the reverse side depicted the naked figure of Zeus in the act of hurling a thunderbolt. The Greek god had the thundering aegis draped over his left arm and an eagle at his feet. The minting authority was identified in a Greek inscription as ΒΑΣΙΛΕΩΣ ΑΝ-ΤΙΟΧΟΥ (King Antiochus). Prinsep attributed this coin to one of the Seleucid rulers of that name, guessing that it might be Antiochus the Great (223–187 B.C.), and put its manufacture in ancient Parthia.[27] There was clearly nothing about this new specimen to suggest that it was actually minted by Diodotus of Bactria, and so it remained unnoticed while Rochette, Prinsep, and others tried to explain away the strange absence of Diodotus I and II from the growing list of discovered kings.

The truth dawned slowly in an interesting exchange of letters and articles among the leading numismatists of Europe. In 1839, *The Numismatic Chronicle* in London received an excited communication from a recent traveler to Paris.[28] Writing under the pseudonym "Parvulus," the Londoner reported having seen a gold coin "bearing the name of a Bactrian king, none of whose coins have as yet been figured, or even mentioned by Mr. Prinsep or Professor Wilson." The coin's legend read ΒΑΣΙΛΕΩΣ ΔΙΟΔΟΤΟΥ (King Diodotus). In addition to the portrait of the king on the obverse, the design on the reverse showed thundering Zeus and a storklike bird. "Parvulus" noted that the coin was destined for the French royal collection, but he was "not aware that any of the

---

26. J. Prinsep, "Notes on Lieutenant Burnes' Collection of Ancient Coins," *JASB* (1833), republished in Prinsep, *Essays*, vol. 1, pp. 25–29, with an update by E. Thomas; also, H. H. Wilson and J. Prinsep, "Observations on Lieutenant Burnes's Collection of Bactrian and Other Coins," in Alexander Burnes, *Travels into Bokhara*, vol. 2 (London: John Murray, 1834), esp. p. 460. Burnes's role in spying out Afghanistan for British interests eventually brought him grief as well as glory; he and his brother Charles were hacked to death in Kabul during an uprising in 1841. See Hopkirk, *The Great Game*, pp. 133–152, 239–242.

27. Drawings of this enigmatic coin appeared in the publications listed in n. 26. The coin has since vanished.

28. "Parvulus," "Gold Coin of Another Bactrian Prince," *NC* 2 (1839–40): 202–203.

principal numismatists of Paris have as yet seen this coin, it having been a very recent importation."[29]

This letter prompted a rather indignant response from across the Channel. On behalf of the French, Adrian de Longpérier expressed "mystification" that anyone could imagine so important a coin's having gone unnoticed in Paris.[30] He further explained that the Diodotus stater had been known there for more than a year and was soon to be published by Raoul Rochette. He of course corrected the description of the storklike bird and noted that if a Diodotus coin had been overlooked by experts anywhere it was in England, where the Burnes tetradrachm had yet to be properly recognized (by its thundering Zeus type) as a Diodotid issue.

When Wilson's *Ariana Antiqua* appeared in 1841, the Diodotus stater in France had still not been published; therefore, Wilson gave full details of the specimen by quoting at length a letter from Rochette:[31]

> The gold medal of Diodotus, recently obtained, corresponds entirely in weight, fabrication, and style with the gold coins of Antiochus II. The portrait also bears so close a resemblance to the portraits of Antiochus, that it is likely the artist copied the head of that prince. The obverse is occupied by the head of the king. The reverse has a naked figure of Jupiter erect. . . . The legend on either margin of the reverse is ΒΑΣΙΛΕΩΣ ΔΙΟΔΟΤΟΥ, perfectly distinct. The coin is in excellent preservation. It was procured, along with other coins of less interest, by an Armenian, at the fair of Nishni Novgorod, for a private collector at St. Petersburg; from him it passed into the possession of M. Rollin of Paris, by whom it has been sold to the Royal Cabinet of Paris.

This, then, was the first Bactrian coin actually bearing the long-sought name of Diodotus, proving at last that this king did indeed exist and strike coinage. It had taken more than a century of busy searching to bring Bactria's first dynasty to light. Curiously, the single gold coin that caused so much controversy and correspondence remains elusive to this day. It rests, of course, in the collection trays of the Bibliothèque Nationale (the former Royal Cabinet) in Paris, where it has been since 1840, but the coin that now passes for it is one obtained in 1880 from a Mr. Feuardent. In other words, years of handling has displaced these coins from their proper slots, resulting in a mix-up that has become more or less perma-

---

29. The coin, as described, weighed 138 grains Troy (nearly 9 grams!) and brought the price of £120. "Parvulus" attributed the piece to Diodotus II but without explanation.

30. A. de Longpérier, "Médailles de la Bactriane," *RN* 5 (1840): 83–84.

31. Wilson, *AA*, pp. 218–219. Rochette uses the Roman name (Jupiter) for the Greek god Zeus.

nent through no real fault of the museum curators.[32] This is a recurring problem in numismatic studies, akin to having excavation pottery or dinosaur bones stored away in the wrong boxes.

Though improperly identified, the first known coin in the name of Diodotus can still be tracked from ancient mint to modern market and, finally, a modern museum. Not so the earlier find, in the name of Antiochus, from Burnes's collection. In his discussion of the Paris coin, Wilson noted (with due reference to Longpérier's work) "that we have in this country [England], without knowing it, a coin of the same prince, in a silver tetradrachm, presented by Sir Alexander Burnes to the British Museum."[33] He corrected the views earlier expressed by himself and Prinsep about this coin, arguing instead that although the legend read "King Antiochus" it must have been struck by Diodotus because of the reverse type. This identification proved to be a crucial point regarding the career of Diodotus. As Wilson understood it,

> As long as that prince professed obedience to the Seleucidan king, he struck coins in the name and with the device [coin-type] appropriate to Antiochus; when he declared himself independent, he continued the same coin, but substituted his own name for that of his liege lord. The silver coin [in London] is, therefore, the Bactrian coinage of Diodotus the satrap; the gold [in Paris], the Bactrian coinage of Diodotus the king.

This provided a breakthrough in the search for the history of Diodotid Bactria. It established at least two phases in the coinages of Diodotus—one in his own name and an earlier in the name of Antiochus II. It required the discovery of a link between these phases, the thundering Zeus coin type, to make sense of the evidence. It was merely bad luck that the coin with Diodotus's name had been found and finally published years after the type in Antiochus's name, which therefore could not be imme-

32. In the recent official catalog of the Bactrian coins in the Bibliothèque Nationale, the coin acquired from Rollin ("Rollin 1840" on its identification ticket) is given as series 5A, specimen 11: Bopearachchi, *Monnaies*, p. 149. This coin has changed places with the true Rollin 1840 stater, now identified wrongly as series 5A, specimen 8 (K.2825-1880/Feuardent). Not only does specimen 8 have the closer weight to that of the heavy 1840 piece, as given by "Parvulus," but a drawing of the actual 1840 stater appears in the forgotten work of J. de Bartholomaei, "Notice sur les médailles des Diodotes, rois de la Bactriane," published as an extract of the *Journal de Numismatique et de Science Heraldique* (*Koehnes Zeitschrift*) in 1843, p. 12 and plate 1.b. This drawing clearly matches the coin now labeled K.2825 (note the neck scratches) and *not* Bopearachchi's specimen 11 (note the cut across the portrait of the king). In all fairness, I did not detect this problem myself when I first examined the BN collection in 1984; only further research finally brought to light the strange peregrinations of the first-known Diodotus stater. See appendix A.

33. Wilson, *AA*, p. 219.

diately appreciated as the earliest known example of Diodotid currency. Curiously, this silver coin has also been an elusive quarry. If, as Wilson claimed, Burnes gave this coin to the British Museum, this important artifact cannot today be located there. It may in fact have been auctioned away as a duplicate specimen in the early twentieth century.[34] Such have been the wayward paths of the first Diodotus coins to reach the modern scholarly community.

EXPANDING HORIZONS

In 1843, J. de Bartholomaei published a Diodotus drachm, thus bringing the total of known Diodotid specimens to three in the first full treatment of these kings and their coins.[35] Unfortunately, this numismatist believed (as had Rochette) that King Agathocles was still somehow part of this first Bactrian dynasty, following Syncellus's account in spite of the prescient objections raised by Prinsep, Lassen, Grotefend, and Wilson. Bartholomaei formed his own opinions in light of the first discovery of a commemorative (or pedigree) tetradrachm issued by Agathocles that bore the coin-type of Diodotus and the obverse legend ΔΙΟΔΟΤΟΥ ΣΩΤΗΡΟΣ (Diodotus Soter).[36] This "magnificent medallion" suggested to him that Agathocles was the successor of Diodotus, not his predecessor as Rochette had argued. In other words, Bartholomaei claimed that he had found in Agathocles the Diodotus II mentioned in Justin's text. He further supposed that Pantaleon, another king known only from his coins, was also a son of Diodotus. This theory produced a family tree with Diodotus I and his two sons/successors Agathocles and Pantaleon, both of whom were allegedly deposed by Euthydemus I.

When a similar coin honoring Diodotus Soter was found in the name of King Antimachus, it became necessary to expand the dynastic tree once again.[37] But over the next decades more of these so-called pedigree coins (which later misled Tarn) came to hand and toppled the history reconstructed by Bartholomaei. These coins were issued by Agathocles or Antimachus, and each commemorated an earlier Bactrian king. As the list

34. Personal communication, British Museum.
35. Bartholomaei, "Diodotes." This drachm, like the earlier tetradrachm and stater, has had a troubled history. Its current disposition is unknown, and even its existence has generally been forgotten by numismatic scholars. See appendix A.
36. See Holt, "Pedigree Coins." The ordinary coinage of Agathocles featured his own portrait and the figure of standing Zeus; some of his smaller coins were bilingual and rectangular.
37. Ibid., p. 70.

of honored kings grew, it became less and less possible to maintain the theory that all of these men lived at about the same time and were part of the same nuclear family. It became untenable, too, that Agathocles and Antimachus were "subkings" under the authority of Diodotus, Euthydemus, and Antiochus. The appearance of Alexander the Great among these "pedigree" issues finally made this clear enough.[38] Eventually, this run of monarchs included nearly every known Bactrian ruler of the third and early second centuries B.C., a valuable reference point for numismatists but nevertheless confusing in other respects. In time, this series of coins naturally pushed the kings who struck them—Agathocles and Antimachus, and the ephemeral Pantaleon as well—to the end of the list. This cleared away the misplaced branches of the Diodotid family tree, leaving father and son the only monarchs at the beginning of Bactrian independence from the Seleucid empire, just as the literary sources had indicated.

While the ongoing and confusing discoveries of these "pedigree" coins dominated much of the Bactrian numismatic debate in the second half of the nineteenth century, progress was registered on other fronts. British officers, most notably Hay and Cunningham, continued to collect new specimens in India. Hay's collection entered the British Museum in 1860, and much of Cunningham's followed in 1888. By this time—the sesquicentennial of modern Bactrian studies—the British collection had grown dramatically; it included twenty-seven Diodotid coins (eleven from Cunningham). The French collection held only four Diodotus specimens, the great surge of its Bactrian acquisitions being still to come in the second half of the twentieth century.

Unfortunately, the great demand for these coins encouraged a considerable trade in forgeries. As knowledge of and interest in the Bactrian coinages increased, so did the skill of the modern forgers. Some counterfeiters manufactured cast copies of actual coins, dumping these copies on unsuspecting collectors while selling the originals to connoisseurs. To supply "new" coin-types, forgers sometimes made "mules" by joining the obverse of one ancient type to the reverse of another. Ambitious forgers also prepared their own dies for striking imitations of ancient coins. Depending upon the skill of the engraver, these false coins could either

---

38. Some experts tried, nonetheless, to see all of these kings as contemporaries: Cunningham, *CASE*, pp. 92–93. On the significance of the Alexander coin, see Alfred von Sallet, "Alexander der Grosse als Grunder der baktrish-indischen Reich," *ZfN* 8 (1881): 279–280.

be laughable junk or museum-quality copies. The forgery trays of the major museums of the world now contain a considerable number of these
specimens. No doubt, too, there are still undetected fakes lying among
the genuine coins as well. This problem complicates the work of the numismatist at every turn. In particular, there were many forgeries made
of the gold staters bearing the name of Diodotus, and even a collector
as astute as Cunningham could be deceived into buying them. These brilliant forgeries would later mislead even scholars such as Newell, and no
doubt many of us are victims still.[39]

In the face of these dangers, however, innovative methods were being developed by scholars to improve the quality and reliability of numismatic research. In the latter decades of the nineteenth century, scientific rigor and technical improvements elevated numismatics to new
levels of precision, especially by way of photography, the cataloging of
major collections, metrology, monogram analysis, and die studies. Photography clearly improved the work of scholars who had long struggled
with line drawings that could not convey the necessary detail for study.
The move to publish the coin collections of major museums quickly put
a wealth of this material into the hands of numismatists and historians.
In 1886, for example, Percy Gardner completed the laborious task of
publishing *The Coins of the Greek and Scythic Kings of Bactria and India in the British Museum*.[40] The scientific analysis of the metals used
in ancient coins, although primitive by present standards, allowed numismatists of the nineteenth century to work out questions of manufacture, exchange rates, and weight standards. These investigations
proved especially useful in understanding the relationships of ancient
currencies.

From the earliest study of Bayer onward, special attention was paid
to the monograms that appeared on Bactrian coins. These markings con-
sisted of one or more Greek (or, on later coins, Kharoshthi) letters. On
the analogy of other Greek coinages, these monograms were variously
interpreted as dates, references to mint officials, or indications of the city

39. See above, esp. nn. 8 and 12. On Bactrian forgeries in general, see Lahiri, *Corpus*,
pp. 62–68. Also of special merit are the following studies: Dominique Gerin, "Becker et
les monnaies bactriennes du Cabinet de France," *BSFN* 38 (1983): 305–309, 321–322;
Mariusz Mielczarek, "On the Finding of a Copy of a Bactrian Tetradrachm" (in Polish),
WN 28 (1984): 194–199.
40. P. Gardner, *The Coins of the Greek and Scythic Kings of Bactria and India in the
British Museum* (1886; rpt. Chicago: Argonaut, 1966). This great work preceded the large
acquisition of coins from Cunningham's collection and did not include the Diodotus coins
bearing the name of Antiochus.

where the coin was minted. Cunningham in particular worked diligently at this problem, which is not yet settled today.[41] At the least, however, it was understood that coins could be sorted and grouped in part on the basis of these markings. More important, scholars learned that sequences of coins could be established by matching the dies from which their obverses and reverses had been struck. Ancient coins were generally made by using negative-image dies between which a blank of metal was placed and then hammered; this striking produced a positive-image coin on both faces. These dies were engraved, of course, by hand, and therefore varied slightly, with the result that two well-preserved coins struck from the same die can usually be identified and thereby linked in the manufacturing process. Since obverse dies were often set in an anvil, they tended to wear out less rapidly than the reverse or "punch" die. Thus, mints issued their coins with a steady substitution of new dies in a pattern that might resemble this:

OBV 1——————OBV 2——————OBV 3—
REV A———REV B———REV C———REV D—

By studying die linkage, a numismatist can often arrange coin specimens in the proper order of their actual striking—for example, a coin with OBV 1/REV A, then a coin with OBV 1/REV B, next OBV 2/REV B, then OBV 2/REV C, and so on. Such series provide important chronological clues and help to establish authenticity or forgery by linkage to other examples. These advanced methodologies were first developed in the 1860s and 1870s by numismatists such as Friedrich Imhoof-Blumer and heavily influenced the later work of Newell and others.[42]

Scholars of the twentieth century therefore inherited a rich intellectual legacy from those of the nineteenth. The era of massive collecting was giving way to an age of contemplation and analysis. New types and kings were still being found, but now there was sufficient material to do more than just line up the Bactrian kings in their proper order. Schol-

41. A. Cunningham, "An Attempt to Explain Some of the Monograms Found upon the Grecian Coins of Ariana and India," *NC* 8 (1845–46): 175–197, and his many later articles republished in *CASE*. For more such attempts, see E. Thomas, "Bactrian Coins," *JRAS* 20 (1862–63): 99–134, esp. 131–132 (the "Diodotopolis" monogram comes from an Agathocles coin). On later efforts to deal with the monogram problem, consult Lahiri, *Corpus*, pp. 52–62; Bopearachchi, *Monnaies*, pp. 31–34, along with the review by F. Holt in *AJN* 3/4 (1992): 215–222, esp. 218–219.
42. See Clain-Stefanelli, *Numismatics*, pp. 42–43. In addition, readers may gain an overall appreciation of the long history of numismatic research by consulting Frances Campbell, "Numismatic Bibliography and Libraries," in the *Encyclopedia of Library and Information Science* (New York: Marcel Dekker, 1984), vol. 37, pp. 272–310.

ars became more concerned with finding a full narrative history within
this numismatic evidence. In 1909, H. G. Rawlinson won the Hare University Prize at Cambridge for his essay on Bactria. Later published as
a monograph, this work assembled the written and material evidence
in a broad appreciation of the Greek experience in the East.[43] In rough
fashion, Rawlinson tried to sort out exactly when and where the various kings reigned, which were subordinate to others, and what motivations shaped their actions. He still considered Antimachus an early
rather than later ruler, guessing that he was "a son, or close relation of,
Diodotus II"; otherwise, he offered a reasonable outline of early Bactrian history.[44]

A stronger case was made a few years later by E. J. Rapson and George
MacDonald. Their chapters in the 1922 edition of *The Cambridge History of India* were brilliant in their day.[45] MacDonald knew the numismatic evidence well and interpreted it so boldly that the findings of later
writers can often be traced to his ideas. Regarding the Diodotids, Mac-
Donald presented a thoroughgoing numismatic analysis far beyond that
of Rawlinson and other predecessors. Using an impressive range of research tools, he analyzed monograms, metrology, die axes, iconography,
and find spots.[46] In his view, Diodotus became satrap of Bactria early in
the reign of the Seleucid king Antiochus I (281–261 B.C.). As satrap, he
supervised the minting of Seleucid royal coins that bore monograms ($\triangle$,
$\triangle$, $\oslash$) representing the name Diodotus (ΔΙΟΔΟΤΟΥ). But as the Seleucids busied themselves elsewhere and barbarian aggression threatened the
Oxus Greeks, Bactria slowly evolved into a self-sufficient state under the
strong guidance of Diodotus. Before this process was completed, however, old Diodotus died (probably still a satrap), leaving his son Diodotus
II in charge of affairs. The son gradually introduced to the Seleucid
coinage a new coin-type, the family canting badge of thundering Zeus.
Next came coins of this type still in the name of Antiochus but with the
youthful portrait of Diodotus II. Finally, Diodotus II added his own
name and broke all ties to the Seleucids; he also allied himself with the
Parthians, contrary to the policies of his father. Some "ten or twelve
years" later, it was argued, Diodotus II perished during the coup d'état
of Euthydemus I.

43. H. G. Rawlinson, *Bactria: The History of a Forgotten Empire* (London, 1912; rpt.
New York: AMS Press, 1969).
44. Ibid., p. 62.
45. "Ancient India," in *CHI*, vol. 1.
46. Ibid., pp. 384–419, esp. 390–396.

In this reconstruction, MacDonald carefully analyzed the commemorative coinage of Agathocles and Antimachus and so doing at last put to rest the mistaken notion that either of these monarchs could be a contemporary relative of Diodotus I or II; Agathocles, Antimachus, and Pantaleon were rightly assigned a much later place in the Bactrian king list (ca. 150 B.C.). This left only two members of the Diodotid family: the satrap (Diodotus I) who struck Seleucid coins but none of his own and the king (Diodotus II) who issued all of the known Diodotid coins. In the work of MacDonald we find the historical and numismatic foundation upon which Tarn and Newell built so boldly. [47] For his part, Tarn added to MacDonald's basic narrative of Diodotid history the extraordinary tale of the queens who controlled the fate of the dynasty. This theory of Bactrian family history arose from Tarn's conviction that the commemorative coins of Agathocles and Antimachus traced an actual pedigree between the Seleucid, Diodotid, and Euthydemid dynasties. As we have seen, the only way to make this work was to postulate marriage alliances using otherwise unknown princesses, and Tarn then gave these women the personalities and motivations necessary to flesh out the narrative. Newell, for his part, elaborated upon the monogram analysis done by MacDonald on the Seleucid and Diodotid coinages of Bactria. To this work he added his discoveries of die linkage between the staters of Antiochus II and those of Diodotus. As we have seen, this meant for Newell that Diodotus I (and not just Diodotus II) struck royal coinage in his own name but otherwise confirmed the narrative reconstruction of a gradual Bactrian secession.

DIVISION IN THE RANKS

Two hundred years after Bayer first published and commented upon a (bogus) Diodotus coin, substantial progress in Bactrian studies had been registered. It took a century merely to confirm the existence of the Diodotids in the numismatic record, but then new finds quickly accumulated during the course of the nineteenth century. These coins answered some questions and raised others as part of the normal process of discovery. As numismatics matured into a more scientific discipline, it became possible to sort out the Bactrian coinages with greater preci-

---

47. Tarn's earlier work on Bactria was conceptual in nature and barely touched upon the Diodotids; it served instead as the framework for the nonnarrative pt. 1 of his *GBI*: see Tarn, "Notes on Hellenism in Bactria and India," *JHS* 22 (1902): 268–293.

sion. Large collections were cataloged, and ancient kings found their proper places in the relative chronology of Bactria. Our knowledge of ancient Central Asia was progressing rapidly.

But the increasing sophistication of numismatic research and the growing body of material on which to apply these new techniques inevitably drove a wedge between those trained to study texts and those trained to study coins. In the eighteenth and nineteenth centuries it was possible for individual scholars and even keen amateur collectors to master the evidence and make important contributions to knowledge, but by the twentieth century specialization had begun to take hold in most research disciplines. Scholars required so much training in one discipline that they had to rely on the conclusions of other experts without themselves knowing all the evidence firsthand. The historian Tarn, for example, called numismatics "one of the wonders of scholarship" but argued that "the numismatist as such has sometimes been unable to place or explain the facts which he has elicited; naturally so, for he is not expected to be a Hellenistic historian."[48] Clearly, he accepted a division in the ranks of Bactrian studies that put specialists out of touch with the raw evidence of other fields. He demonstrated in his own history some of the dangers inherent in this state of affairs, for his complaint about the numismatist could be turned upon the historian. After all, Tarn knew the texts of the Hellenistic Age but not its coinage and so tended to "explain" far more than the numismatic evidence ever suggested. No one could expect him to be a numismatist, he assumed, and therefore, like other historians, he piled upon the numismatists' cautious and complex work a narrative structure that it simply could not bear.[49]

Since the days of Tarn and Newell, books and articles about Bactria have generally been written by one kind of specialist or another. In the many publications of Narain we find the most widely read and appreciated interpretation of Bactria and, in particular, India since Tarn's generation. Narain's forte has always been the analysis of coins, and he has recently insisted upon his own background in numismatics and archaeology, quite apart from the training and methodology of Tarn and other subjective historians.[50] On their side of the professional fence, Hellenis-

48. *GBI,* p. viii.

49. As in the recent case of Hellenistic hoard statistics discussed above (chap. 2).

50. Consult Narain, *IG,* esp. pp. 1–19, "The Greeks of Bactria and India," in *CAH*[2] 7, pp. 388–421, incorporating some new theories based on fresh archaeological discoveries, and his spirited defense of his earlier works in "Approaches and Perspectives," *Yavanika* 2 (1992): 5–34.

tic historians continue to work in a world of segregated evidence. As just one example, consider again the great debate among historians about the rebellion of Diodotus from the Seleucid empire (chap. 3). The second edition of *The Cambridge Ancient History* (1984) devoted a special appendix to this problem that helped to polarize modern opinion around two possible reconstructions: a revolt by Diodotus I against Antiochus II (the "high" chronology) or a secession during the Seleucid War of the Brothers (the "low" chronology).[51] Historians have brought to bear on this important debate a number of mostly obscure ancient texts that in some small way or another may touch upon the problem, but not one Hellenistic historian has here referred to the considerable numismatic evidence that underlies this debate.

Since the days of Bayer there have been two kinds of evidence for the history of Bactria: a few written texts and the material clues provided by numismatic and archaeological discovery. Although the prospects for discovery have been realized far beyond Bayer's expectations, the essential dialogue between the two communities of specialists involved has all but ceased. The result has inevitably been stagnation for two generations and a sterility of argument that frustrates rather than fertilizes the various fields of inquiry. On their side, historians have virtually given up on the Diodotid problem. In 1978 Claire Préaux, wondering which Diodotus minted which coins and whether both issued royal currency, lamented that "la numismatique ne répond pas à nos questions."[52] Indeed, many numismatists had also abandoned the chase. Fewer and fewer were trying to sort out the Diodotus issues, to map out the progression of monograms, or to establish a series of telling die links. The best researchers bypassed these problems. Now, in the latest published Bactrian catalogs, scholars no longer even try to sort out the coinages of Diodotus I and II.[53] The verdict on this enduring problem offers us little hope: two of the finest Hellenistic historians of this generation have now declared the whole matter "a mess hardly capable of being unrav-

---

51. See chap. 3, n. 37.

52. C. Préaux, *Le monde hellénistique* (Paris: Presses Universitaires de France, 1978), vol. 1, p. 107. For the prolific Polish scholar Josef Wolski, too, the verdict seems final: "Il est superflu de poser la question de l'origine de Diodote, nous n'en savons rien." See Wolski, "Le problème de la fondation de l'état gréco-bactrien," *Iranica Antiqua* 17 (1982): 138. In an earlier study he remarked, "As to the numismatic evidence, it is of no value for establishing the exact chronology, although it may contain many surprises for the future." See "The Decay of the Iranian Empire of the Seleucids and the Chronology of the Parthian Beginnings," *Berytus* 12 (1956–57): 36–37.

53. For example, Bopearachchi, *Monnaies*, pp. 41–45, 147–153.

eled," and a leading numismatist has just confessed that "we still have no reliable solution to this problem."[54]

False coins, hopes, and histories have taken their toll. Two hundred years after Bayer's inauspicious beginning, we thought that we knew everything about the Diodotids of Bactria. From their wars to their wives, the Diodotids seemed fully in focus in the pages of Tarn and Newell. Today we complain that we, historians and numismatists alike, can know nothing.[55] Both texts and coins are deemed a hopeless tangle. But perhaps we have forgotten the Bactrian paradigm for Hellenistic history—that in the days of Rochette and Prinsep the absence of the right information seemed to doom the whole search for the elusive Diodotid dynasty when in fact the evidence was already in hand. So, too, scholars today stand on the threshold of discovery in needless despair; we have stumbled past the very clues we most want to find.

54. Historians: Sherwin-White and Kuhrt, *Samarkhand to Sardis,* p. 107; numismatist: N. Smirnova, "Bactrian Coins in the Pushkin State Museum of Fine Arts," *Ancient Civilizations* 2 (1995): 337, and "On Finds of Hellenistic Coins in Turkmenistan," *Ancient Civilizations* 3 (1996): 265 n. 27.

55. A particularly severe judgment emerges from the interesting and insightful critique of Bactrian studies by Olivier Guillaume, *L'analyse de raisonnements en archéologie: Le cas de la numismatique gréco-bactrienne et indo-grecque* (Paris: Editions Recherches et Civilisations, 1987), now available in an English translation by O. Bopearachchi (Oxford, 1990). Guillaume uses recent (logicist) archaeological theory to test the assumptions that underlie the work of numismatists, on the one hand, and historians, on the other. He critiques first the cataloging of the Bactrian coins by numismatists and then their use as evidence by historians. Many valid points are raised, exposing methodological flaws and the danger of specialists' not understanding the evidence used by others. In the end, however, Guillaume's work condemns itself because it, too, begins with a weak sample of catalogs and histories and fails to examine the intermediate steps that link historical constructions to cataloging procedures. The complaint that historians and numismatists assume connections in their evidence without proof is valid, but so would be the criticism that Guillaume postulates without proof a direct connection between one set of catalogs and another set of histories. After all, two of the major catalogs examined in Guillaume's sample appeared *after* the two histories (Tarn and Narain) that he argues were influenced by them.

CHAPTER 5

Thundering Zeus

SEVEN POUNDS OF THE PAST

Ancient coins salvaged from the soil of Central Asia have been gathered in sufficient numbers to help answer many of our hardest questions about Diodotid Bactria: When and how did Diodotus I rise to power? Did he indeed declare himself a king? What role did his son play in the development of an independent state? How many mints did these men operate? What steps did they take to further the monetization of Central Asia? Why did they choose certain types and symbols for their gold, silver, and bronze coinages? How long did each hold power?

Much has, however, been lost. Of the many tons of precious metal that the Diodotids put into circulation in Central Asia, only seven pounds remain.[1] The rest lies hidden still or, more likely, transformed in the melting pots of later civilizations.[2] Precious metals find new uses with each

---

1. There is a vast literature on ancient coin production, including the following works: Tony Hackens, "L'apport de la numismatique à l'histoire économique," pp. 151–169 in T. Hackens and Patrick Marchetti, eds. *Histoire économique de l'Antiquité* (Louvain-la-neuve: Séminaire de Numismatique Marcel Hoc, 1978); D. M. Metcalf, "What Has Been Achieved Through the Application of Statistics to Numismatics?" *PACT* 5 (1979): 3–24; François de Callatay, "Les trésors achéménides et les monnayages d'Alexandre: Espèces immobilisées et espèces circulantes?" *REA* 91 (1989): 259–274; J. W. Muller, "Estimation du nombre originel de coins," *PACT* 5 (1981): 157–172; and W. E. McGovern, "Missing Die Probabilities, Expected Die Production, and the Index Figure," *ANSMN* 25 (1980): 202–223.

2. For examples of this phenomenon, see Dio Cass. 68.15.3; Suetonius *Augustus* 41; and the Hellenistic case of Alexander's gold coffin, probably made in part from old coinage and later melted down into coin again, as related by Strabo 17.1.8.

new age: many ancient coins have doubtless been dispersed into modern electronics, jewelry, and teeth. Bronze and copper coins tend to be small, earth-colored, and often not worth the trouble to look for when dropped or scattered. More than shiny coins made of precious metals they tend to pass from the domain of man to nature, and there they often become unidentifiable blobs.[3] As with our other sources, coins must endure the filters of man and nature—the base metals vulnerable to natural corrosion and concealment, the precious metals to human need and greed.

Thus, from an original output surely in the millions, we must count ourselves fortunate to find the few hundred coins surviving today with the thundering Zeus type of Diodotus I and II. Just 150 years ago only three Diodotid coins, with a total weight of but a single ounce, were known. Today there are some twelve ounces available for study in London, nearly eight in New York, seven in Paris, four in St. Petersburg, four in Berlin, three in Oxford, at least two in war-ravaged Tadjikistan, one in Washington, D.C., and another in Lahore.[4] Scattered among the world's great numismatic collections are these fractions of the full harvest, costly to track down and study but at least safely gathered for the future.[5]

Many of the most important Bactrian coins are not yet available for study in a public museum (see appendix A). It is therefore imperative that numismatic studies not be limited to museum collections alone. A vast amount of numismatic material now in private hands can be accessed through auction catalogs or the kindness of individual dealers/collectors, who tend to be as eager as academics to share information and to expand our knowledge. The American Numismatic Society in New York maintains an exemplary record of coins passing in trade, including the Bactrian material, although this endeavor seems impossible to keep up-to-date. Unlimited time and travel funds would not allow the most de-

---

3. Among the stray finds at Ai Khanoum were 224 coins (plus 10 unstruck flans), of which nearly all were bronze and 50 were unidentifiable: Bernard, *AK* 4, p. 5. None of the hoards at Ai Khanoum (or elsewhere in the Oxus Valley) contained bronze coins. For general background, see P. J. Casey, *Understanding Ancient Coins* (Norman and London: University of Oklahoma Press, 1986); and P. J. Casey and Richard Reece, eds., *Coins and the Archaeologist,* 2d ed. (London: Seaby, 1988).

4. The Diodotid holdings of these collections are among those cataloged in appendix A, with the bronzes in appendix B.

5. There are, sadly, some major exceptions. The extraordinary Afghan national collection in Kabul has recently been looted. On this disaster, see Nancy Dupree, "Museum Under Siege," *Archaeology* 49 (March/April 1996): 42–51; John Burns, "In Kabul's Museum, the Past Finds Its Ruin in the Present," *New York Times* (November 30, 1996).

termined researcher to gather every piece of numismatic evidence. Part of the puzzle will always be missing.

The seven pounds of coins examined in this study are vitally important to Hellenistic history. In the past, this Diodotid silver and gold coinage presented a complex and seemingly contradictory pattern of key features that long beguiled historians and numismatists alike. We find on these precious metals a single reverse type (thundering Zeus) but two names (Antiochus and Diodotus), as many as three different portrait styles, four denominations (stater, tetradrachm, drachm, and hemidrachm), dozens of mint marks, and often a wreath symbol. Then, of course, we face the various bronze issues with different types altogether. Historians such as Tarn chose to ignore the implications of this numismatic complexity in order to fit everything into an imaginative narrative tale that stressed personality and politics. More recently, historians have either avoided the numismatic evidence entirely or assumed that it must fall somehow into a simple linear pattern that connects the reigns of all the principal players (Antiochus I, Antiochus II, Diodotus I, Diodotus II, and then Euthydemus I) as so many beads on a string. But while the historians' approach was clearly naive, the numismatists were themselves hard-pressed to offer a solution that made sense of all the coins.[6] As a result, each of the following possibilities has been argued in print:

1. Diodotus I struck the coinage in the name of Antiochus, and his son minted the Diodotus coinage.

2. Diodotus I struck all of the Antiochus coinage and some of the Diodotus coinage and his son issued the rest.

3. Diodotus II struck *all* of the Diodotid coinage.

4. Both father and son struck coins under the names Antiochus and Diodotus.[7]

Each of these solutions to the Diodotid puzzle was formulated by a historian or numismatist using an inadequate sample of the available

6. See, e.g., A. N. Lahiri, "The Diodotus Coins," *IHQ* 33 (1957): 222–228. Published in the year of Tarn's death and critical of Narain's treatment of the Diodotid coins, this article surveys the general enigma of the coins. For other discussions, consult *BMC, Bactria*, pp. xx–xxi; *TQ*, pp. 73–75; and J. Wolski, "L'éffondrement de la domination des Séleucides en Iran au IIIᵉ siècle av. J.-C.," *Bulletin Internationale de l'Académie Polonaise des Sciences et Lettres* 5 (1947): 64.

7. Representative proponents of each of the four views include (1) Lahiri, *Corpus*, pp. 110–111; *BMC, Bactria*, p. xxi (with some allowances for scenario 2); (2) *ESM*, pp. 248–249 (with some allowances for scenario 1), followed by *GBI*, p. 323; (3) MacDonald, *CHI*,

evidence, and each of them is wrong. To find the truth, the bulk of the material amassed over the past centuries must be placed upon the scales. Historians and numismatists must try to examine every available coin, seeking connections between individual specimens, identifying related series of coins, organizing these into larger groups, and then straining to see the whole. In this manner, each nexus allows the expert to build toward a complete skeleton of the Diodotid mintage, much as a paleontologist reconstructs from fragments of bone the lost body of a dinosaur.

The analogy of bone to coin is a useful one, because the methodologies of these two specialized fields are similar. A bone here or there can tell the paleontologist important things, but real answers rest upon assemblages of interconnected bone. We see ancient creatures "come alive" in the ways in which their bones fit together and articulate an animal that no longer exists in any other form. Rarely does the expert find such a skeleton intact; the pieces must be brought together from various places, and often a missing section here or there can never be recovered. To assemble as much evidence as possible for making educated inferences, the expert travels to different sites and museums around the world. Collecting by other experts or by amateurs assembles the body of material evidence from which all progress must grow. It is no simple hobby, and even the lively commercial trade in fossils (or coins) does not negate the serious scientific nature of the overall endeavor. The paleontologist squinting at a tray of bones or plaster casts of bones addresses the same kinds of problems that perplex the numismatist who examines coins and casts of coins. As parts of the whole, how do these pieces fit together, and what does this tell us about the past?

For the Diodotid numismatic "dinosaur," the principles of taxonomy guide us in sorting the pieces and shaping a final picture. Seven pounds of the past, painstakingly gathered and scientifically arranged, will indicate the general pattern of a numismatic history that once weighed in the neighborhood of the fleshed-out dinosaurs themselves. For example, the gold and silver coins all bear the same coin-types: the ruler on the obverse and thundering Zeus on the reverse (see plates 7–16). The bronze coinage in the name of Diodotus (see plates 18–20) has different types: a male deity (Zeus or Hermes) on the obverse and a female deity (Artemis

---

p. 393; (4) Narain, *IG*, p. 17, and Mitchiner, *IGISC*, vol. 1, p. 36. Some scholars, such as Wolski, "L'éffondrement de la domination des Séleucides," have toyed with a fifth possibility: that all of the coins of Diodotus II were recalled and restruck, with the result that we now have only the mintages of Diodotus I. This is extremely unlikely, to say the least.

hunting or Athena armored) on the reverse. Smaller bronze units (see plates 21 and 22) give abbreviated types (the eagle of Zeus and the quiver of Artemis), the familiar attributes of these deities standing in for the Olympians themselves. But while these features define the Diodotid issues in general, there is also much variation involving technical elements (e.g., weights, die axes) and artistic elements (e.g., engraving and lettering style). As noted above, the inscriptions and monograms also distinguish parts of the coinage. Like a paleontologist separating vertebrae from limb bones, the numismatist must sort the coins into distinctive subgroups based upon the slightest of shared characteristics.

For the silver and gold coinage, this taxonomic process (appendix A) yields six clear strands that may be thought of as so many sections of a skeletal structure.[8] Half of these (series A, C, E) were issued in the name of Antiochus and the other half (series B, D, F) in that of Diodotus. Two of them (series A and B) show an older portrait, the latter idealized, and the other four a younger one. Half of them (series A, C, D) were struck with the reverse inscription carefully aligned under Zeus's arm; on the others it is outside his arm. All except one (series E) include at least one gold issue, and all have a wreath symbol at some point in their evolution, with the wreath symbol on all of the gold.

No simple linear arrangement of these series makes sense. For example, putting them together (A–F) as the progressive issues of one mint seems to put the portraiture in proper order but makes a mishmash of the legends, legend alignment, and symbols. We would have a coinage first in the name of Antiochus, then Diodotus, then Antiochus again, and finally Diodotus. If they are arranged according to name, then the portraiture wanders back and forth between youthful and elderly. If, instead, we posit a parallel arrangement representing the output of two mints, it is possible to connect these series so that matching characteristics all fit together in time and place (see fig. 4). Each mint has two lines of production showing the old and young portraits of, presumably, Diodotus I and II, respectively. Series E and F, for example, connect beautifully: the same portraiture follows from one to the other; both have the same legend alignment *outside* the arm of Zeus; both have fluctuating die axes; and the control mark progression on series E carries over to series

---

8. Following the conventions of numismatics, I shall designate each of these six strands as a *series* (identified here by letters). The constituent parts of a series I shall call *groups* (marked here by numbers). Each group represents a step in the development of a series (e.g., A1 through A8 or B1 through B3).

FIGURE 4:   OVERVIEW OF SILVER AND GOLD
DIODOTID MINTAGE

"Antiochus"

MINT A: 𝌆   MINT B: 𝌆

Old	Young	Old	Young
A1 (none)			
A2 (◎)			
A3 (⌂)			
A4 (E)			
A5 (Σ)			
A6 (⋏)	C1a (⋏)		
	C1 (⋏⊖)		E1 (ᛘbarᚺ)
			E2 (ᛘ⌐ ⚔)*
			E3 (⌐⚔)*
			E4 (⌐ I ⋀⚔)
A7 (Ͷ)	C2 (Ͷ)		E5 (Ͷ⚔)*
			E6 (Ҡ ⚔)
A8 ○	C3 ○		E7 ○ (⊤⋀⚔)
			E8 ○ (⊤ ⊣ᛘᛘ)*
			E9 ○ (⌐ ᛘᛘ⌐)*

- -

"Diodotus"

	D1 ○ (P)		F1 ○ (⌐ ᛘᛘ⌐)
	D2 ○ (P)		F2 ○ (⌐ ᛘᛘ)*
	D3 ○ (Σ)		F3 ○ (ᛘᛘ)*
	D4 ○ (Ͷ)		F4 ○ (ᛘᛘ ᚺ)
	D5 ○ (A)		F5 ○ (ᛘᛘ M ᚺ)*
	D6 ○ (B)		
	D7 ○	B1 ○ *	F6 ○ *
	D8 (ᛘ)	B2 (none)	F7 (ᛘ)
		B3 (◡)	F8 (ᛝ⊥)

* Variable die axis.

F. All evidence points to a linkage between them, showing the evolution
from the younger Diodotus's coinage in the name of Antiochus to his
coinage in the name of Diodotus. To clinch the case, there is die linkage
(on drachms and tetradrachms as well) between E9 and the earliest
groups of series F.[9] Thus, series E and F form a continuous output from
a particular Bactrian mint. The wreath symbol was added prior to the
change of name, and it stayed on the coinage through a substantial gold
mintage (F6) and then was dropped.

Precisely the same, simultaneous pattern may be found on series C and

9. The same obverse die was used to strike series E, group 9 (examples 2 and 3), series F, group 1 (examples 1 and 2), and series F, group 2 (example 1); also, on the
tetradrachms, series E, group 9 (example 1) and series F, group 3.

D. These are the products of a different mint, where the engravers aligned the reverse legend below the arm of Zeus and maintained a constant 6:00 ($\downarrow$) die axis. Struck in parallel sequence with series E and F, the coins of series C and D show the same portraiture, the same introduction of the wreath before the change of name, the same abandonment of the wreath after a huge gold mintage, and even a common control mark ($\bigwedge$) near their end. What is more, the obvious connection between series C and D may be confirmed through die linkage. The tetradrachm of D1 is said to share an obverse die with the "first row, middle specimen," of Mitchiner's type 67; this is C3, example 9 (BM 1888-12-8-50), which is itself die-linked to example 8 (AK Exc Hoard, coin 9).[10] Die identity with this last coin, unearthed in controlled excavations, insures the authenticity of all these linked specimens. We have therefore established that series C and D run parallel with series E and F, each independently but simultaneously progressing from a coinage in the name of Antiochus to a coinage in the name of Diodotus. Moreover, the absence of die linkage between series C and E or series D and F confirms the existence of two separate mints.

Series A and B bear an older portrait. Series A has the legend alignment and consistent die axis associated with the mint of the younger man's series C and D, while series B has the alignment and variable die axis consistent with the mint of the younger's series E and F. There is good reason, in fact, to connect these series in just this way. After all, A6–8 have a close parallel in C1–3. A similar but less compelling connection exists between B1 and F6.

This arrangement of the six identifiable series of thundering Zeus coins follows demonstrable lines of time and place. The elder portrait at first precedes the younger, the Antiochus issues precede the Diodotus, the control marks fall into clear progressions, the coins attributable to the different mints are consistently parallel but not cross-linked, the wreath coinages fit into a single unbroken period, and the necessary transition from Antiochus to Diodotus can be verified at both predicted points. Thus do seven pounds of the past yield a unified and rational skeleton of the original Diodotid mintage.[11]

10. See the description in NFA (1987) no. 494.

11. Note should be taken of an important article published in a new Japanese journal that appeared after the acceptance of this manuscript for publication: Sergei Kovalenko, "The Coinage of Diodotus I and Diodotus II, Greek Kings of Bactria," *Silk Road Art and Archaeology* 4 (1995–96): 17–74. Analyzing a slightly smaller sample of Diodotid coins, Kovalenko has produced an interesting reconstruction that I nevertheless cannot accept in many particulars. Many of the die links identified are questionable if not demonstrably

So far, the original number of coins struck in each series and group cannot easily be estimated, nor can we safely identify a specific time period for the minting of each group. Although our sample seems reliable enough, especially given the great number of collections that have been consulted, many unknown factors influenced the production rates of ancient coins. The dies, prepared by hand, were necessarily hard and brittle alloys of bronze or steel; their useful life spans varied. Some were used even though cracked or worn while others were soon abandoned with little wear.[12] In spite of these problems, various statistical methods have been developed to estimate the size of a given ancient mintage, generally positing an output of from ten thousand to thirty thousand coins per obverse die.[13] For series A this would yield an estimate of from .80 to 2.4 million tetradrachms (represented today by some eighty coins), over half of which come from group 6 of this series. Does this mean that group 6 was produced for a very long time (equal to all the other groups of series A combined) or that it represents a phenomenal rush of coins in a short period? The condition of the coins themselves suggests that the former hypothesis is more likely than the latter. Assigning each group a fixed span of time, say, a year, will not work overall. Series E, for instance, seems to average three groups for every one of series A and C over the same general period of time. Some groups probably stretched over more years than others, giving us a rough notion of chronology but no absolute dates. In conjunction with the other sources, however, a theoretical overview is possible.

THE ELDER DIODOTUS

What, then, does this new analysis of the numismatic evidence tell us about the men behind the money? Diodotus I was surely responsible for

---

wrong: e.g., p. 34 (the drachms) and the forty-five tetradrachms on pp. 20–23 allegedly struck from only six obverse dies. He has tried in vain (pp. 25–26 and 36–37) to rehabilitate some of the forgeries condemned by Jenkins. His readers should be wary of numerous misprints ("Whaler" for Wahler throughout, "Mogdahan" for Moghadam, etc.). His own arrangement of issues leaves him at a loss to explain the simultaneously young and old portraits, the occasional disappearance of the wreath at his "wreath mint," the portraiture on the "pedigree" coins, and so forth. These knotty difficulties have been resolved in my own reconstruction of the coinage, outlined here and in appendix A. Kovalenko is nonetheless to be commended for his research, the most comprehensive to appear so far in the article literature.

12. Warren Esty and Giles Carter, "The Distribution of the Number of Coins Struck by Dies," *AJN* 3/4 (1991–92): 165–186.

13. D. G. Sellwood, "Some Experiments in Greek Minting Technique," *NC* 3 (1963): 217–231; O. Mørkholm, "The Life of Obverse Dies in the Hellenistic Period," pp. 11–21

minting series A. These coins must have been struck over many years, indeed for the bulk of his career as an emerging Hellenistic dynast. His portrait slowly ages during these years, with occasional plumping. He long used a single mint that produced fine tetradrachms with a consistent die axis and careful alignment of the reverse legend under the arm of Zeus. There is, of course, no swift introduction, as once supposed, of successive Diodotid features (type, portrait, then name) onto the standard Seleucid coinage of Bactria. That fairly rapid sequence, seen only in the forgeries of Diodotid coins, must be abandoned here and removed from Bactrian history. Diodotus the satrap, in one step, put a special portrait and type on the coinage he struck in the name of his sovereign, Antiochus II. He then issued that coinage, almost entirely in silver tetradrachms, for a very long time. Only at the end of that huge mintage, perhaps after a decade or more, did he issue a little gold (group 8). In fact, given the great amount of thundering Zeus Antiochus coinage, it is difficult to understand how anyone could imagine a rapid, die-linked evolution to coins in the name of Diodotus.

Obviously, Diodotus the satrap began his career as the agent of the Seleucid king, and from that context arose his earliest mint activities. We have seen that Antiochus I Soter struck a full range of coinage in Bactria that included gold (staters), silver (tetradrachms, drachms, hemidrachms), and bronze. The Bactrian output of the succeeding king, Antiochus II Theos (261–246 B.C.), was much reduced: some gold staters and a very few silver drachms and hemidrachms but one tetradrachm and little bronze.[14] There is no evidence of any later Seleucid mintage from Bactria, and therefore a profound change clearly occurred at or before the end of Antiochus II's reign. At Ai Khanoum this same phenomenon can be traced in the stray finds. Representing Antiochus I alone there were sixty-two coins, while for Antiochus II there were only two. This was followed by twenty-six stray finds of Diodotid coinage and forty-nine for Euthydemus I.[15] There is no material or literary evidence to suggest a gap in the production of Bactrian coinage due to civil strife or economic collapse. We must assume that the limited mintage of Antiochus II leads directly into the long mintage of Diodotus's series A tetradrachms.

in C. N. L. Brooke et al., eds., *Studies in Numismatic Method Presented to Philip Grierson* (Cambridge: Cambridge University Press, 1983).

14. See chap. 3 on the pre-Seleucid and early Seleucid coinages of Central Asia. For Antiochus II, consult *ESM*, pp. 243–245, and Houghton, *Coins of the Seleucid Empire*, p. 119. See also Brian Kritt, *Seleucid Coins of Bactria* (Lancaster: CNG, 1996).

15. Bernard, *AK* 4, pp. 6–8, 41–54, 154.

During the reign of Antiochus II, then, his satrap Diodotus altered the
Seleucid coinage being struck in Bactria. He introduced a new portrait that
may have been his own, wearing a royal diadem. At the same time, he replaced the standard Seleucid type of seated Apollo, choosing instead the
vigorous thundering Zeus. And yet this was still the coinage of King Antiochus, as the inscription clearly proclaimed. What did this new coinage
signify? The boldest possible change (the diademed portrait) is the most
difficult aspect for us to judge today, because we have no independent portraiture of Diodotus with which to compare it. The face does not seem to
be that of Antiochus, and so we may suppose that it is Diodotus's own.
Unfortunately, we cannot know what Bactrians of the third century B.C.
saw in this portrait—whether a daring declaration of independence by
their satrap or an ambiguous rendering of a distant sovereign. The type,
too, has several connotations. Zeus provided an obvious reference to the
name "Diodotus," and for this reason the new type has often been called
the canting badge of the Diodotid dynasty. There are, however, some connections to the Seleucids as well. Seleucus (I) Zeus Nikator put the
bearded portrait of Zeus on many of his coins; it is the very image found
on the Diodotid bronze coinage struck (probably) at Ai Khanoum.[16] If
one wished one could probably see this coinage as safely Seleucid.[17]

Yet there is no question that Diodotus I was behind this new mintage
and that the changes could also be interpreted as exaltations of his local
status.[18] But why? Other satraps had been known to take such numismatic liberties under the Achaemenids, Alexander, and even the Seleucids. Already in Bactria there had been local emissions of coins, including the famous case of Sophytes.[19] The Parthian coinage in the name of
an Andragoras discussed above may have been issued contemporaneously
with Diodotus's series A tetradrachms.[20]

16. *ESM,* p. 38, on the choice of Zeus by Seleucus I. Note the cult title "Seleucus (I)
Zeus Nikator" in *OGIS* 245. For the bronze Diodotid coinage, see chap. 6.

17. Similarly, the head on Alexander the Great's silver coins could be that of Herakles
or Alexander himself. Likewise, his reverse type can be seen as either a Greek Zeus or a
Near Eastern Ba'al: chap. 1, n. 6; A. R. Bellinger, *Essays on the Coinage of Alexander the
Great* (New York, 1963; rpt. New York: Durst, 1979), pp. 14–24. Scholars are still arguing about this portraiture and iconography.

18. The obvious linkage of this currency to that of a younger Diodotus who minted
in his own name makes it clear that his predecessor, the satrap Diodotus, initiated this new
coinage and that the type was deemed appropriate for the fully independent king.

19. Holt, *Alexander and Bactria,* pp. 96–98; O. Mørkholm, *Early Hellenistic Coinage
from the Accession of Alexander to the Peace of Apamea (336–188 B.C.)* (Cambridge: Cambridge University Press, 1991), p. 73.

20. See chap. 3, n. 39.

In this context, the early coinage associated with Diodotus I may not be so revolutionary at all. The type and portrait may beg the question of his growing independence, but this could surely be considered a Seleucid coinage in the name of King Antiochus. Unlike Sophytes and Andragoras, Diodotus was not placing his own name on the coins. This was significant enough that the Bactrian king Agathocles later distinguished this Antiochus/thundering Zeus coinage from that of Diodotus (I) Soter and Diodotus (II) Theos.[21] Whatever the portrait and type signified, the name itself made these issues of series A as much Seleucid as Diodotid in the eyes of *later* Bactrians.

The inauguration of the thundering Zeus coinage (A1) may be provisionally dated between 255 and 250 B.C., replacing the Seleucid Apollo type early in the reign of Antiochus II. This accords well with the general time frame given by the various literary sources for the emerging independence of the eastern Seleucid satraps. This state of affairs changed little until the opening of a second mint and the striking of new coins marking the viceroyalty of his son Diodotus II (at A6, C1, E1). Some of these coins bear the younger portrait and introduce smaller denominations. Tentatively, we may associate this dynastic step with the political situation of ca. 246 B.C., namely, the troubled accession of Seleucus II and the invasion by Ptolemy III of Egypt. Still, there was no absolute break with the Seleucids—only the hedging of bets given the drift of events in East and West.

The smooth evolution of this Bactrian coinage (delineated fully in appendix A) leads to some rather interesting innovations near the end of series A. The clearly aging Diodotus added a conspicuous victory wreath or crown in group 8, which saw as well the first striking of gold after years of silver tetradrachms. This wreath has heretofore been treated by experts simply as an occasional control mark on the Diodotid coinage, even though it is obviously not a monogram of the usual type employed

21. These commemorative issues of Agathocles (and, to a lesser extent, Antimachus) have been discussed above (chap. 4) and are considered in further detail later in this chapter. These special coins seem to inaugurate a ruler cult in Bactria that stressed first Antiochus Nikator and Diodotus Soter, then Euthydemus I Theos and most of the other Bactrian kings (including Alexander the Great). We might prefer, of course, that the honored Antiochus be Seleucus's son rather than the less prominent Antiochus II, but there are many nuances that surely escape us in the elaboration of this new practice (including the epithet given to this Antiochus). Against the complaint that Agathocles should have commemorated the Apollo type of Antiochus II is this fact: Agathocles modeled this special series of coins upon the *tetradrachms* of the honored kings, and the Bactrian tetradrachms of Antiochus II overwhelmingly bear the thundering Zeus type issued by Diodotus.

by these rulers. It is, of course, a potent symbol in its own right. On later Bactrian coinages, for example, we find Herakles crowning himself (reign of Demetrius I) and, thus crowned, later crowning a subsequent ruler's name (reign of Euthydemus II).[22] Clearly, then, the wreath on later Bactrian coins did have special meaning, as it had earlier for Seleucus I.[23] The significance of the wreath as a Diodotid symbol and not merely a mint mark can be confirmed by examining the later commemorative coins of Agathocles and Antimachus. As noted above, these kings issued special series of tetradrachms that imitated the types of their royal forebears. These coins faithfully copied all of the details of the original designs *except the monograms*. Yet, the three commemorated thundering Zeus types of the series all have the wreath. It is apparent from this that the wreath was an integral part of the original types and not simply a control mark.[24]

The recent discovery of a new prototype for the commemorative series makes this point even stronger.[25] King Agathocles introduced these posthumous imitations of the earlier Bactrian coinages by striking a Diodotus Soter and Antiochus Nikator commemorative prototype, both with Agathocles's own characteristic control mark (⚶). The Diodotus Soter commemorative prototype imitates B1, while the newly found Antiochus Nikator commemorative prototype imitates Diodotus's A7. This commemorative prototype, however, naturally replaces the N monogram of the original with the ⚶ control mark of Agathocles's own mint. Yet, when Agathocles later established the true commemorative series (which, unlike the prototypes, clarified the issuing authority with a genitive absolute), Agathocles chose to imitate A8—the last issue of Diodotus in Antiochus's name. This issue, of course, bears the wreath. Here, too, then, the wreath is an essential element of the design, with Agathocles's own monograms (⚶ and later ⊞) moved out of the way to the right field. The appearance of the wreath on all of the coins of the fully elaborated commemorative series proves that it was not a mint mark. No other commemorative types depict the control marks of the originals, and one should wonder in any case why later kings would bother adding such

22. See, e.g., Lahiri, *Corpus*, p. 31.
23. *ESM*, pp. 108–111.
24. Kovalenko considers the wreath a mint mark that inexplicably comes and goes on the coinage of his second Diodotid mint: "The Coinage of Diodotus I and Diodotus II," pp. 28, 43, 45. He furthermore does not explain its presence on the commemorative coins of Agathocles and Antimachus.
25. In the private collection of Riaz Babar. See O. Bopearachchi, "L'indépendance de la Bactriane," *Topoi* 4 (1994): 513–519, esp. 516–517.

defunct symbols to the commemorative series. The wreath obviously meant something more to them.

To appreciate the meaning of this wreath, we must note that it was introduced simultaneously on all of the Diodotid coinages, father's and son's at both mints, and that it appears on the very first issues of gold. These are the patent numismatic signs of some great military victory. We may never be sure of the circumstances, since the coinage carries no Roman-style reference to the vanquished. From the literary evidence we have learned of only one such military triumph by Diodotus I. Sometime around 240 or the early 230s B.C., he confronted the forces of Arsaces and drove them from Bactria. Our sources describe this Arsaces as a barbarian, a nomadic bandit whose predatory raiding had to be stopped. In the Hellenistic world, victories over such foes greatly increased the prestige of the Greek commander.

The crowning glory of Antiochus I was his defeat of the Gauls in ca. 270, the popular action for which he received the cult title Soter (Savior),[26] and, as we have seen, the Greeks established a Soteria (Savior) festival to honor the defense of Delphi against invading Celts.[27] An even better parallel can be found in the defeat of the Gauls by Attalus I of Pergamon, an event roughly contemporary with Diodotus's action against Arsaces. Pergamon in Asia Minor (modern Turkey) had been advancing toward full independence from the Seleucids since the time of Philetairos (ca. 300–263 B.C.). Under this governor it eventually issued coins that ambiguously displayed the idealized portrait of the deceased Seleucus I with a new coin-type, the Athena of Lysimachus (later the type of the Attalid dynasty), plus the name of Philetairos *without* royal title.[28] The chosen successor of the eunuch Philetairos was his nephew, Eumenes I, who put his uncle's portrait in the place of the Seleucid king's.[29] These actions fell just short of declaring full independence, a step taken only when Attalus I "became the first of these men to call himself king *after overcoming the Gauls in battle.*"[30] This victory also earned Attalus the

26. Appian *Syr.* 65; Sherwin-White and Kuhrt, *Samarkhand to Sardis,* pp. 32–34; B. Bar-Kochva, "On the Sources and Chronology of Antiochus I's Battle Against the Galatians," *PCPS* 119 (1973): 1–8.

27. G. Nachtergael, *Les Galates en Grèce et les Sotéria de Delphes: Recherches d'histoire et d'épigraphie hellénistiques* (Brussels: Académie Royale de Belgique, 1977).

28. See the groundbreaking study by E. T. Newell, *The Pergamene Mint Under Philetaerus* (New York: American Numismatic Society, 1936); cf. Mørkholm, *Early Hellenistic Coinage,* pp. 128–129.

29. Ulla Westermark, *Das Bildnis des Philetairos von Pergamon: Corpus der Munzpragung* (Stockholm, 1960).

30. Strabo 13.4.2 (emphasis added); cf. Livy 38.16 and Polybius 18.41.7–8.

cult title Soter. Thus on one frontier of the Seleucid empire we find a well-documented case that helps us to understand another. With exemplary caution, local dynasts exercised virtual autonomy under cover of eclectic coin-types and ambiguous loyalties. Only a celebrated military success, preferably the act of "saving" Greeks from marauding barbarians, could justify at long last the royal title for a new, self-made dynasty.[31]

This raises an important question: did Diodotus I declare himself king outright in the wake of this victory? In his condensed version of these events, Justin states, as we have seen, that he did and that his power then grew during the takeover of Parthia by Arsaces. The coins, however, tell a slightly different tale. The only coins with a victory wreath, a portrait of Diodotus I, and the name "Diodotus" belong to series B. These coins cannot be made to follow A8 directly for many reasons. There is no die linkage; indeed, the portraiture changes significantly to an idealized visage rendered in a new style. The king's hair, from the brow back to the nape, takes on a special saw-tooth pattern that is quite extraordinary on the Diodotid currency. The only other coin remotely resembling this one in this feature is specimen 19 of F7, a British Museum drachm of Diodotus II struck contemporaneously with series B. The series B reverse, too, shows novel characteristics. On these coins alone, the aegis exhibits snakes that rear up in a threatening gesture above the arm of Zeus. One coin (example 1) has a die axis of 12:00 (↑), a peculiarity found only on issues of the younger Diodotus. All were struck at the second mint (otherwise to be associated with Diodotus II), and they fall after the mintages of Diodotus II in his own name that are die-linked to series E. The logical conclusion is that series B constitutes a posthumous issue for Diodotus I struck by his son, a practice common enough in the Hellenistic Age.[32] Since it therefore appears that Diodotus I did not strike series B, we must assume that he never actually took the royal title for himself, at least not on his coins. This finding negates all of the proposed "solutions" to the Diodotid puzzle enumerated above: (1) that all the coins in the name of Antiochus were struck by the father, while the son issued the Diodotus coins, (2) that Diodotus I struck all of the Antiochus coins

---

31. On the Attalids in general, see E. V. Anson, *The Attalids of Pergamon*, 2d ed. (Ithaca: Cornell University Press, 1971). Perhaps the pronounced "Greekness" of the Bactrian royal coinage (e.g., the "commemorative" coins) has its parallel in the outpouring of Greek art in Pergamon emphasizing their victory over barbarians.

32. Consider, again, the parallel case of Pergamon (nn. 28 and 29). Indeed, the Hellenistic Age was born in this way with many posthumous issues of Alexander and the early Diadochoi (above, chap. 1, n. 6).

while he and his son minted the Diodotus coins, (3) that Diodotus II issued all of the coins; and (4) that both father and son issued coins in both names.[33]

The coins of Diodotus I strongly reinforce the general scenario revealed to us by the literary sources, all the more so if Justin simply misunderstood which Diodotus first took the royal title. It was not long after Arsaces was driven into Parthia and took power there that Diodotus I suddenly died. Before the demise of the Bactrian dynast, we are led to believe, Arsaces feared both the Seleucids and Diodotus I. If this denotes a cooperative military action against Arsaces, then there is little wonder that Diodotus still deferred the final act of putting his name on the ambiguously "Seleucid" coins that he had been minting for some fifteen to twenty years.[34] His son, however, proved much less cautious from the moment of his accession in ca. 235 B.C.—and much less capable of staying alive in the dangerous world of Alexander's heirs.

THE YOUNGER DIODOTUS

Ambition and opportunity, the ubiquitous midwives of Hellenistic monarchy, were busy on the eastern frontier. Bactria and Parthia were breaking free of the Seleucid empire, each unsure of the other and yet alert to the awful consequences of independent action. At this critical moment, Diodotus I died a king in all but name. His son carried the next generation ahead, crossing the line on which his father had balanced for so many years. The transition to outright kingship was smooth and swift, as we can see in the archaeological, literary, and numismatic records. Fortunately, the coins also explain why this was so.

We can see now that Diodotus II had accumulated years of experience as his father's co-ruler in Bactria. Together they had struck a fully integrated coinage, all in the name of Antiochus. At the primary mint (A) the son had issued a relatively modest coinage alongside his father's— just enough, perhaps, to advertise his own portrait and to enhance his

33. Although close to solution 4, this reconstruction disputes the view of Narain (*IG*, p. 17) and others, who insist that both father and son occasionally issued coins in both their own names and that of Antiochus. See n. 7.

34. That Diodotus was still issuing coins in the name of Antiochus rather than the new Seleucid king, Seleucus II Callinicus, should cause no surprise. Again, the parallel case of the Attalids shows that Philetairos was able "to acknowledge Seleucid suzerainty while at the same time avoiding any demonstration of loyalty to the actual king, Antiochus I," by maintaining a numismatic reference to Seleucus I instead: Mørkholm, *Early Hellenistic Coinage*, p. 128.

status as heir apparent (series C). This step, perhaps taken during the turmoil of the Seleucid empire in ca. 246 B.C., guaranteed the future position of Diodotus II in this fluid state of affairs. This was not yet a Diodotid monarchy, but it was already the beginning of a Diodotid dynasty. The promoted but still secondary status of Diodotus II at mint A can be seen today in the smaller numbers (and denominations) of his series C coins. In fact, the only fractional silver produced at this mint during the long hegemony of Diodotus I is represented today by the few drachms and hemidrachm bearing the youthful portrait of his son (C2 and 3).

The main task of Diodotus II at this time was to open a second Bactrian mint as part of his vice-satrapal position, all on the royal model we have seen for Seleucus I and his son Antiochus I.[35] Economic and political developments could have motivated the creation of this second mint. Bactria was not a small region, and the need for another mint should not surprise us: Macedonia, even before Alexander's reign, had at least two royal mints (one at the capital, Pella, and another near the mines at Amphipolis) less than eighty miles apart. The second Diodotid mint clearly complemented the first by issuing mostly small silver denominations. This new operation, however, had its problems. The quality of this coinage does not match that of the coinage of the experienced parent mint. The dies were sometimes poorly engraved and continued to be used even when badly cracked and worn.[36] Also, the proliferation of control marks betrays a greater effort to monitor the work of this subsidiary operation.[37] Yet, as Diodotus II assumed these new duties, he gained administrative experience and a status approaching that of his aging father. While small change in the numismatic picture, he was becoming highly visible in the increasingly independent realm of Bactria.[38]

The younger Diodotus shared in his father's celebration of victory (over Arsaces?) by adding, too, the new wreath symbol to his coins (C3

35. Series E: the possible location of this mint will be considered in the next chapter.

36. See, e.g., E2 example 1 and E5 example 2 (evidence of two coins struck off-flan). Note the prescient commentary of E. T. Newell in *ESM,* p. 247 (his coins 721 and 722).

37. The need for so many control marks may explain the origins of the characteristic legend alignment *outside* the arm of Zeus at mint B. Indeed, the type was sometimes distorted to accommodate these marks, as in the severe bowing of Zeus's back on series E and F. On F5 the monograms seem to have crowded out the eagle itself.

38. The relative importance of this small change to the monetization of Bactria will be considered further in the following chapter. On the role of the "crown prince" in Hellenistic history, consider the Seleucid cuneiform evidence from Babylonia: S. M. Sherwin-White, "Babylonian Chronicle Fragments as a Source for Seleucid History," *JNES* 42 (1983): 265–270.

and E7–9). At mint A, he also struck the associated gold issues. These important coins were followed without interruption of any kind by the royal coinage of Diodotus II at both mints. His father dead at the end of A8, the son immediately renounced all vestiges of Seleucid loyalty and replaced the name of Antiochus with his own.[39] The use of the name "Antiochus" had long been a matter of numismatic momentum, carried over beyond the death of Antiochus II because it was familiar on the Bactrian issues and hedged the bets of Diodotus I. In fact, keeping that name on the coins after the accession of Seleucus II was itself a subtle statement of growing independence.[40] Diodotus II dared to take the decisive step at the death of his father, putting his name on the coinage and then looking to the Parthians for support should the Seleucids now take action.

The transition was numismatically as well as archaeologically uneventful, marked only by the name on Diodotus II's issues. Mint B continued to produce its usual coinage with multiple monograms. In fact, we can see the unbroken succession of magistrates who "signed" this mintage and carried over some obverse dies to the sole reign of Diodotus II. At mint A the same progression is evident with obverse die linkage and, here, the continued use of a single monogram, legend alignment under Zeus's arm, and strict die-axis control. These were apparently not large issues for the first few years, each group being represented today by only one to four examples.[41] This production pattern changed rather dramatically with the parallel issues of D7 and F6. Noteworthy, too, are the numerous gold staters that entered the Bactrian market at this time. Simultaneously, Diodotus II apparently paid homage to his father's "reign." At the second mint, which had never struck the coins of the elder Diodotus, the son authorized a group of tetradrachms and heavy staters bearing the idealized portrait of his predecessor. This series B took

39. This seems to be the sense of our written sources. Deena Pandey has wrongly argued that Diodotus II was a weak and ineffectual ruler who, out of fear, reverted to the Antiochus legend *and* allied himself with Parthia: "Notes on Indo-Greek Coins," *JNSI* 28 (1966): 198–199.

40. See n. 34.

41. Kovalenko has tried ("The Coinage of Diodotus I and Diodotus II," p. 45) to arrange the issues of my series D, groups 1–6, by assuming that the Greek letters on them are actually numbers signifying the ongoing count of issues in sequence A, B, N, P, Σ, and T. He notes: "The last letter is T. So one can suppose that there might have been no less than nineteen issues of this sort" over a period that "was not long." But in normal Greek practice, the letter T as a numeral represents three hundred (not nineteen), just as N equals fifty, P equals one hundred, and Σ equals two hundred. We cannot suppose three hundred issues over any length of time, much less a short one. These mint marks are surely not numbers, and there is no need yet to force them into that sequence.

its place among the last coins struck by the dynasty; the rise of Euthydemus I seems to have ended the reign of Diodotus II (D8/F8/B3).

It is possible that the posthumous issues honoring Diodotus I had
something to do with the challenge of this Euthydemus. The royal authority of Diodotus II rested in part upon the legitimacy of his father, reinforced by Hellenistic notions of doing great deeds and so becoming a
king by acting as king.[42] Diodotus I had certainly achieved great things,
but there is no numismatic evidence that he struck coins in his own name
as outright monarch of Bactria. His son therefore did so posthumously,
out of piety perhaps but also self-interest. The idealized portrait and heavy
staters (which seem never to be cut) established the obvious heroic rank
of Diodotus Soter as the legitimate "royal" predecessor of Diodotus II.

This series B mintage commenced soon after the accession of the
younger Diodotus, at the time of a huge production of gold issues from
both mints. If it is not celebratory in nature, the sudden striking of gold
in great quantity often betokens a crisis. It can mean that a ruler must
buy loyalty at a premium or that his silver reserves have been depleted.[43]
The situation in ca. 230 B.C. (D7/B1/F6) suggests that Diodotus II faced
such problems. His initial output of gold staters quickly suffered a reduction in weight standards, probably to stretch his gold reserves as far
as possible. The weights were rapidly reduced at both mints, resulting in
the cutting of the earlier, heavier staters still in circulation.[44] Why the
posthumous staters of Diodotus I (B1) escaped this defacing process is
difficult to say, unless it was out of deference to the deceased. These unusually heavy issues may simply have been hoarded, explaining their pristine condition today.

As for the cause of this crisis, we must naturally look to the rise of
Euthydemus I for answers. The early coins of Euthydemus I include several Diodotid monograms, notably the last three employed by Diodotus
I at mint A (Σ, $\mathcal{A}$, N) and the combination ($\mathcal{A}$ plus letter) used there
by Diodotus II.[45] This is not much to guide us, but it does hint that early

---

42. See chap. 1, n. 8.

43. Colin Kraay, "Greek Coinage and War," pp. 3–18 in W. Heckel and R. Sullivan,
eds., *Ancient Coins of the Graeco-Roman World: The Nickle Numismatic Papers* (Waterloo, Ontario: Wilfrid Laurier University Press, 1984).

44. This pattern has been examined in appendix A, showing incremental reductions
from the normal Attic standard down to 8.3 grams in D7 and F6 (but not the posthumous
staters of B1).

45. On the Euthydemid issues bearing monograms $\mathcal{A}$ and $\mathcal{A}$ N, we often can observe
a portrait style (particularly in the rendering of the hair) peculiar to Diodotus II's series B
coins honoring his father. See chap. 7 for further discussion.

on Euthydemus I had a stronger connection to mint A than to mint B. This makes sense given the special long-standing relationship between Diodotus II and mint B. We observe also that not long after introducing the posthumous Diodotus I coins (B1) Diodotus II abandoned forever the wreath that had adorned the thundering Zeus issues since ca. 240 B.C. We must ask why. This wreath had been important iconographically to both father and son in an age that required military victory to justify claims of power. Diodotus II, especially, needed that legitimacy to defend his throne against other challengers. This was the way of Hellenistic power and politics. Yet the victory wreath was summarily dropped. The reason must lie in a change of policy that in no way diminished the dynastic link to Diodotus I (the posthumous issues continued without the wreath) but required a playing down of this victory symbol.

It has been suggested above that the military victory that this wreath celebrated was the defeat of Arsaces by Diodotus I. If correct, we have the answer to the question at hand: the literary sources claim that after his accession Diodotus II reversed his father's policies by forming an alliance with Arsaces of Parthia. Such a pact might explain the decision of the Bactrian king to remove from his coinage the blatant reference to his new ally's defeat at his father's hands.

From their western perspectives, the ancient literary sources and their modern commentators have put the Seleucids at the heart of this whole affair. According to Tarn and others, the Diodotids always acted in terms of the perceived threat from Syria—the father trusting Seleucus II for help against Arsaces, the son trusting Arsaces for help against Seleucus II. But the local situation in Central Asia is sufficient to explain the facts without making the reign of Diodotus II a Bactrian referendum on the Seleucid dynasty. What the new Bactrian king needed in ca. 230 B.C. was not a defensive alliance against Seleucus II but the help of Parthia in his effort to stop a local rival.[46]

An alliance with Arsaces (whatever Diodotus thought of the man) was meant to put Euthydemus I in jeopardy. The coalition did not have its desired effect, however, as the coins and texts make quite clear. Arsaces was not much inclined to expend actual resources against the Bactrians. In fact, a civil war there probably suited his purposes in the long run. In

---

46. Thus, while Tarn (*GBI*, p. 74) and others (e.g., Rawlinson, *Bactria*, p. 65) supposed that it was the alliance with Parthia that prompted the rebellion of Euthydemus I, the coins lead me to think that it was the rebellion of Euthydemus that prompted the alliance with Parthia.

any case, Arsaces was soon preoccupied on his opposite frontier, meeting the attack of Seleucus II in ca. 228 B.C. He did so with confidence that a divided Bactria could not threaten his flank. Euthydemus also benefited from these events, since he likewise could focus his energies against Diodotus II without fear of Arsaces. As we have seen, Ai Khanoum suffered a major attack ca. 225 B.C. that likely saw the end of the Diodotids in Bactria. Like all Hellenistic kings, Diodotus II had gambled—but poorly.

All of this now makes perfect numismatic sense. There is no reason to animate these events with imaginary queens or to explain everything in terms of western Seleucid history.[47] The approach made so popular by Tarn may be put aside in favor of direct analysis of the archaeological, numismatic, and literary record.[48] That record places the Diodotids squarely in the milieu of Hellenistic state building and illuminates both their rise and their fall. The very forces that had raised Diodotus I and II to power, quickened now by their own example, spelled doom for the dynasty. In that spirited world of spoils and spear given birth at Babylon, men like Seleucus, Diodotus, and Euthydemus competed feverishly for new kingdoms. Noble origins were important, but ambition and opportunity mattered most. The legitimacy claimed by Diodotus II could not save him, just as it had not saved the family of Alexander the Great. Probably in battle, that arbiter of so much in Hellenistic civilization, the thunder of the Diodotid Zeus fell silent forever on the Bactrian frontier.

---

47. This is not to imply that Bactrian queens should be dismissed as unimportant. On the Bactrian and Indo-Greek coins we find several of note (e.g., Laodice, Agathocleia, and Calliope). The point is that the latter are at least *attested* in the sources. For their coins, see Bopearachchi, *Monnaies,* pp. 209, 251–253, 325.

48. It should be noted that Tarn's whole interpretation of the later rise of Eucratides the Great in Bactria follows his usual methodology, whereby he imagines Eucratides to be a cousin (by supposed marriage) of the Seleucid ruler Antiochus IV. His approach relies heavily upon a (supposed) linkage of events in Syria and Bactria: *GBI,* pp. 183–224. These conclusions have now been challenged by more direct analysis of the evidence. See, e.g., Holt, "Pedigree Coins."

CHAPTER 6

The World of Bronze

HERMES AND ZEUS

The principal numismatic medium for the rediscovery of ancient Bactria has always been the precious metals.[1] In part this reflects the more "narrative" nature of silver and gold coinages, which bear the rulers' portraits, dynastic badges, sequences of control marks, commemorative features, and defining royal symbols of an age. The bronze coinages tend to be less eventful in design, bearing instead the images and attributes of deities transcending the historical moments that so occupy us.

The role of bronze in numismatic research has also suffered from the market dynamics of modern coin collecting.[2] The less valuable the coin, the less likely it is to be prominently marketed or pursued by a museum. Many bronze specimens on the world market do not attract the attention of major auction houses and dealers; these pieces generally trade below the level of the lavishly illustrated auction catalogs that help us in the hunt for ancient numismatic evidence. Even when listed, bronze coins are often not illustrated, and without this vital information one coin cannot easily be distinguished from another or studied in any re-

---

1. In general, consult the excellent periodic surveys published since 1967 by the International Numismatic Commission under the ongoing title *A Survey of Numismatic Research;* also see the specific works listed above, chap. 4, nn. 17 and 42. Cunningham, *CASE,* is the first numismatic work to devote serious attention to the Bactrian bronze.

2. The exception, proving the rule, is the collector who chooses to pursue bronze issues and thus makes a considerable contribution to scholarship. The recent case of Brian Kritt, *Seleucid Coins of Bactria* (Lancaster: CNG, 1996), is a notable example.

liable detail. The result is a diminished sample of usable numismatic material. Compared with the seven pounds of precious-metal Diodotid coinage available today for study, there are less than two pounds of bronze.

It is also true, of course, that bronze coins reach us from a different point of origin. Instead of the dazzling hoards so common for the precious metals, bronze specimens generally trickle to the modern marketplace or museum as the result of small stray finds.[3] Only systematic archaeological excavations reverse this pattern of discovery, yielding more bronze stray finds than precious-metal ones.[4] The work at Ai Khanoum validates this point, but the rarity of such excavations in Afghanistan only underscores the problems we have today with the search for bronze coin evidence.

The combined impact of these factors can be easily seen in numismatic science. In 1886, when the British Museum first published its large Bactrian collection, there was but one Diodotid bronze coin in its inventory.[5] The Bibliothèque Nationale in Paris did not acquire its first Diodotid bronze specimen until 1934, and today the eighteen Diodotid coins in that first-class museum include only four of bronze.[6] It also comes as no surprise that one-third of all known Diodotid bronze coins have derived from Ai Khanoum in recent decades.

These bronzes were the elusive coinage of everyday life. They did not travel as far as silver and gold, but they certainly traveled faster. Instead of being hoarded they passed frequently from hand to hand in the bustle of small business.[7] Such pieces were more often used and more eas-

3. Compare the recent deluge of precious-metal coins evident in F. Holt, "Eukratides of Baktria," *AncW* 27 (1996): 72–76. Subsequent auction sales point to a wellspring of Bactrian hoard material.

4. This has been shown to be true of Ai Khanoum (chap. 5, n. 3), but other examples are easy to find. Olynthus (excavation seasons 1928, 1931, 1934, and 1938) yielded 4,009 legible stray bronzes but only 393 stray silver and no gold: D. M. Robinson and P. Clement, *Excavations at Olynthus,* vols. 9 and 14 (Baltimore, 1938). For Athens, see John Camp, *The Athenian Agora: Excavations in the Heart of Classical Athens* (London: Thames and Hudson, 1986), p. 130, and John Kroll, *The Athenian Agora,* vol. 26, *The Greek Coins* (Princeton: American School of Classical Studies at Athens, 1993).

5. *BMC,* Bactria, p. 3 no. 7.

6. Bopearachchi, *Monnaies,* pp. 147–153. Of the total 1,127 Bactrian and Indo-Greek specimens in the BN, only 332 are of bronze: p. 447. Most museums and private collections have this "collector's ratio" of bronze to precious metals, whereas the "archaeological ratio" exclusive of hoards will generally be at the opposite extreme.

7. The *velocity* of a coinage is considered by monetary experts as a prime measure of monetization, since it reflects actual levels of transaction via the coin. The *range* of bronze coinage is limited by its fiduciary nature, whereas precious-metal issues are valuable even beyond the boundaries of the states that mint them.

ily lost and then harder to find in the trampled dirt of an ancient city or town. Reclaimed thus by nature, the bronze coin weathers the ages very poorly. Chemicals in the earth and air attack the surface of the metal, and moisture accelerates the transformation from coin to scrap. Accretions develop, cuprite warts emerge, and blotches of red or green may appear. In many cases the bronze coin corrodes beyond recognition, and not only collectors and curators but even skilled archaeologists may give it scant attention. Even some advocates of the "New Archaeology," which treats every shred of evidence (even stray seeds and bone splinters) with the utmost care, seem all too willing to sacrifice bronze coins. At Kourion, for example, the excavation director speaks of a "power struggle" over the handling of stray coins: "I needed the coins cleaned as soon as possible for purposes of dating and identification; but the conservators, as is their wont, lobbied for the safest and slowest methods. The reader will perhaps not be surprised to learn that the dig director won out, particularly since the coins were hardly art treasures and were in very bad shape."[8] Bronze coins have long been valued as chronological indicators and little more; old habits die hard.[9]

As with the more plentiful and better-preserved silver and gold, the few bronzes reaching us for study have an inherent ambiguity in terms of their identifying legends (see plates 17–22). Some types bear the name "Diodotus," others "Antiochus." The bronzes, however, have no royal portraits to help us sort them out, nor do they normally have control marks. Taken alone, this token bronze coinage could never be attributed to one king or the other, but from the series and groups of precious metals worked out in chapter 5 and appendix A we may now assume that all bronzes struck in the name of Diodotus were issued by the younger ruler. Those in the name of Antiochus, depending upon their mint of origin, could have been issued by either man or, for that matter, by Antiochus I or II. Absolute certainty on this point is, so far, out of the question.

What we find stamped on these coins is a pattern of patron deities, notably the pair of Hermes and Zeus, sometimes linked as well with Athena and Artemis. To avoid confusion with the precious-metal issues

8. See David Soren and Jaime James, *Kourion: The Search for a Lost Roman City* (New York: Doubleday, 1988), pp. 113–114.

9. An exemplary study of bronze coins from an archaeological context may be found in the work of Paul Bernard at Ai Khanoum, where the evidence has more than just chronological importance. He notes there the very corrosive effect of the humid subsoil upon these bronze finds: *AK* 4, p. 17.

(A–F), appendix B lists the Hermes types as series G and H and the Zeus types as series I. As with the silver and gold, groups distinguish any variations within each series, and an effort has been made to fit these together into a meaningful picture of bronze coin production (see fig. 5). On the bronze issues, however, it is possible for groups within the same series to have seemingly different types. This is not unusual for Hellenistic bronze issues. For example, scholars have heretofore treated the Diodotid Zeus/Artemis bronzes as distinct from the issues bearing the eagle/quiver type. This is not the case at all. What we are seeing is the eagle *of Zeus* and the quiver *of Artemis,* their well-known attributes standing in for the deities themselves on the tiniest denominations. Thus, these are actually part of the same series of coins. Likewise, we must recognize that *all* of the bronzes bearing the name "Diodotus" were issued in a remarkably balanced and orderly way. Each series gives us a male deity obverse with female deity reverse, he (Zeus or Hermes) with bust facing right and she (Artemis or Athena) standing or striding in full figure (except, for reasons of space, on the tiniest coins mentioned above). This was clearly a carefully managed program of denominations and coin-types.

These bronze pieces were generally struck with a 6:00 die axis onto precast flans that were cut from a molded bronze "tree." These flans are generally thick, their edges beveled to facilitate removal from the casting molds. Four bronze denominations may be distinguished in terms of weight and size (diameter): doubles, ca. 8.40 grams (20–24 millimeters), singles, ca. 4.20 grams (14–18 millimeters), halves ca. 2.10 grams (10–12 millimeters), and quarters ca. 1.05 grams (8–10 millimeters).[10] The spending power of these denominations and their various exchange rates with the precious metals cannot be known.

The earliest series (G) of bronze coins shows the head of the Greek god Hermes, facing right, wearing a petasos. These specimens have a reverse type of Hermes's caduceus and were all struck in the name of Antiochus.[11] Coins with Hermes and a reverse type of standing Athena all bear the name Diodotus (series H). These coins seem part of one progression that bridges the change of name, suggesting a mintage of

10. Bopearachchi, *Monnaies,* pp. 45–46.
11. The caduceus appears also as a symbol on the silver coinage of Sophytes: Mitchiner, *IGISC,* vol. 1, p. 23. A recent bronze acquisition of the British Museum, perhaps from Ai Khanoum, has an animal (stag?) obverse and a caduceus reverse. This coin, struck in the name of an Antiochus, was originally attributed to Antiochus I but later to Antiochus II. Its relationship to the Diodotids is therefore uncertain. See P. Bernard and O. Guillaume, "Monnaies inédites de la Bactriane grecque à Ai Khanoum (Afghanistan)," *RN* 22 (1980): 31–32, and Bernard, *AK* 4, p. 34.

FIGURE 5:   OVERVIEW OF BRONZE DIODOTID MINTAGE

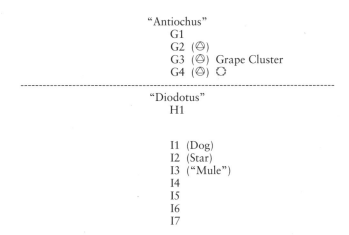

Diodotus II as in the case of series C and D and series E and F in the precious metals. As on the silver and gold issues, too, the bronzes add a wreath symbol (G4) to the last mintage in the name of Antiochus. With the sole reign of Diodotus II, the bronze coins of series H add the name "Diodotus" and a new, more complex reverse type of warlike Athena with helmet, spear, and shield.

The coins of series I were all struck by Diodotus II in his own name. They show a bearded Zeus wearing a laurel crown on the obverse and the goddess Artemis running with a long torch on the reverse. On the earliest issue (I1), a dog bounds ahead of Artemis as they take up the hunt. This animal is quickly abandoned in favor of a star (I2). In addition to this curious change we find an extraordinary issue (I3) that replaces the head of Zeus with the portrait of a king.[12] This numismatic "mule" clearly pairs the wrong set of dies. Some careless mint worker has used a stater or drachm obverse die, bearing the king's portrait, instead of the proper die with bearded Zeus. Some scholars have confidently identified this errant obverse die as belonging to Antiochus II on the basis of the portraiture.[13] This could be the case, but no actual die linkage has yet been found, and the image does not really seem a good match with the coins of Antiochus II. In fact, the portrait could conceivably be that of, say, Antiochus

---

12. First published by Bopearachchi, *Monnaies,* pp. 42, 151–152.
13. Most notably Bopearachchi himself (see n. 12).

I or, more reasonably, that of Diodotus I or II. The bronze "mule" shows a hairstyle (with longer tresses than those of Antiochus II) consistent with the gold of series B and one drachm of F7, all minted by Diodotus II.

Much, of course, has been made of this "mule." Even if we *knew* that the portrait was from an Antiochus II die, this would not mean that this bronze coin was issued by Diodotus I immediately upon his revolt from the Seleucids. Indeed, everything observed so far in the coinage makes this impossible. Diodotus I issued no coinage in his own name, least of all at the outset of his independence; many issues in the name of Antiochus preceded the first in the name of Diodotus. We must assume, if the portrait is Seleucid, that a very old die was still at hand in this Bactrian mint. This would not be impossible,[14] but it appears more likely that one of the dies cut by Diodotus II would have been near to hand. This possibility alone has chronological implications—it would date the striking of bronze series I to the latter part of the reign of Diodotus II because of the portrait style.

At all events, the presence of *any* royal portrait on this coin distinguishes this as a precious-metal die, not a bronze one. Thus, at some time at least, the mint producing these series I Diodotid bronzes also housed the dies that struck silver and gold coinages. We are therefore dealing with a major operation and not just a local one producing bronze types alone. This observation supports the view that these bronzes were issued from at least one of Bactria's main mints and perhaps one dating to the Seleucid era.

The last groups (4–7) of series I are issues of tiny quarters weighing scarcely a gram and usually much less. These coins, unknown before 1977, are sometimes no larger than Lincoln's *head* on a U.S. cent. For this reason, they do not carry the full designs found on the larger denominations. The eagle of Zeus, which die engravers should have had long experience in cutting, took the place of the god's laureate bust on the obverse. The eagle's unusually long neck and beak on many of these I4 quarters find their closest parallel on some of the silver coins of F7 and F8, perhaps reflecting the work of a particular die engraver. Artemis was represented on the reverse by her quiver and sometimes her bow as well.[15]

14. In other words, this error coin does not tell us which Seleucid last ruled over Bactria, only perhaps that Antiochus I or II (?) once struck coins there. This we know quite well already. On the storage of old dies, see *Inscriptiones Graecae* II² 1408 ll. 11–13. On ancient minting errors, see Diogenes Laertius 7.1.18.

15. The uncertain designs on series I, groups 6 and 7, have been noted in appendix B; no clarification or explanation can yet be offered.

Taken together, the mintage of series I as we now know it is composed of 60 percent doubles, 11 percent singles, no halves, and 29 percent quarters. Of these sixty-three specimens, nineteen were excavated at Ai Khanoum and two at Gyar-Kala. For series H we have 51 percent doubles, 11 percent singles, 36 percent halves, and 2 percent quarters, with twelve of the fifty-five coins from Ai Khanoum, two from Gyar-Kala, and five from Takht-i Sangin. If considered together, series H and I mesh beautifully, with similar production of doubles and singles and counterbalanced concentrations of halves and quarters. Series G consists of only seven specimens (six doubles and one single).

How, then, are these three bronze series related? The earliest must be series G in the name of Antiochus, which evolves directly into series H in the name of Diodotus. Series I could follow series H or be contemporary with it as the local emission of a separate mint; after all, the silver and gold issues suggest that Bactria maintained two major mints from the viceroyalty of Diodotus II through his independent reign. We might therefore assign the Hermes types to one of these mints and the Zeus types to the other. This remains one possibility, but the archaeological and findspot evidence is inconclusive; more urban sites, in particular the minting cities themselves, must be excavated to find true patterns of regional bronze production and circulation. We are fortunate to have the results from Ai Khanoum to guide us, but care must be taken lest the evidence from this one major site skew our interpretations. What seems a meaningful concentration of certain issues there (e.g., I2) might look altogether different if we had other *excavated* sites with which to compare it. The absence of certain issues at certain sites (for example, of series I at Takht-i Sangin) may be more significant, but series H and I are equally represented among the finds from Gyar-Kala.

Ai Khanoum also seems to demonstrate a rather even distribution of coins from series H and I. The numbers are not really large enough to permit strong statistical conclusions, but some general observations are warranted. For example, if one of these series was struck at Ai Khanoum and the other elsewhere, we should expect to find a heavier concentration of the local bronze issues rather than a homogeneous distribution.[16]

---

16. Unless the two mints were very close together or the distant mint produced a far larger supply of coins that circulated in sufficient numbers to match the local mintage at Ai Khanoum. Obviously, these bronzes were currency throughout the realm and not just in particular cities. This conclusion finds some support in the finds of Diodotid coins at Gyar-Kala (Merv), where two examples each of groups H and I have been reported: N.

If neither was struck at Ai Khanoum, then an even distribution there by way of steady commerce would be quite reasonable. But we know that the city did operate a bronze mint in the time of Eucratides and almost certainly in the Seleucid period.[17] Also, the discovery at Ai Khanoum of so many small Diodotid bronzes, heretofore unknown, suggests the possibility of local manufacture.[18] It would follow that if any of these bronzes were struck at Ai Khanoum, then, given the even distributions of types, probably some part of each series was minted there.

The evolution of these series might therefore run as follows: If the recent study of Seleucid bronzes by Brian Kritt is correct, then the control mark found on Diodotid G 2–4 should be associated with Ai Khanoum.[19] Kritt argues that Ai Khanoum had become the main Bactrian mint as early as ca. 285 B.C. during the viceroyalty of Antiochus I. The parent mint (at Bactra?) was phased out of operation after a relatively brief run (ca. 290–280 B.C.). Ai Khanoum, nearer the sources of Bactrian ores, then struck a varied array of Seleucid types ending with some Antiochus II bronzes with Hermes/caduceus types. These issues were followed by the bronzes identified here as series G.[20] Perhaps, then, when Diodotus II began issuing fractional silver as his father's viceroy (series C and E), he also minted at Ai Khanoum the Hermaic bronzes in the name of Antiochus (G 2–4). G1, without the monogram and with variable die axis, may be an issue of the new mint (our mint B). This mint B may be Bactra, a city perhaps emerging anew under Diodotus II, but we cannot be certain on this point. This would seem to make Ai Khanoum another minting city—if not also the capital—of Seleucid and early Diodotid Bactria.

Series G at Ai Khanoum culminated in the wreath coinage (G4) simultaneously with the gold and silver wreath coinages (C3 and E7–9). With the death of Diodotus I and the accession of his son as king, the name "Antiochus" was dropped and the bronze coin-type modified. Diodotus II chose to continue the familiar obverse, at first still with the cloaked Hermes. The reverse design changed completely, dropping the

---

Smirnova, "On Finds of Hellenistic Coins in Turkmenistan," *Ancient Civilizations* 3 (1996): 260–285.

    17. See Bernard, *AK* 4, pp. 12–15 and (for the Diodotids) 55–57.

    18. As indicated above, this cannot be conclusive until other urban sites are excavated in Afghanistan. Bernard, *AK* 4, pp. 12–15, suggests that both types (Zeus/Artemis and Hermes/Athena) could have been struck at or near Ai Khanoum.

    19. Kritt, *Seleucid Coins of Bactria*.

    20. Ibid. This summary is not meant to oversimplify the complex arguments of the author. Kritt includes some issues (stag/caduceus) not included here. See n. 11.

monogram and all additional symbols in favor of the Athena type. The circulation of H1 coins does not seem restricted to Ai Khanoum, and therefore they were probably struck at all mints during the first years of Diodotus II's sole reign. This would make series I a later bronze issue rather than a contemporaneous one. In other words, the difference between series H and I is temporal rather than spatial.

This may be confirmed by the countermark on two series H coins.[21] Such countermarks guaranteed the currency of a particular coin, revalidating or revaluing an issue that might otherwise be outdated or suspect (see plate 23). Thus, at Ai Khanoum and Takht-i Sangin, where these specimens were excavated, two series H doubles of normal weight and size needed restamping to authorize their continued use in the local economy. In one case, the excavation director has speculated that some financial emergency prompted this action, and he notes the connection between the thunderbolt wielded by Zeus on the Diodotid silver and gold and this special countermark symbol.[22] The surmise of some unknown economic problem (not restricted to Ai Khanoum) may well be correct, perhaps associated with the revaluation of the gold staters observed in D7 and F6. It is also possible that the change of bronze types from Hermes/Athena to Zeus/Artemis at first required that some older issues (series H) be countermarked with a symbol of the newer issues (series I) before the mintage could be more widely accepted. This shows the proper sequence of mintage.

The varied series I coins were probably the last bronze issues of Diodotus II. Some of these featured a dog at Artemis's feet, others a star in right field. The "mule" is best associated with this period, as is the engraving style of the eagle on the I4 quarters. The bronze progression to smaller denominations also fits this scenario quite well. If this is the best arrangement we can make of Diodotus's bronze money, we must next ask what this evidence reveals to us about life in Diodotid Bactria.

PATTERNS OF EVERYDAY LIFE

In terms of evidence, bronze is to the numismatist what broken pottery is to the archaeologist—a window onto the mundane world of everyday

21. H1, examples 3 and 18 (a thunderbolt in each case).
22. Bernard, *AK* 4, pp. 56–57. The thunderbolt may also be seen on the sandals of the huge statue of Zeus at Ai Khanoum and a bronze plaque from the indented temple: Francfort, *AK* 3, p. 56 (no. 26).

ancient life. Books and lectures are more likely to be illustrated with pristine gold portrait coins and lavishly painted funerary vases, but much of what we really know rests upon the detritus of daily living. Small bronze coins dropped in the marketplace or outside the temple and water jugs broken in the kitchen or beside the public fountain are the ancient equivalents of the pennies and plastic that will someday write our own modern story.[23]

The picture we derive from the Diodotid bronze coinages has a plainer, less royal quality than the narrative silver and gold. In fact, the bronze must be linked to the precious metals to acquire an eventful chronology. But in terms of larger historical processes such as the economic and cultural interaction of Greeks and non-Greeks in Bactria, nothing breaks the millennial silence more eloquently than these unassuming lumps of bronze. As low-value units of daily exchange, these coins filtered deeper down throug the ranks of Bactrian society. This was literally the baseline for the final monetization of the East, bringing a money economy to more and more people outside the privileged Greek enclave. While precise exchange rates remain unknown, this Bactrian bronze had considerably less purchasing power than the silver and gold denominations. In his early study of this problem, Cunningham proposed an exchange rate of 48:1 for bronze and silver.[24] This meant, for example, that a single drachm was worth 48 units, a hemidrachm worth 96 quarters, a tetradrachm worth 384 halves, and a stater worth 480 of the largest doubles. Clearly, a large number of low-value transactions needed this bronze currency to make them feasible. In modern terms, we might think of a wealthy man with a pocketful of hundred-dollar bills trying to buy a newspaper from a street vendor. Put another way, the mass of poor people would have had little opportunity to participate in a monetary economy based solely on a currency of hundred-dollar notes and higher. In Diodotid Bactria, where some commodities clearly were valued at no more than a half or a quarter, broad-based monetization was scarcely possible with silver and gold alone. It took bronze coinages to reach down to the nonelite.

---

23. A personal experiment bears this out. An accounting of all coinage in my own home has just revealed 3,308 cents, 184 nickels, 81 dimes, and 19 quarters. Similarly, I have found by chance on the streets and sidewalks of my suburban neighborhood, in a six-month period, 56 cents and 1 quarter. According to records of the U.S. Department of the Treasury, the U.S. Mint conducted a survey in 1987 to determine coin circulation and loss rates. There were 129 billion cents in circulation, compared with 16.4 billion dimes (the second most numerous denomination). The attrition rate for cents was 5.6 percent per year.

24. Cunningham, CASE, pp. 305–337.

This profound process of coin-based monetization, too long considered a uniform phenomenon attributable to the lifetime of Alexander the Great, had a cultural as well as an economic dimension. Money carries with it the economic power and cultural values of those who design and distribute it. Today, those who would take advantage of U.S. currency must also be party to its cultural canon: the leaders to be admired (Washington, Jefferson, Lincoln, Roosevelt), the languages adopted (English and Latin), the religion sanctioned (Christianity), the ideals pursued (Liberty), the symbols embraced (eagle, fasces, olive branch), and the monuments hallowed (Monticello, Lincoln Memorial). As means and message, our coinage appears overwhelmingly to promote one culture within a pluralistic society. The "one out of many" (E PLURIBUS UNUM) to be seen in this currency is decidedly white, European, male, and Christian. The same kind of bias can be found on the Bactrian coinage. This money carried with it the values of the conquering Greeks, making it among the most potent of all agents of Hellenization. And that transformative power was, of course, inversely proportional to the size and value of the coin. Ancient silver and gold often circulated over the heads of most farmers and poor tradesmen, who relied upon a bronze token coinage in order to participate in the Greeks' world of monetary rents, tolls, taxes, and fixed-price trade.[25] Monetization and Hellenization, two key developments of the Hellenistic period, can best be studied today on the lowly bronze coin of the realm.

We have seen that Seleucus I and his son Antiochus first supplied a substantial bronze coinage for Bactria. The finds at Ai Khanoum reveal a telling Seleucid legacy in this regard. After these strong first steps, however, the monetary situation becomes less clear. Only a few bronze issues can be attributed to the lifetimes of Antiochus II and Diodotus I.[26] Thus, the profuse output of bronzes by Antiochus I apparently sufficed for several decades as Bactria moved slowly from barter to bronze at the lowest economic levels.[27]

25. Compare the situation in Hellenistic Egypt: N. Lewis, *Greeks in Ptolemaic Egypt* (Oxford: Clarendon Press, 1986), p. 17. These peasants rarely saw silver; instead, they used copper valued against silver at a ratio of five hundred to one. On such matters in general, see K. Greene, *The Archaeology of the Roman Economy* (Berkeley: University of California Press, 1986), and F. Braudel, *Civilization and Capitalism, 15th–18th Century*, vols. 1 and 2 (New York: Harper and Row, 1981 and 1982).

26. Series G, groups 1–4, and perhaps the two unique bronze pieces discussed in n. 11 and appendix B, n. 19.

27. On the occasional overproduction followed by underproduction of bronze coinages at Ai Khanoum and other Hellenistic sites, see the remarks of Georges Le Rider in his re-

It is also possible that some economic condition obviated the need for fresh supplies of bronze and small silver from ca. 260 to 246 B.C. If not simply an oversupply by Antiochus I, then perhaps we have here the hint of something like a new policy for military recruitment. After all, the payment of soldiers constituted a primary demand for coined money in the ancient world.[28] While slowly breaking from the Seleucids, Diodotus I may have found it difficult to maintain the long-standing supply of Greek military colonists from Asia Minor and the Aegean. He himself may originally have been recruited from the West, as was most certainly the case with the Euthydemid family that would destroy his son Diodotus II.[29] In the next generation, however, there may have been a hiatus. One solution was to intensify in Bactria a *kleros* system whereby military service would be rewarded with land grants rather than salary. Depending upon the rank of the *kleruch* (soldier-settler), the land allotment varied in size and value; usually the estate was worked by local tenants, leaving the warrior free to perform his duties. This system, best-known in Hellenistic Egypt, required far less hard currency to maintain. Since the *kleros* was generally hereditary, the Hellenistic kings could rely upon a steady pool of soldiers from these families. Naturally, some native troops could also be counted upon, especially the local horse-rearing aristocracy of Bactria-Sogdiana. Supported thus by their estates, soldiers did not need to be paid exclusively in coin (which would then have needed small change to be useful beyond payday) or recruited as mercenaries, for whom portable cash wealth was life itself.[30] Under these conditions, Bactria might manage for some while with the bronze and small silver already in circulation.

Eventually, of course, fresh low-denomination currency would be required.[31] As small old coins wore out or were lost over the years and as

view of Bernard, *AK* 4, published in *RN* 29 (1987): 238. Bactria seems to follow a cycle of heavy and light bronze production from the Seleucids to Eucratides I.

28. The classic formulation of this thesis is by Colin Kraay, "Greek Coinage and War," pp. 3–18 in W. Heckel and R. Sullivan, eds., *Ancient Coins of the Graeco-Roman World* (Waterloo, Ontario: Wilfrid Laurier University Press, 1984).

29. The family of Euthydemus I emigrated from Magnesia in Asia Minor, probably the Greek city on the Meander River: Polybius 11.39.1, with discussion in Bernard, *AK* 4, pp. 131–133. See also chap. 7 and appendix D.

30. For background, see G. T. Griffith, *The Mercenaries of the Hellenistic World* (Cambridge, 1935; rpt. Chicago: Ares, 1975), and B. Bar-Kochva, *The Seleucid Army: Organization and Tactics in the Great Campaigns* (Cambridge: Cambridge University Press, 1976). On the *kleros* system, see R. Billows, *Kings and Colonists: Aspects of Macedonian Imperialism* (Leiden: Brill, 1995), esp. chaps. 5 and 6.

31. A shortage of small change was cause for great concern, and such travails often were noted in ancient chronicles alongside famine and scabies. In general, see Christopher Howgego, "Why Did Ancient States Strike Coins?" *NC* 150 (1990): 1–25.

the elaborated *kleros* system moved beyond its initial generation, the Bactrian economy would need fresh money in its marketplaces. Diodotus I, like every other Hellenistic adventurer turned ruler, had to look to the future of the state he was founding. This explains why, as argued in the previous chapter, Diodotus II was elevated to the status of heir apparent and allowed to establish a second mint for Bactria in ca. 246 B.C. Under his supervision, a small wave of new drachms and hemidrachms swept into the Bactrian economy (series C and E) along with a few bronze doubles and singles (series G, groups 1–4). This was the next necessary step in stimulating the monetization of the region under way since the time of the Seleucids.

The increasing monetization of Bactria can be measured best during the sole reign of Diodotus II, as doubles and singles were supplemented first with halves (series H) and finally with quarters (overwhelmingly series I). These bronze quarters made it possible to transact business on a very small scale indeed. If not so attractive today to the collector, these tiny coins nevertheless played a vital role in the development of the Bactrian state. They were probably the first Diodotid issues to reach the hands, purses, and mouths (a convenient carrying place in antiquity) of the nonelite in Bactria.[32] This bronze currency of daily business found its way everywhere into the social interactions of diverse populations. It called forth new ways of thinking, new images of authority, new methods of meeting old obligations. It was the product of the monarch but the daily possession of the masses. In this humble money we find the meeting place of disparate cultures, that mysterious phenomenon that so defines the history of the Hellenistic world.

Low-denomination money was at the forefront of cultural change in Bactria. It was where the non-Greek saw the state through Greek eyes and where the Greeks eventually acknowledged the important place of non-Greek culture within that state. In time, the acceptance of non-Greek numismatic elements (Brahmi and Kharoshthi legends, square shape, Indian weight standards) would begin on this low-value coinage and work its way upward to the silver (but never the gold) denominations. This reflects, it seems, the cultures of those who were expected to handle these currencies. These changes would be accelerated by the fact that, overall, a tetradrachm-based economy prevailed north of the Hindu Kush and a drachm-based economy to the south.

---

32. On the habit of carrying ancient money in one's mouth while shopping, see Aristophanes *Ecclesiazusae* 815–822 and *Wasps* 787–793.

At first, the coinage of the Greek rulers of Bactria reflected only the tastes of their own elite soldiers and administrators.[33] The Seleucids and Diodotids chose from the pantheon of their own native land, preferring Apollo, Zeus, Hermes, Artemis, Athena, and others to Samkarshana, Vashudeva-Krishna, and the Indian goddesses, Buddhist shrines, and other eastern types later to adorn an Indo-Greek currency.[34] In the third century B.C., as more and more native Bactrians handled the Greek bronze coins of King Diodotus II, how did they and their overlords see (differently) the images in their hands?

The head of Zeus (series I) of course captured the dynasty's patron deity, a miniature drawn from the bearded and laureate figure better known to the well-to-do on the gold and silver issues. This type may have copied a prominent cult statue in one or more of the chief Bactrian cities.[35] Excavators discovered the remains of just such a statue at Ai Khanoum, a colossal figure of (seated?) Zeus in a Mesopotamian-style temple from the time of Eucratides I.[36] On the small quarters of series I, Zeus's eagle appears in his stead. On many statues and imitative coin-types known to the Greeks, this eagle perched on the outstretched hand of Zeus as the god sat upon his great throne.[37] The vigorous pose of the Diodotid Zeus, however, put the eagle out of hand; the eagle, too, moves forward aggressively with wings outstretched at the feet of the god. It is this pose, perhaps again based upon a particular cult statue or painting, that the eagle assumes on the smallest Diodotid bronzes.[38] Though seen

33. The selection of coin-types was very important to these ancient people, who, much more so than today, looked closely at the coins in their possession. Aristotle remarks in passing that "everybody inspects his coins": *History of Animals* 1.6.20 (491a).

34. M-Th. Allouche-Le Page, *L'art monétaire des royaumes bactriens* (Paris: Didier, 1956), offers a fine survey of types that is too often overlooked. Useful discussions may also be found in the standard numismatic catalogs (listed above, chap. 1, n. 38) and, for the larger Seleucid context, J. Zahle, "Religious Motifs on Seleucid Coins," pp. 125–139 in Per Bilde et al., eds., *Religion and Religious Practice in the Seleucid Kingdom* (Aarhus: Aarhus University Press, 1990).

35. One of the best Hellenistic examples is the statue of Tyche, sculpted by Eutychides of Sikyon on a commission from Seleucus I. This famous statue (a copy of which is in the Vatican Museum) personified Antioch, the Seleucid capital, and was often portrayed on coins minted there. We may today think of the Lincoln Memorial, with the president's statue inside, as portrayed on the U.S. cent.

36. Francfort, *AK* 3, pp. 56, 121, 125.

37. This served as the silver type for Alexander the Great and was thereafter copied extensively: M. Price, *Alexander,* cf. the Bactrian imitations by Agathocles in the "commemorative" series (Bopearachchi, *Monnaies,* series 12).

38. See M. Price, "Paintings as a Source of Inspiration for Ancient Die Engravers," pp. 69–75 in L. Casson and M. Price, eds., *Coins, Culture, and History in the Ancient World* (Detroit: Wayne State University Press, 1981).

and interpreted in ways unknown to us, these small representations of
Greek art passed into the hands of the general Bactrian population, especially those living near cities and shrines.[39] If indeed, as alleged by Plutarch, the people of Bactria learned to honor the Greek gods after Alexander, then surely bronze coinage played an important role in the
introduction of these non-Greeks to the pantheon of the newcomers.[40]

A remarkable glimpse of this complex process may be seen on the other
side of the coin. If interpreted correctly, we find in series I the meeting—
and lack of meeting—of ancient minds. The choice of Artemis as a Greek
coin-type was natural for Diodotus II. She was universally worshipped
by the Greeks, who saw her as both a city goddess and the patroness of
wild beasts and uncultivated haunts. Twin sister of Apollo and goddess
of the moon, she was a huntress with legendary skills in archery. She
brought fertility to land and beast and special protection to women in
childbirth. Her popularity among the Greeks was matched by her ready
assimilation by Iranian peoples to the Persian goddess Anahita.[41] This
connection brought Artemis/Anahita into divine association with water
and waterways, including rivers and irrigation. A better patron goddess
for a Bactrian city such as Ai Khanoum could not have been found. It
may be only coincidence, but the choice of Artemis as one female type
for this city has a faint echo down through the ages. The ancient Greek
name of this polis has vanished from history, but its current appellation
derives from Turko-Uzbek and means "Lady Moon." Local legends offer
several explanations and identify various important women as the epony-
mous hero of the site. For example, local village women still bring votive offerings to a "Lady Moon," protector of mothers and infants. Another "Lady Moon" was associated with irrigation canals and yet another
with control over the rivers that flowed by the walls of the city. Such
"modern" folktales reverberate with ancient echoes of Artemis/Anahita,
goddess of the moon, mistress of the fertilizing waters, and guardian of
women in childbirth.[42]

39. For the local assimilation from coins of Greek gods such as Zeus, see E. Errington
and J. Cribb, eds., *The Crossroads of Asia: Transformation in Image and Symbol in the
Art of Ancient Afghanistan and Pakistan* (Cambridge: The Ancient India and Iran Trust,
1992), esp. pp. 74–88.

40. Plutarch *Moralia* 1.328(D). On Zeus in particular, see A. N. Lahiri, "Religio-Mythical
Bearing of the Representation of Zeus on Indo-Greek Coins," *JNSI* 42 (1980): 58–65.

41. See William Hanaway Jr., "Anahita and Alexander," *JAOS* 102 (1982): 285–295.

42. On the close connections between Artemis/Anahita and the local traditions of Ai
Khanoum, see P. Bernard and H-P. Francfort, *Etudes de géographie historique sur la plaine
d'Ai Khanoum (Afghanistan)* (Paris: CNRS, 1978), pp. 17–26.

Artemis/Anahita well suited the needs of Diodotus II because she was familiar to both main cultural groups under his sway. At least one famous statue of Anahita, at Bactra, predated the arrival of the Greeks.[43] But several numismatic anomalies suggest a brief sociocultural miscommunication in this regard. First, we recall the subtle deviation of types in series I. The mint clearly elected to represent on the quarters the key deities Zeus and Artemis by means of token, if not totem, attributes. The logical options from the larger denominations of Diodotid bronze coins were signifying the deities by way of their weapons (Zeus's thunderbolt and Artemis's arrows) or by their affiliated animals (Zeus's eagle and Artemis's dog), but the rigorous symmetry otherwise apparent in the selection of bronze types falters at this point. We get, instead, a mismatch: his animal, her weapon. Why did the mint not pair Artemis's hound (I1) with the ubiquitous eagle of Zeus?

There was in Bactria a very good reason to avoid any bronze mintage bearing a dog as its principal type. We happen to know, in fact, that the Greek and non-Greek populations of Bactria were at odds over the role of the dog in religious practice. In a clash of worlds, the two ethnic groups saw totally different things in this common creature. According to Strabo, the Alexander historian Onesicritus described only the "worst" habits of the native Bactrian people, namely, that they allowed special dogs to devour the old and infirm.[44] Alexander the Great detested this ancient practice, and the Greeks in Bactria resolved to eradicate it.[45] Whatever the means employed to eliminate these scavenging animals, the locals apparently venerated their dogs and persisted as far as possible in this custom.[46] There is even evidence that, in spite of Greek efforts, the Bactrian

---

43. Artaxerxes II of Persia (405–359 B.C.) spread her cult and statues: Berossus *apud* Clement of Alexandria *Protreptikos* 5.65.3. The statue at Bactra, as described in the sources, was not the particular model for the pose of Artemis on the Diodotid bronzes.

44. See appendix D; also attested much earlier in the *Vendidad* (6.44–45, 8.10) and much later in Chinese sources, for which see Frantz Grenet, *Les pratiques funéraires dans l'Asie centrale sédentaire de la conquête grecque à l'Islamisation* (Paris: CNRS, 1984), p. 227.

45. Porphyry *De Abstinentia* 4.21; cf. Holt, *Alexander and Bactria*, p. 96. The problem was a local one. Alexander certainly did not dislike dogs in general; he allegedly founded a city in honor of his favorite dog, Peritas (Plutarch *Alex.* 61.3), perhaps one of the famous Indian dogs that so impressed the Macedonians (Pollux *Onamasticon* 5.42; Strabo 15.1.31; Quintus Curtius 9.1.31; Diodorus 17.92.2). One of these powerful Indian dogs may appear on a carved stone, imported or plundered from India, that was found in the Ai Khanoum excavations: Francfort, *AK* 3, pp. 78–79.

46. An otherwise unknown Bactrian, Hyspasines son of Mithroaxos, dedicated in ca. 178 B.C. an ex-voto "Hyrcanian dog" to Apollo at Delos: F. Durrbach and P. Roussel, *Inscriptions de Délos* (Paris: Champion, 1935), no. 1432, Aa 11, ll.26–27, and cf. 442. B, ll. 108–109 with 443 Bb, l. 33. See appendix D.

"burial dogs" were again at work when Ai Khanoum fell in the second century B.C.[47] It is little wonder that the design of Diodotus II's tiny quarters did not display Artemis's hound as the major type, since the population likely to use such coins would have seen in them a distinctly non-Greek iconography. If, as our written sources attest, the dog was a sore point between these cultures, then the choice of bronze types might well reflect a decision to avoid the controversy.[48] Rather than eagle and dog or thunderbolt and arrows we find an incongruous but innocuous mix of eagle and quiver.

This might also explain why Artemis's hound enjoyed such an apparently brief stay on the doubles of series I. It is possible that the Greek authorities abandoned this part of the design for cultural and religious reasons. After all, how might native peoples have interpreted the image of a torch-bearing woman with a "devourer-dog" at her feet? This was not part of the iconography of Anahita, and so the Greeks may have clarified the whole matter with a new design (I2). Here the dog disappeared but a star was added to the sky near the goddess. This reinforced the image of Artemis with her torch, hunting at night. It furthermore recalled for the Greeks the celebrated star myth of Artemis, who slew Orion with her arrows and made him a constellation.[49] The missing dog reminds us that different cultures often see the same images in totally different ways.

The earlier striking of series G and H was much more consistent from beginning to end and probably much less controversial. The male deity chosen for these issues was Hermes, Greek god of merchants.[50] On the

47. For Ai Khanoum, see Grenet, *Les pratiques funéraires,* pp. 73–75; P. Bernard, "Campaign de fouilles 1976–1977 à Ai Khanoum (Afghanistan)," *CRAI* (1978): 440–441. In light of these unburied skeletons, one wonders about the report of Eucratides's death in Justin 41.6.5: "*corpus abici insepultum iussit*" ([the parricide] ordered that the body be thrown aside unburied).

48. For an interesting parallel, see Joe Cribb, ed., *Money: From Cowrie Shells to Credit Cards* (London: British Museum, 1986), p. 76 (nos. 262–264). A gold solidus issued by Justinian II in A.D. 692 was rejected in Muslim Syria because the coin carried representations of the emperor and of Christ. Caliph Abd al-Malik adopted the type in A.D. 695, but even this proved unacceptable. In A.D. 698 the failed coins were replaced by dinars bearing simply the declaration of the Islamic faith.

49. The story is as old as Homer (*Odyssey* 5.121–124). The enduring popularity of Artemis's mythology in the East may also be reflected in a small stone palette found in Pakistan and now in the British Museum: 1936.12-23.1 (dated first century B.C.). It illustrates the story of Actaeon's punishment, killed by his own dogs, because he spied on (here, an Indianized) Artemis during her bath. See Errington and Cribb, *The Crossroads of Asia,* p. 154 (illustrated); and H-P. Francfort, *Les palettes du Gandhara* (Paris: Boccard, 1979), pp. 13–14. Note Artemis's tubular quiver, as represented on Diodotus's coinage.

50. Also honored at Ai Khanoum, along with Herakles, in an ex-voto inscription from the gymnasium. See appendix D and Veuve, *AK* 6, pp. 28, 111–112.

other side of King Diodotus II's series H bronzes was Athena, destined
to become the most popular of all coin-types in this region. She would
grace the mintages of seventeen reigns *beyond* the demise of the Diodotid
dynasty.[51] As with the female deity on series I, Athena stands in full pose
on the series H coins. She clearly wears a helmet, holds a spear, and rests
her shield upon the ground.[52] This posture, with left leg forward and bent,
is derived from statuary like that of the (later) Pergamene Athena now
in the Staatliche Museum in Berlin.[53] It seems likely that a similar cult
statue stood somewhere prominently in the realm of Diodotus II.

As already noted, some coins of both series H and I may have been
issued from the mint at Ai Khanoum. A second mint may have been at
Bactra, known to have been the satrapal capital of Bactria in Alexander's
day and still (or again) the principal city in the region during the reign
of Euthydemus I. Nonetheless, Ai Khanoum was well-situated for minting bronze in particular because it lay near the sources of Bactria's native ores. The plain of Ai Khanoum had been the home of a Bronze Age
metalworking colony of the Harappan civilization in India. Copper
mines, not to mention other mineral ores (iron, lead, and some silver)
and precious stones (rubies and lapis lazuli), lay nearby in the mountains
of Badakhshan. In the Hellenistic period, Ai Khanoum remained a center of metallurgical activity. When the city fell, its treasury still contained unstruck bronze flans. Non-Greek squatters then scavenged the
city for its stockpiled metals, leaving behind scales, plumbs, weights, ingots, and other evidence of their own metallurgical activities.[54] Local mineral wealth added to the strategic and agricultural importance of Ai
Khanoum, making it a natural regional administrative center and a principal mint of Bactria.

---

51. Athenian "owls" were known in Bactria before the arrival of the Greeks; see above,
chap. 2, n. 37, plus H. Troxell and W. Spengler, "A Hoard of Early Greek Coins from
Afghanistan," *ANSMN* 15 (1969): 1–19; and H. Nicolet-Pierre and M. Amandry, "Un nouveau trésor de monnaies d'argent pseudo-athéniennes venu d'Afghanistan (1990)," *RN* 36
(1994): 34–54. After Alexander and before Diodotus, imitation Athena types were struck
in Bactria and neighboring regions: Mitchiner, *IGISC*, vol. 1, pp. 19, 21–22, 24. The
Diodotus II bronze issues therefore have the most popular male (Zeus) and female (Athena)
deities as types but not in the same issues. They are paired with deities (Artemis and Hermes) who are poorly represented on the coinages of later Bactrian and Indo-Greek kings.
52. The same type was later used on the silver coinage of Demetrius II: Bopearachchi,
Monnaies, p. 195.
53. A second-century B.C. copy of a fifth-century original, illustrated, e.g., in P. Green,
ed., *Hellenistic History and Culture* (Berkeley: University of California Press, 1993), p. 75.
54. Bernard and Francfort, *Études de géographie, p. 36;* C. Rapin, "La trésorerie hellénistique," *Revue Archéologique* (1987): 41–70; Francfort, *AK* 3, p. 93 (silver mines); Ball,
Gazetteer, vol. 2, sites 372, 780, 1089.

It is possible, as noted above, that Ai Khanoum was the only mint during the last years of Seleucid rule and the first years of Diodotid hegemony. If Ai Khanoum also served as Bactria's capital in that period (though this is not a necessary condition of its minting activity), then we may surmise that the threat of Arsaces prompted Diodotus I to establish his son, with a subsidiary mint, at Bactra. This strengthened the region in the direction of Parthia but may have led to the eventual rapprochement between Diodotus II (as king) and Arsacid Parthia. Certainly by the time of Euthydemus I, Bactra once again served as the royal capital. We know that Ai Khanoum had suffered attack during Euthydemus's rise to power. Though quickly repaired, there is no evidence that Ai Khanoum was later approached by the forces of Antiochus the Great during his epic two-year siege of Bactra, the impregnable center of Euthydemus's spear-won state.[55]

Thus do the bronze coinages of Diodotus II bring us down to the basics of ancient Bactrian society. Though difficult and dangerous to interpret, we must nevertheless elicit what we can from these few coins in the hope of someday writing a full history of this forgotten time and place. Local traditions and ancient cultural conflicts seem to stare back at us from these often-overlooked types, but only fresh discoveries will tell us where we have guessed right—and wrong. No coin is so small or so base that it might not bring back to life the cities and subjects of Diodotid Bactria.

55. See chap. 7 for discussion of these events, with sources in appendix D.

CHAPTER 7

The Monarchy Affirmed

EUTHYDEMUS AND ANTIOCHUS

We have seen the shadowy Diodotids of Bactria take their place among the ambitious heirs of Alexander the Great. The age in which they flourished and then foundered was born out of the brilliant conquests of Alexander and the brutal contests of his self-made successors. The silence at Babylon in 323 B.C. gave way to three centuries of warlike din, and some of that thunder reverberated from the Bactrian frontier, where a father and son named Diodotus were elevated and eliminated as part of this pattern of Hellenistic royal power.

The man who, in his turn, toppled the Diodotid dynasty remains another enigma to us. From what position he arose and what explained his stunning success we cannot say. Tarn, of course, considered him the son-in-law of Diodotus I who used his satrapal position and connections to the Seleucid queen to overthrow Diodotus II.[1] More recently, R. Morton Smith has out-Tarned even Tarn in his speculations about dynastic politics.[2] Playing the old game of imaginary queens, Smith has woven a detailed "history" in which the widow of Antiochus II influenced her daughter (Diodotus I's wife) to forge an alliance between Diodotus and the widow's youngest son, Antiochus Hierax. This Antiochus, accord-

---

1. *GBI*, p. 74. The possibility of a satrapal position for Euthydemus has long been considered; see Narain, *IG*, p. 19 with notes.
2. R. M. Smith, "The First Bactrian Coinage: An Introduction," *Cornucopiae* 4 (1979): 6–13.

ing to Smith, is the Antiochus named on the Diodotid coinage. Later, according to Smith, Diodotus's widow (sister of Seleucus II) "mediated the
compromise" between Diodotus II and Seleucus II. This younger Diodotus was "probably a spoiled young man chafing under his mother's tute-
lage," and so he repudiated his Seleucid alliance and joined forces with
the Parthians. Diodotus II had to be stopped in such madness, so "probably with the connivance of his mother" the king was assassinated by
Euthydemus I, "apparently chosen for the 'coup d'état' by the queen-
mother." Euthydemus was allegedly given Diodotus's sister as a legiti-
mating bride.

This scenario once again makes pawns of the known principal players and empowers instead their imagined wives and widows. Here
Diodotus II dons an emasculated personality worthy of Nero, and Euthydemus appears as a timid puppet who dared not even mint his own
coinage until 201 B.C., when Antiochus the Great had gone away and a
more powerful "restraining influence was probably removed by the death
of the queen-mother-in-law."[3] In place of this whole approach to the
poorly attested events of Bactrian history, we are obligated to focus upon
the few facts that do survive. In this case, our sources are relatively full
and require no stretch of the imagination to understand the aftermath
of the Diodotids' rise and fall.

Marking the centennial of Seleucus I Nikator's conquest of Central
Asia, Antiochus III ("the Great") attempted a reconquest between 212
and 205 B.C.[4] Marching eastward through Media and Parthia, Antiochus
and his army entered Aria on their way to Bactria.[5] It was the intention
of the Seleucid king to end the insurrection begun by the Diodotids and
perpetuated by Euthydemus I. Hardly the impotent Seleucid loyalist
imagined by some modern writers, this Euthydemus amassed a large military force (including an impressive ten thousand cavalry) to defend his

3. Ibid., p. 9. This theory is based in part on the notion that each monogram on the
coins represents one year of issue, which is patently false for Euthydemid coins.
    4. Our main source (see appendix D) is Polybius, in books 10 and 11 (with Wal-
bank's *Commentary*). See also H. H. Schmitt, *Untersuchungen zur Geschichte Antiochos
des Grossen und seiner Zeit* (Wiesbaden: Historia Einzelschriften, 1964). Sherwin-White
and Kuhrt, *Samarkand to Sardis*, pp. 197–198 offer a revisionist interpretation of these
campaigns.
    5. Notice, in the context of earlier discussions of the mutability of precious metals,
that Antiochus stripped many temple furnishings at Ecbatana (Media) in order to melt down
the gold and silver for coinage; this had previously been done by Alexander, Antigonus,
and Seleucus the son of Nicanor: Polybius 10.27.10–13.
    6. The details are given by Polybius 10.49.1–15, our most complete account of any
military action in the history of Hellenistic Bactria.

right to rule as king over independent Bactria.[6] The Bactrian cavalry was sent ahead to guard the ford of the Arius River, but Antiochus deftly led a picked force of cavalry and light-armed infantry across the river when the Bactrians had retired for the night. When Euthydemus's cavalry realized their error the next morning, they quickly charged the invaders in the hope of driving them back across the Arius.[7] Antiochus mounted a spirited defense and earned special praise for his personal bravery. A wound to his mouth deprived the king of several teeth, and his horse was speared and killed during the battle. Such deeds were the hallmark of Hellenistic kingship, and Antiochus would never again enjoy so much royal acclaim as on the day he defeated the Euthydemid cavalry.[8]

Meanwhile, the king of Bactria was camped some miles away with the rest of his troops and could claim no regal honor from this engagement. His cavalry had been routed in his absence, leaving him little choice but to retreat. Polybius describes Euthydemus as "shocked" by this setback, but there is no reason to suppose panic or cowardice. Antiochus had arrived sooner than Euthydemus expected and crossed the Arius without the Bactrians' knowledge. In fact, Euthydemus's first intimation of these events was the amazing sight of his battered cavalry returning to camp. Euthydemus had badly miscalculated the advance of Antiochus, as Polybius makes clear, and this meant that he was not on the battlefield at the decisive moment.[9] This, too, was a paradigm for Hellenistic power. Error, not cowardice, had driven Euthydemus from the defense of his own frontier. The kingdom he had wrested from the Diodotids now rested upon the walls of Bactra.

For two years (208–206 B.C.), Antiochus and his army besieged the formidable capital of Bactria.[10] The details of this epic struggle are lost to

---

7. Where was the Bactrian infantry? Tarn, *GBI*, p. 124, believed that Euthydemus dared not test the loyalty of his Greek troops by leading them "against their lawful king," Antiochus. This presumes that the cavalry was non-Greek, the infantry Greek, and the latter Seleucid loyalists. Who, then, staunchly defended Bactra for the next two years? Clearly, the loyal infantry was with its lawful king, Euthydemus, some distance away from the Arius battle. See also the speculations of A. Simonetta, "Some Hypotheses on the Military and Political Structure of the Indo-Greek Kingdom," *JNSI* 22 (1960): 56–62.

8. Polybius 10.49.14; cf. 11.39.16 (see appendix D).

9. The king's conspicuous presence in battle was considered important, as in the response of Antigonus Gonatas when informed that he was outnumbered: "How much is my own presence worth?" See Plutarch *Moralia* 183D ("Sayings of Kings and Commanders").

10. Polybius 11.39.1–16 renews the story of these campaigns for the year 206 B.C. On the fame of this siege, see Polybius 29.12.8.

11. On the impressive remains at Balkh, whose later walls still stand, see Ball, *Gazetteer,* pp. 47–49 (site 99). No clear evidence of this particular siege has been found in the levels so far exposed.

us, absent from the pages of Polybius and still archaeologically invisible.[11]
How the whole operation ended, however, is well known. Antiochus the
Great, unable to capture the city, sent an envoy to Euthydemus to ne-
gotiate a settlement. Teleas, the Seleucid ambassador, was a native of
Magnesia in Asia Minor, not coincidentally the hometown of Euthydemus himself.[12] Thus, the king of Bactria—or perhaps his father before
him—had been one of those Greeks from the West who answered the
call of ambition, wealth, and adventure that so characterized the Hellenistic world. Having taken those risks and risen to the status of king,
Euthydemus defended his right to rule Bactria. The case he made to
Teleas, surely part of an official version of this meeting, seems interesting. First, he denied that he was a rebel deserving punishment by Antiochus. Instead, he argued, he had won the kingdom by destroying the
descendants of those who *had* revolted, the Diodotids. Euthydemus took
the position that Bactria had become an independent state under
Diodotid leadership and that his own rule over it was no act of rebellion
against the Seleucids. In other words, the Diodotids' success had voided
the claims of Antiochus, and therefore the Seleucids "should not begrudge
him the title and powers of king."[13]

The second theme of Euthydemus's defense took a more practical turn.
Teleas was reminded of the nomads who might easily take advantage of
the situation should this conflict drag on at Bactra. Some modern scholars have read into this warning a "whiff of blackmail" or even the threat
of a military alliance,[14] but surely the message was a straightforward re-
minder, as Polybius states, that the two kings—and the Hellenism they
championed—were equally endangered by these outsiders. The country
for which Euthydemus and Antiochus were contending might all too easily lapse into barbarism unless the Greeks settled their differences. Such
words conjured the age-old specter of Spitamenes and Arsaces, playing
upon the Greeks' natural fears and recalling the struggles of Alexander,
Seleucus I, Antiochus I, and most recently the Diodotids. All that had
been won in Central Asia might be jeopardized by the nomads who now
gathered on the borders of Bactria, drawn (not summoned) by the civil

---

12. On Teleas, see E. Olshausen, *Prosopographie der hellenistischen Königsgesandten*,
vol. 1 (Louvain: Studia Hellenistica, 1974), pp. 229–230. There are several cities named
Magnesia in Asia Minor. Each author, from Bayer and Cunningham to Tarn and Narain,
has chosen one or another of these cities; however, Bernard, in an appendix (5) to *AK* 4,
pp. 131–133, argues vigorously in favor of Magnesia on the Meander.

13. Polybius 11.39.2–3.

14. Blackmail: Walbank, in CAH², vol. 7(1), p. 82; alliance: *GBI*, pp. 82, 117 (followed by Rostovtzeff, *SEHHW*, vol. 1, p. 543).

wars of Alexander's successors.

A nomadic invasion of Hellenistic Bactria was deferred for another generation by the tireless efforts of Teleas. Shuttling back and forth between Euthydemus and Antiochus, he hammered out a basic agreement that finally ended the siege. Euthydemus's son Demetrius helped to ratify the settlement and was promised by Antiochus one of his daughters in marriage—the only such princess actually mentioned in our sources, although her name and the wedding itself are not attested.[15] By written treaty and sworn alliance, Euthydemus remained king of Bactria. He surrendered his elephant corps to Antiochus and provided ample foodstuffs to the Seleucid troops, who had apparently suffered no less than the besieged.[16] Notably, Euthydemus paid no monetary tribute. Antiochus then departed for India, where he renewed with Sophagasenus the alliance made between their forebears, Seleucus I and Chandragupta Maurya.[17] Little had changed in the relationship between India and the Seleucid empire over the course of a century, but Bactria was clearly another story. The monarchy established there by the Diodotids was given the official sanction of Antiochus himself, proving that no man or army could arrest the forces unleashed by Alexander's death at Babylon.[18]

In some fashion, of course, we would hope to find this historical evolution reflected in the numismatic record. When Euthydemus declared himself king at the expense of the Diodotids, he naturally issued coins in his own name and bearing new designs. His portrait, with royal diadem, graced the obverse; in it we can trace the advancing years of the king, from a youth with angular features to a plump old man losing his

15. Polybius 11.39.9; see chap. 4, n. 4.
16. Elephants had long been a major preoccupation of Hellenistic kings, as noted in chapters 2 and 3. See appendix D, inscriptions 1 and 6. See also Polybius 11.39.11–12 and H. H. Scullard, *The Elephant in the Greek and Roman World* (Ithaca: Cornell University Press, 1974). The Bactrians apparently made good their losses: Francfort, *AK* 3, pp. 7–8.
17. See F. Holt, "Response." pp. 56–64 in P. Green, ed., *Hellenistic History and Culture* (Berkeley: University of California Press, 1993).
18. Sherwin-White and Kuhrt, *Samarkhand to Sardis,* pp. 199–200, argue that Antiochus achieved a genuine reconquest of the East. Certainly they are right to offer a greater appreciation of the anabasis than is usually offered by modern scholars; however, the enhanced reputation that Antiochus enjoyed in the West must be balanced against the real situation in the East. If the Seleucid intended to remove Euthydemus from power and reduce Bactria to a satrapy, then he failed. In spite of his initial success at the Arius River, Antiochus was persuaded by the words of Euthydemus and the walls of Bactra to accept a compromise that left the Seleucids little (or no) actual control over the region. See P. Bernard, "L'Asie centrale et l'empire séleucide," *Topoi* 4 (1994): 477–480.
19. This aging sequence is illustrated in F. Holt, "A History in Silver and Gold," *Aramco World* 45 (May/June 1994): 8–9. Tarn, *GBI,* p. 75, characteristically read Euthy-

teeth and hair.[19] Euthydemus chose the Greek hero Herakles for his reverse type. At first this Herakles was shown seated upon a pile of rocks
and resting his famous club upon a smaller column of stones. In time,
the club moved to the knee and then the thigh of Herakles; a lion skin
eventually draped the rock formation on which the hero rested.[20]

The artistic evolution of this coin-type helps us to organize the coinage
with remarkable precision (see plates 24 and 25). Coupled with the aging portraiture of the king, these stylistic changes follow certain technical changes as well. For example, there was a change in die axis, and the
die cutters finally abandoned the reverse border of dots. Taken together,
this evidence shows that Euthydemus's silver and gold coinage was produced in two major phases.[21] The earlier coins (set A) were struck at several mints; these gave way to a highly refined series of coins (set B) from
a single mint. The principal monogram for set A was $\oplus$, while the exclusive monogram for set B was K .

It is significant that we can date this whole transformation of Euthydemus's coinage to the time of Antiochus's two-year siege of Bactra
(208–206 B.C.). During this critical period, Euthydemus began to con-
solidate all mint activity and, at about the same time, struck a rare gold
octodrachm issue. This magnificent coin stands at the end of the set A
series and has been associated with the lifting of the siege in 206 B.C.
that affirmed the independence of Bactria.[22] A similar transition manifests itself on the bronze coinages of Euthydemus, which show the
bearded head of Herakles on the obverse and, with the king's name, a
galloping horse on the reverse. His earlier issues were struck on the thick,
beveled flans characteristic of the Diodotid bronze mintage; likewise,

---

demus's whole character and motivation in this portrait: "One has only to look at his face
to see why he seized the crown: he meant to rule because he could." For a *possible* portrait of Euthydemus, see the discovery of a stunning third-century B.C. diademed clay bust
at Takht-i Sangin: B. Litvinsky and I. Pichikyan, "Monuments of Art from the Sanctuary
of Oxus (North Bactria)," *AAASH* 28 (1980): p. 64.

20. The model for Euthydemus's coin-type may be found in the popular statuary of
Herakles and certain Seleucid coin-types from the Asia Minor homeland of Euthydemus's
family: Bernard, *AK* 4, p. 131; cf. Chaibai Mustamandy, "Herakles, Ahnherr Alexanders,
in einer Plastik aus Hadda," pp. 176–180 and frontispiece in J. Ozols and V. Thewalt, eds.,
Aus dem Osten des Alexanderreiches (Cologne: Du Mont, 1984).

21. F. Holt, "The Euthydemid Coinage of Bactria: Further Hoard Evidence from Ai
Khanoum," *RN* 23 (1981): 7–44, esp. 21–24; cf. A. D. H. Bivar, "The Bactra Coinage of
Euthydemus and Demetrius," *NC* 11 (1951): 22–39, and Bopearachchi, *Monnaies*, pp. 47–49.

22. Bopearachchi, *Monnaies*, p. 158 (series 11); cf. G. Le Rider, "Monnaies grecques
récemment acquises par le Cabinet de Paris," *RN* 11 (1969): 26.

these coins have no mint marks. Later, Euthydemus employed bronze flans that were thinner and had rounded edges. These issues carry monograms, including the K common to the set B precious-metal coins. One of these bronze issues, with $\triangle$ | monogram, also bears an anchor symbol on the reverse.[23] This anchor has nothing to do with landlocked Central Asia; it is the badge of the Seleucid dynasty.[24] The momentary appearance of this well-known symbol on Euthydemus's coinage should be dated to ca. 206 B.C., when, in exchange for his independence, the Bactrian ruler acknowledged the nominal suzerainty of Antiochus III. With the departure of the Seleucid army, there would have been no reason to make such a gesture, and certainly this coin would not have been struck while Euthydemus was still at war with Antiochus. Thus, it is a chronological hinge—like the gold octodrachm—between the two phases of Euthydemus's coinage.

We can therefore readily identify the mintages produced in Bactria between the fall of Diodotus II and the siege of 208–206 B.C. These early issues included the thick, beveled bronzes without control marks and the silver and gold coins of Euthydemus's set A (mostly A); after the siege, the set B issues (K) predominate.[25] This evidence tells us some important things. For example, many of Euthydemus's early bronzes have been found at Ai Khanoum, but none of the bronze issues dated during or after the siege have been discovered there. This suggests that Ai Khanoum itself may have produced many of the earlier coins but not the later ones. The war with Antiochus could easily have suspended most minting operations except at Bactra, giving rise to a consolidation of coinage manufacture that persisted after the immediate danger had passed. In terms of the monograms, this localizes $\triangle$ |, K, and others at Bactra from ca. 208–206 B.C. onward. It is just possible, then, that we should associate A with magistrates at Ai Khanoum, as hinted at already for the mintages of Diodotus I and II. In fact, the early coinages of Euthydemus were heavily A mintages, some (as with the Diodotids)

23. In the BN: Bopearachchi, *Monnaies*, p. 162 (series 22, coin 34), with comments in Holt's review, *AJN* 3/4 (1992): 219–220.

24. According to Appian *Syr.* 56, Seleucus I used the anchor (which had portended his royal future) as his personal seal; the symbol appeared also on Seleucid coins: O. Mørkholm, *Early Hellenistic Coinage from the Accession of Alexander to the Peace of Apamea (336–188 B.C.)* (Cambridge: Cambridge University Press, 1991), p. 73.

25. In the early days of Bactrian studies, these monograms were looked upon not only as abbreviations for city names (see above, chap. 4) but also as possible dates. For one example of these dead-end speculations, see A. F. Rudolf Hoernle, "Monograms of the Baktro-Greek King Euthydemos," *Indian Antiquary* 8 (1879): 196–198, assigning the massive mintages of A and K to the individual years 218 and 192 respectively.

bearing an associated Greek letter including Ⴈ. Whether this means that Euthydemus first arose in the area of Ai Khanoum we cannot yet say, but the similar patterns of monograms are noteworthy.[26] An overlap of control marks also exists between the early coinage of Euthydemus and the last issues of Diodotus II at mint B (Bactra?). These issues of Euthydemus include drachms, tetradrachms, and even gold staters with Diodotus's control mark ဩ from F8.[27] The gold coins continue the pattern of weight reduction observed in the Diodotid mintages and so fall nicely in the run of mint B issues: Diodotus II's F6, F7, F8, to Euthydemus's 1, 2, and 3. Significant, too, is the fact that Euthydemus chose this moment to mint his first and, the octodrachm excepted, only gold coins. This signifies the decisive victory of Euthydemus in his rise to undisputed mastery over Bactria. The transfer of Diodotus's last control mark, from his last mint, onto the first gold issues of Euthydemus bears witness to the end of one dynasty and the beginning of another. Some twenty years later, Euthydemus would face—and survive—a similar challenge to his own authority. On that occasion, he again struck a significant gold issue. The coins, like the literary texts, confirm that Euthydemus had negated the rival claims of first the Diodotids and then the Seleucids. In so doing, however, he validated all that the Diodotids had done to make Bactria a separate and successful Hellenistic state.

The settlement between Euthydemus I and Antiochus the Great was therefore a watershed event in Bactrian history. It marked a century of Seleucid interest in the eastern reaches of Alexander's old empire, and yet it acknowledged the inexorable rise of independent states so typical of the Hellenistic period. It can be seen as the final step in what the Diodotids had started, bringing to its logical conclusion the legacy of father and son. Like the walls of Bactra, the work of Diodotus I and II stood resolutely between Antiochus the Great on one side and Euthydemus I on the other.

SILENCE IN BACTRIA

The careers of these two kings after 206 B.C. foreshadowed the future of the Hellenistic world. After his venture into India, Antiochus the

26. See also N. Smirnova, "Bactrian Coins in the Pushkin State Museum of Fine Arts," *Ancient Civilizations* 2 (1995): 340 and n. 31.

27. Bopearachchi, *Monnaies,* pp. 154–155 (series 1–3). A particularly fine example of the stater has recently surfaced: Harlan Berk Sale (Sept. 1995) no. 5 (8.14 g).

28. Schmitt, *Antiochos;* Sherwin-White and Kuhrt, *Samarkhand to Sardis,* pp. 201–219; *CAH²* 8, pp. 249–289.

Great returned west to the Mediterranean.[28] With his new elephants and his new fame, he invited comparisons to Alexander and Seleucus I Nikator. Among those who took notice were the Romans, whose legions were just finishing their own epic saga with the defeat of Hannibal the Carthaginian.[29] When Antiochus risked a modest invasion of Greece in 192 B.C., the Roman republic responded in force. The Seleucid king was driven back to Asia Minor, where he suffered a major defeat at the Battle of Magnesia in 190 B.C. Thereafter, the Seleucid empire lost possession of much military power and all of Asia Minor by the terms of the Peace of Apamea (188 B.C.).[30]

This fiasco was not by any means the finish of the Seleucids, but it did establish the future course of events. The relentless expansion of Roman influence into the eastern Mediterranean would continue to humble the royal successors of Alexander. One by one, the major Hellenistic states passed into the dominion of Rome as conquered provinces: Antigonid Macedonia in 146 B.C., Seleucid Syria in 64 B.C., and Ptolemaic Egypt in 30 B.C.[31] It was into the grip of this "new world order" that Antiochus had led his own empire after leaving Euthydemus king of Bactria.

For his part, the Bactrian monarch and his new Hellenistic kingdom would never face the threat of Rome's legions, except by way of fiction or a few lost soldiers.[32] The danger to Bactria lay in another direction. Recent numismatic studies have suggested just how seriously Antiochus and Euthydemus had been menaced by the nomads to the north of Bactria. It has long been recognized that Sogdiana, the region just beyond the Oxus River, achieved its independence from Bactria by the early decades of the second century B.C. This development may be seen in the coinage, where a group of people beyond the political control of the Greeks began to issue their own so-called barbarous imitations of the royal Bactrian currency.[33] These imitations diverge from the Bactrian pro-

---

29. On Rome and Carthage, see J. F. Lazenby, *Hannibal's War: A Military History of the Second Punic War* (Warminster: Aris and Phillips, 1978) and Brian Caven, *The Punic Wars* (New York: St. Martin's Press, 1980).

30. A. H. McDonald, "The Treaty of Apamea (188 B.C.)," *JRS* 57 (1967): 1–8; A. H. McDonald and F. Walbank, "The Treaty of Apamea (188 B.C.): The Naval Clauses," *JRS* 59 (1969): 30–39.

31. For these important developments, consult the works cited in chap. 1, n. 7.

32. Fiction: H. Warner Munn, *The Lost Legion* (Garden City, N.Y.: Doubleday, 1980). Fact: Z. Usmanova, "Inscriptions from Kara-Kamar," *VDI* (1990): 145–147 (including a curious Latin inscription attesting a Gaius Rex of the Fifteenth Legion in Bactria).

33. The seminal study was made by Allotte de la Füye, "Monnaies incertaines de la Sogdiane."

totypes in terms of engraving style, weight standard, and facility with the Greek language.[34] Some issues actually carry non-Greek inscriptions, most notably in Aramaic.[35]

These earliest Sogdian imitations may now be dated to the period of Antiochus's siege of Bactria.[36] This suggests that the barbarian threat about which Euthydemus warned was much closer and more organized than previously imagined by scholars. Sogdian independence under non-Greek leadership would indeed have weighed heavily upon the minds of the two men warring at Bactra. In the archaeological record we can see evidence of new fortifications along the northern perimeter of Bactria and at Ai Khanoum from ca. 200 B.C.[37] Euthydemus and his successors may also have begun to recruit non-Greek troops, perhaps in the same way that Rome later absorbed the strength of the nearer barbarian tribes in order to stave off others. Indeed, the coins show that the independence of Sogdiana was unbroken from the time of Euthydemus down to ca. 150 B.C., when the nomadic Yueh-Chi tribes finally invaded the Oxus Valley.[38] In the same year that barbarian Rome destroyed the great cities of Carthage and Corinth, tribal nomads in 146 B.C. swept away the great city at Ai Khanoum.[39] The fate of the Hellenistic world was thereby sealed forever on its eastern and western frontiers.

The balance of Greek power in Central Asia then shifted south of the Hindu Kush, where Euthydemus's descendants established new Indo-Greek states that lingered until about A.D. 10. In the Oxus heartland of Bactria itself, the last Greek king (Heliocles I) was gone by 130 B.C.[40] Thus, a century after the rise of independent Bactria under the Diodotid dynasty, the Greek kingdom had collapsed in the face of tribal invaders.

---

34. Caution must be exercised for the more subjective criteria, such as "Greek artistic style." For a study of errors in the Greek inscriptions, see F. Holt, "Mimesis in Metal: The Fate of Greek Culture on Bactrian Coins," pp. 84–100 in F. Titchener and R. Moorton, eds., *Mimesis: The Reciprocal Influence of Life and Arts in Graeco-Roman Antiquity* (forthcoming).

35. F. Widemann, "Un monnayage inconnu de type gréco-bactrien à légende araméene," *Studia Iranica* 18 (1989): 193–197.

36. O. Bopearachchi, "The Euthydemus Imitations and the Date of Sogdian Independence," *Silk Road Art and Archaeology* 2 (1991–92): 1–21.

37. Leriche, *AK* 5, pp. 93–95; G. Pugachenkova, "The Antiquities of TransOxiana in the Light of Investigations in Uzbekistan (1985–1990)," *Ancient Civilizations* 2 (1995): 11–16.

38. Bopearachchi, "Euthydemus Imitations," pp. 12–13; P. Bernard, "Maracanda-Afrasiab colonie grecque," pp. 331–365 in *La Persia e l'Asia Centrale da Alessandro al X secolo* (Rome: Accademia Nationale dei Lincei, 1996).

39. For the date, see P. Bernard, "Campagne de fouilles 1978 à Ai Khanoum (Afghanistan)," *CRAI* (1980): 442–443.

40. See the chronological discussion by Bopearachchi, *Monnaies,* pp. 74–141.

This political crisis had a fascinating social and cultural dimension. In some important ways, the work of the Seleucids, Diodotids, and Euthydemids transcended the total eclipse of their Hellenistic state. Before and after the political fall of Greek Bactria, strong cultural interactions were at work. We may even be able to witness some of this interchange in the workshops of the royal mints, where the last Greek kings of Bactria seem to have employed non-Greek artisans.[41]

In contrast to the old notion that the Yueh-Chi tribes exterminated the Greeks, suddenly and savagely replacing Hellenism with barbarism, it now seems that the transition of power was ameliorated by at least a generation of intense social and cultural contact.[42] By the time the last Greek king was gone from Bactria, the kingdom was already under the powerful influence of the tribes settled in neighboring Sogdiana. By the same token, traces of Hellenism can be seen in Central Asia for centuries beyond the fall of Greek Bactria. As the nomadic invaders settled the area and created the great Kushana empire, their culture betrayed much Greek inspiration. Viktor Sarianidi's extraordinary excavations of a necropolis at Tillya-Tepe (the Golden Mound) provide ample evidence of this phenomenon. Among these finds of the first century A.D. were the famous Bactrian Aphrodite, a dress clasp showing Dionysus and Ariadne, a pendant with Artemis/Anahita, and a cameo of a Greek king of Bactria (Eucratides?).[43]

If we look into but one of these lavish Kushana tombs, we can glimpse the many cultural threads that were finally woven together by the successors of the Greek rulers in Bactria. Grave 3 held the remains of a young female whose possessions are a veritable catalog of ancient Mediterranean, Mesopotamian, Asian, and Indian artifacts.[44] She wore the elaborate, gold-spangled costume and jewelry of her once-nomadic ancestors. A silver mirror from Han China lay on her chest, and a Parthian royal coin had been clenched in her fist. A gold Roman coin, struck by the emperor Tiberius in Lugdunum (modern Lyons), rested among her funeral

---

41. See Holt, "Mimesis in Metal," for the evidence.
42. Tarn, *GBI*, p. 301, writes of the sharp antithesis between Greek and barbarian and argues that "the Greek coinage of Bactria remained fine to the end, and then the great Bactrian artists vanished from the world. . . . "
43. For general treatments of these discoveries, see V. Sarianidi, "The Golden Hoard of Bactria," *National Geographic* 177 (March 1990): 50–75, "The Treasure of the Golden Mound," *Archaeology* 33 (1980): 31–41, and "The Treasure of Golden Hill," *AJA* 84 (1980): 125–132.
44. On what follows, consult V. Sarianidi, *The Golden Hoard of Bactria* (Leningrad: Aurora Art Publishers, 1985), pp. 27–34, with splendid illustrations.

offerings, along with a lidded silver vessel whose weight was inscribed, in Greek, on the bottom (see plate 26). Her clasps were an eclectic blend of Asian, Persian, Greek, and Roman styles; her signet rings were Graeco-Roman. An oval pendant showed Athena in full armor, the goddess's name inscribed in Greek along the edge (see plate 27). An ivory comb had come from India, and an intaglio of Persian or Greek manufacture was adorned with a carved zebu (Indian ox). A world of ancient art went to the grave with this anonymous Kushana girl.[45]

The life and death of those buried at Tillya-Tepe brought together all the historical and cultural strands that had trailed away from the confrontation of Antiochus and Euthydemus. In this long drama, the Diodotids had played their part as heirs to the opportunism unleashed at Babylon in 323 B.C. We have traced these events as best we could through archaeology, texts, and coins. These sources have many limitations, but the prospects of new evidence and keener insight have never been brighter. For this as for so much else in Hellenistic studies, Bactria remains an extraordinary window onto the workings of the ancient world. Instead of Tarn's "brotherhood of man," the kings of Bactria pursued the harsher ideals of Alexander and his earliest successors: aggression, opportunism, chauvinism, conspicuous consumption, and, above all, independence. These were the motive forces behind Hellenistic state building, war, exploration, and economic expansion, and they were also the reasons for so much political instability and revolution. Without underestimating the very real achievements of the Romans, the Yueh-Chi, or the Indians, we must remember that the Hellenistic Greeks never faced a greater danger than themselves. The Hellenistic Age was by all accounts one of the most creative of historical eras; it was also one of the most self-destructive. Bactria remains the paradigm for this extraordinary legacy of Alexander's last breath at Babylon.

45. As an introduction to the larger context of Kushana history and culture, see John Rosenfield, *The Dynastic Art of the Kushans* (Berkeley: University of California Press, 1967); B. Staviskij, *La Bactriane sous les Kushans: Problèmes d'histoire et de culture* (Paris: Maisonneuve, 1986); Gavin Hambly, ed., *Central Asia* (New York: Delacorte, 1969); and Richard Frye, *The Heritage of Central Asia: From Antiquity to the Turkish Expansion* (Princeton: Markus Wiener, 1996).

A Catalog of Diodotid
Coinage in Silver and Gold

This catalog presents the numismatic material upon which much of this book is based. It is as complete as I have been able to make it and certainly far more comprehensive than any inventory ever published. There can be no doubt that fresh finds will have to be incorporated into this evolving framework as part of the normal advance of knowledge outlined in chapter 4; meanwhile, this catalog should mark a significant stage in that process.

Listed here are the Diodotid coins to be found in the British Museum (London), the Bibliothèque Nationale (Paris), the American Numismatic Society (New York), the Smithsonian Institution (Washington, D.C.), the Staatliche Museen (Berlin), the Museum of Fine Arts (Boston), the Danish National Museum (Copenhagen), the Punjab Museum (Lahore), the National Museum of Georgia (Tbilisi), the Tadjikistan Museum (Dushanbe), the Pushkin State Museum of Fine Arts (Moscow), the Staatliche Münzsammlung (Munich), the Fitzwilliam Museum (Cambridge), the Ashmolean Museum (Oxford), the Indian Museum (Calcutta), the Hermitage (St. Petersburg) and other public institutions. Some of these collections I have examined personally, others by way of published catalogs or casts and photographs kindly supplied by their curators. The holdings of several important private collections (some now dispersed) have also been included, most notably those of William Wahler, Arthur Houghton, Aman Ur Rahman, Adrian Hollis, and Harry Fowler. In addition, hundreds of auction catalogs from Europe and the United States have been combed in search of Diodotid specimens still circulating in trade; many dealers have provided photographs and other information for unpublished specimens.

To serve numismatists as a quick reference guide, this appendix will include gold and silver issues beginning with those in the name of Antiochus (series A, C, and E) and then those in the name of Diodotus (series B, D, and F).[1] Appendix B

---

1. It is argued here that Diodotus I issued series A and that Diodotus II was responsible for minting series C and E as his father's viceroy and series B, D, and F as sole king of Bactria.

will present the bronze issues and appendix C the probable gold forgeries. Following the conventions of numismatics, each of these six series (identified by letters) will be composed of groups (marked by numbers). Each group represents a link in the development of a series. The known specimens in each group are identified by the particular collection's accession number and provenance notes, an auction catalog date and number, or some other appropriate designation. Unless otherwise noted, all coins in this appendix are silver tetradrachms with a 6:oo die axis ($\downarrow$). As a matter of convenience, I shall provide in the notes a running concordance with the other major cataloging systems—Bopearachchi, *Monnaies*, and Mitchiner, *IGISC*. Thus, my series A, group 1, corresponds to Mitchiner's 67d (though one coin of his 67c, the Shortt specimen, also belongs in my A1) and to Bopearachchi's series 2F. Also as a matter of convenience, the following abbreviations will be useful in these listings of coins: OBV(erse), REV(erse), r(ight), l(eft), EX(ample)S, A(merican)N(umismatic)S(ociety), B(ibliothèque)N(ationale), B(ritish)M(useum), C(lassical)N(umismatic)G(roup), N(umismatic)F(ine)A(rts), g(ram), A(i)K(hanoum), exc(avation), AV (gold), AR (silver), AE (bronze), DR(achm), H(emi)D(rachm), TF (stray find), F(ixed)P(rice)L(ist).

COINS IN THE NAME OF ANTIOCHUS

There are three series (A, C, E) of thundering Zeus coins struck in the name of Antiochus. Series A, composed of eight groups, represents a very long and uniform mintage of tetradrachms and a single gold stater. All specimens of this series show a distinctive royal portrait, a die axis consistently maintained at 6:oo ($\downarrow$), and an inscription on the reverse that always aligns under (not outside) the arm of Zeus:

SERIES A, GROUP 1

OBV: Head of Diodotus I r., wearing diadem. Border of dots.
REV: ΒΑΣΙΛΕΩΣ ΑΝΤΙΟΧΟΥ Zeus striding l., hurling thunderbolt in
               r. hand; outstretched l. arm draped with aegis; eagle at l. foot of
               Zeus. Border of dots. No visible control marks.
EXS: 1)   BM 1860-12-20-2 (Hay Collection); 16.65 g.
          2)   BM 1922-4-24-1 (Whitehead Collection); 15.60 g.

SERIES A, GROUP 2[2]

OBV: As above.
REV: As above, but with control mark ⓪ in l. field above eagle.
EXS: 1)   BM 1939-3-18-1 (Kabul); 15.87 g.
          2)   F. Kovacs Stock (1997); 16.91 g.

---

2. See Bopearachchi 2J and Mitchiner 64c. I accept here the reading of the monogram proposed by Bopearachchi, *Monnaies*, p. 147 n. 3, rather than the one found in Mitchiner's catalog. The new Kovacs specimen shows the monogram quite distinctly.

The fabric of these pieces very closely resembles that of the previous group as well as the specimens in groups 3 and 4 below.

SERIES A, GROUP 3[3]

OBV: As above.
REV: As above, but with monogram ⌐⌐ above the eagle.
EX: 1)   Houghton Collection no. 1295; 16.34 g.

SERIES A, GROUP 4[4]

OBV: As above.
REV: As above, but with control mark E above the eagle.
EXS: 1)   Empire Coins 10 (May 1989) no. 89; 16.12 g.
      2)   BN 1974.392 (LeBerre Collection); 16.61 g.
      3)   Hollis Collection, previously.[5]
      4)   AK Exc Hoard 2, coin 3; 15.73 g.[6]
      5)   BN 1963 [R.3681.25] (LeBerre Collection); 16.49 g.
      6)   BM (Miller Collection); 15.39 g.

These six tetradrachms form a very closely styled mintage. The obverse die linkage between examples 4 and 5 suggested by Petitot-Biehler has been challenged by Bopearachchi, but these specimens are clearly the work of a single artist.[7] Similarly, coins 2 and 3 probably share an obverse die. More important, the catalog description of coin 1 claims an obverse die link to the Houghton tetradrachm of A3.

SERIES A, GROUP 5[8]

OBV: As above.
REV: As above but with monogram Σ above the eagle.
EXS: 1)   BN (Rollin 1843); 15.69 g.[9]

3. Not represented in either Bopearachchi or Mitchiner; published in Arthur Houghton, *Coins of the Seleucid Empire from the Collection of Arthur Houghton* (New York, 1983), p. 119. Specimens from this source are henceforth designated "Houghton Collection."
    4. Cf. Bopearachchi 2G and Mitchiner 64G.
    5. Illustrated in Mitchiner, *IGISC*, vol. 1, p. 39 (coin 64g), this coin is no longer owned by Mr. Hollis (personal communication, 1987).
    6. Claire-Yvonne Petitot-Biehler, "Trésor de monnaies grecques et gréco-bactriennes trouvé à Ai Khanoum (Afghanistan)," *RN* 17 (1975): 23–57, esp. 25. This important article has been translated into English as part of O. Guillaume, ed., *Graeco-Bactrian and Indian Coins from Afghanistan* (Delhi/Oxford/New York: Oxford University Press, 1991). This coin is among those recently looted from the Kabul Museum.
    7. See n. 6 and Bopearachchi, *Monnaies*, p. 148 n. 5.
    8. Bopearachchi 2I and Mitchiner 64f.
    9. This coin underwent a University of Michigan chemical analysis in 1970, with the following results reported to me by personal communication: silver (99.2 percent), copper (0.62 percent), gold (0.07 percent), arsenic (0.01 percent). This rare analysis of a Bactrian

2)   Ashmolean Collection; 15.96 g.[10]
3)   B. Peus (1973) no. 253; 16.64 g.
4)   Kunduz Hoard, coin 5; 16.32 g.[11]
5)   Kunduz Hoard, coin 4; 16.75 g.
6)   AK Hoard 3, coin 20.[12]
7)   AK Hoard 3, coin 24.
8)   CNG Sale 37 (1995) no. 435; 16.54 g.

This group exhibits much die linkage. Coins 1 and 2 and perhaps coin 3 were struck from the same obverse die. Coin 3 shares a reverse die with coin 4, which in turn shares an obverse die with coin 5. The reverse of coin 5 appears nearly the same as that of coin 6. All specimens in this group show the same artistic rendering of Diodotus's hair, especially below the diadem and behind the ear. This feature appears plainly on the last example of the preceding group, giving further cohesion to series A.

SERIES A, GROUP 6[13]

OBV: As above.
REV: As above, but with monogram ⚹ above the eagle.
EXS: 1)   E. J. Waddell Sale (1988) no. 33; 16.35 g.
      2)   Hermitage Museum.[14]
      3)   AK Hoard 3, coin 21; 15.87 g.[15]
      4)   Houghton Collection no. 1294; 15.84 g.[16]
      5)   BN N.6432 (Allotte de la Füye); 15.85 g.
      6)   Naville Sale 12 (1976) no. 1950; 16.15 g.[17]
      7)   BM 1858-7-31-1 (Crereton Collection); 16.33 g.

---

coin indicates the fineness of the early Diodotid silver issues: cf. Lahiri, *Corpus,* p. 18; and J. A. Buckley, "An Analysis of Thirty-One Coins from the Hellenistic Period," *Archaeometry* 27 (1985): 102–107.

10. Sotheby (1958) no. 281 (Haughton Collection), incorrectly listed twice by Mitchiner as both 64f and 67e.

11. *TQ,* p. 14. This is the source for all references to the Kunduz Hoard in this inventory; these coins have also been lost in the looting of the Kabul Museum.

12. F. Holt, "The Euthydemid Coinage of Bactria: Further Hoard Evidence from Ai Khanoum," *RN* 23 (1981): 7–44, esp. p. 14. Henceforth, coins from this hoard will be identified as AK Hoard 3.

13. Bopearachchi 2E and Mitchiner 64d and e. Like Bopearachchi, *Monnaies,* p. 147, I do not consider Mitchiner's 64e as a separate monogram type. Note also that Mitchiner's 67c is clearly an incomplete reading of the control marks and has been classed in my series C, group 1. I have excluded from this inventory coins for which I have no photographs, casts, or adequate descriptions lest the same specimen be listed twice by mistake (e.g., R. C. Senior Sale List 4 [1982] no. 45; see "Uncertain Attributions" at the end of this appendix).

14. Published in B. Staviskij, *To the South from the Iron Gates* (in Russian) (Moscow: Sovetskii Khudozhnik, 1977), p. 25.

15. Later appeared in Peus Catalogue 298 (1979) no. 116.

16. Previously SNGLockett 3109, from Naville Sale I (1921) no. 2945.

17. Previously Zschiesche und Koder Sale 5 (1913) no. 688.

8) Reported in trade (1989); 15.90 g.[18]
9) Naville Sale 10 (1925) no. 903; 16.43 g.
10) Boston Museum of Fine Arts no. 307; 16.46 g.[19]
11) Leo Hamburger Sale (1930) no. 417; 14.81 g.
12) Sotheby Sale (1977) no. 51.
13) F. Kovacs Stock (1997); 15.80 g.
14) F. Kovacs Stock (1997); 16.28 g.
15) ANS 1995.51.50 (Fowler Collection); 16.34 g.[20]
16) Wahler Collection no. 457, previously; 15.18 g.[21]
17) Smithsonian Institution 85-9-106 (Markoff-Moghadam); 15.28 g.[22]
18) Smithsonian Institution 85-9-107 (Markoff-Moghadam); 14.58 g.
19) Bukhara Hoard, coin 1; 16.4 g.[23]
20) Bukhara Hoard, coin 2; 15.7 g.
21) Bukhara Hoard, coin 3; 16.1 g.
22) Bukhara Hoard, coin 4; 15.9 g.
23) Wahler Collection no. 455, previously; 16.53 g.[24]

18. Personal communication from Frank L. Kovacs, to whom I owe a debt of gratitude for much assistance over the years.
19. Previously Jameson Collection no. 1672.
20. Previously Donner 1982; to be published with other specimens in the ANS *Sylloge* by O. Bopearachchi, who kindly has shared this information with me. I am indebted to the late Harry Fowler, as well as to the ANS staff (especially Carmen Arnold-Biucchi and Frank Campbell), for their assistance.
21. The extraordinary private collection of the late William Wahler, who kindly shared insights and information with me over the years, has been dispersed. This coin previously appeared in Sotheby Sale (1971) no. 285, where it was listed at 15.21 g.
22. From personal inspection and enlarged photographs this coin and coin 16 (Wahler no. 457) appear to be the same specimen in all visible respects. They are struck in exactly the same position on the flan and exhibit identical scratches, dents, and other anomalies (e.g., below the chin, above the aegis, and on the rim near Zeus's head). Note also should be taken of the inscription, where the sigma has been broken. Yet, these cannot be the same coin, because coin 16 was still in the Wahler collection after coin 17 had been given to the Smithsonian Institution. The likelihood of identical coin strikes and wear is remote, whereas casting could easily be the answer. This raises suspicions, of course, about cast forgeries (see Lahiri, *Corpus*, pp. 62–65). The appearance of coins 15 and 18 adds to this concern. They share with coins 16 and 17 their flan positioning and some of their peculiarities, especially along the rim of the reverse and the inscription (identically deformed sigma). Coin 15 is much heavier and "cleaner," while coin 18 is the lightest and least distinct. It is possible that coins 16, 17, and 18 are copies of coin 15. Whether these are ancient or modern cast forgeries remains uncertain: O. Bopearachchi, *Indo-Greek, Indo-Scythian and Indo-Parthian Coins in the Smithsonian Institution* (Washington, D.C.: Smithsonian Institution, 1993), pp. 8, 69. The authenticity of coin 15 is supported by obverse die linkage to coins 13 and 14.
23. Published (with exs. 20–22) by E. V. Rtveladze, "La circulation monétaire au nord de l'Oxus a l'époque gréco-bactrienne," *RN* 26 (1984): 61–76; also E. V. Rtveladze and M. Nijazova, "First Hoard of Greco-Bactrian Coins from Bukhara" (in Russian), *Obshchestvennye Nauki v Uzbekistane* (1984–86): 54–58. Not all specimens are illustrated, so attributions here must rely upon the published descriptions.
24. Appeared in Munz und Medaillen Sale 411 (1979) no. 4 and subsequently in NFA Sale (1989) no. 745.

24) AK Hoard 3, coin 23; 16.16 g.[25]
25) AK Hoard 3, coin 22.
26) Wahler Collection no. 456, previously; 15.35 g.[26]
27) ANS 1944.100.74363 (Newell Collection); 16.32 g.
28) Wahler Collection no. 454, previously; 16.38 g.[27]
29) Cederland Sale 100 (1995) no. 187.
30) AK Exc Hoard 2, coin 5; 15.93 g.
31) Berlin 565/1875; 16.82 g.
32) NFA Sale 11 (1982) no. 247; 15.77 g.[28]
33) Kunduz Hoard, coin 6; 16.47 g.
34) AK Exc Hoard 2, coin 7; 15.82 g.
35) Burnes (1833).[29]
36) Persic Gallery Sale 27 no. 85; 15.7 g.
37) Persic Gallery Sale 28 no. 64; 16.7 g.
38) Schlesinger Sale 13 (1935) no. 1521; 16.6 g.
39) AK Exc Hoard 2, coin 6; 15.90 g.
40) BM 1888-12-8-51 (Cunningham Collection); 16.63 g.
41) Berlin (Loebbecke Collection 1906); 16.39 g.
42) F. Kovacs Stock (1997); 14.94 g.
43) F. Kovacs Stock (1997); 16.22 g.
44) F. Kovacs Stock (1997); 16.31 g.
45) F. Kovacs Stock (1997); 16.77 g.
46) F. Kovacs Stock (1998); 16.27g.
47) F. Kovacs Stock (1998); 16.42g.

These forty-seven tetradrachms constitute a substantial mintage that greatly exceeds the emissions of groups 1–5. Furthermore, they include relatively few die links, which also indicates a large and well-dispersed mintage. Except for the suspicious case of coins 16 through 18 (see n. 22), only examples 13, 14, 15, and 33 and 34 are certainly linked; coin 32 may join these, given its similar obverse die break at the end of the diadem. Many examples show nearly identical features (e.g., coins 39 and 40), but die identity cannot be proven. The portrait of the king undergoes a brief plumping during this mintage, leaving Diodotus with a distinct double chin by the end. Also, the rendering of his hair shows for a time a more pronounced series of curls at the top of his head (seen clearly on coins 23 through 30). These characteristics could reveal aging during a particularly long striking of coinage or perhaps a less ambiguous depiction of the king himself. This portraiture runs smoothly into that of the next group.

25. Appeared in Munz Zentrum Sale 39 (1980) no. 723.
26. Later, Sotheby/NFA Sale 10 (1993) no. 905.
27. Leu Sale 36 (1985) no. 175 and, subsequently, Persic Gallery Sale 32 no. 46.
28. Previously, Naville Sale 10 (1925) no. 904, and Norman Davis Collection no. 258; cf. Norman Davis and Colin Kraay, *The Hellenistic Kingdoms: Portrait Coins and History* (London: Thames and Hudson, 1973), pp. 129–130, 133.
29. Discussed above (chap. 4); current disposition unknown.

SERIES A, GROUP 7[30]

OBV: As above.
REV: As above but with control mark Ͷ above the eagle.
EXS: 1) Berlin (Loebbecke Collection 1906); 16.54 g.
      2) BN N.6431; 16.08 g.
      3) BM 1888-12-8-49 (Cunningham Collection); 16.41 g.
      4) Persic Gallery Sale 26 no. 66.
      5) Rahman Collection no. 1009.[31]
      6) F. Kovacs Stock (1997); 16.66 g.
      7) Edgar Owen Sale 29 (1996) no. 66.
      8) BM 1860-12-20-1 (Hay Collection); 16.65 g.
      9) AK Exc Hoard 2, coin 4; 14.88 g.

This group captures well the advancing age of the king and bridges nicely to the elderly visage on the following group. A few Diodotid drachms with this control mark (Ͷ) have a distinctly different and younger portrait; these are assigned to another series (C). The few known staters with control mark Ͷ are demonstrably false and must therefore be purged from this inventory of ancient evidence.[32]

SERIES A, GROUP 8[33]

OBV: As above.
REV: As above but with a wreath (Ω) above the eagle.
EXS: 1) Harlan Berk Sale 95 (1997) no. 174.
      2) NFA Sale 31 (1993) no. 354; 16.36 g.
      3) Classical Coins Sale 34 (1995) no. 227; 16.64 g.
      4) F. Kovacs Stock (1996); 16.48 g.
      5) Tadjikistan Museum H-473/1; 16.53 g.
      6) ANS 1944.100.74362 (Newell Collection); 16.03 g.
AV 7) Taxila Exc coin 39.[34]

30. Bopearachchi 2H and Mitchiner 64b.
31. Published by O. Bopearachchi and Aman Ur Rahman, *Pre-Kushana Coins in Pakistan* (Islamabad: Iftikar, 1995); part of the second Mir Zakah hoard, it is listed at "8.65 g," an obvious mistake for this tetradrachm.
32. Jenkins, "A Group of Bactrian Forgeries," *RN* 7 (1965): 56. Mitchiner, *IGISC*, vol. 1, p. 39 (type 63) nevertheless lists the false variety, using a specimen condemned by Jenkins. Similarly, the stater in the name of Diodotus with Ͷ control mark (Mitchiner type 70b) seems to be spurious; see Bopearachchi, *Monnaies*, p. 149 n. 12, and A. R. Bellinger, "The Coins from the Treasure of the Oxus," *ANSMN* 10 (1962): 63. A curious attempt to rehabilitate the forgery condemned by Jenkins has been made by S. Kovalenko, "The Coinage of Diodotus I and Diodotus II, Greek Kings of Bactria," *Silk Road Art and Archaeology* 4 (1995/96): 25–26. Jenkins's original case seems quite convincing contrasted with a set of circular stylistic arguments.
33. Not represented in either Bopearachchi or Mitchiner. Bopearachchi's series 1A and 2B bear only the distinct younger portrait that I have assigned to another series (C).
34. John Marshall, *Taxila*, 3 vols. (Cambridge, 1951; rpt. Varanasi: Bhartiya, 1975), p. 798. This stater was discovered in a hoard of punch-marked coins and jewelry (Bhir Mound, 1913), referred to in chapter 2.

This group, culminating in a genuine gold issue, brings to a close the long series A represented by eighty-one tetradrachms and one stater. Group 8 is die-
linked (coins 1 and 2) with the last two examples from group 7 (coins 8 and 9).
Coins 5 and 6 of group 8 may also share obverse and reverse dies. The obvious
and often die-linked evolution of this series makes it an important piece of the
overall picture.

SERIES C, GROUP IA

OBV: Head of younger Diodotus (II) r., wearing diadem. Border of dots.
REV: ΒΑΣΙΛΕΩΣ ΑΝΤΙΟΧΟΥ Zeus striding l., hurling thunderbolt in
r. hand; outstretched l. arm draped with aegis, eagle at l. foot of
Zeus. Border of dots. Control mark ⚭ above the eagle.
EXS: 1) F. Kovacs Stock (1997); 14.96 g. (fourrée).
2) F. Kovacs Stock (1997); 15.68 g.

These two coins (reported to me after the initial editing of this book) must be
inserted here as an important bridge between Series A of Diodotus I and Series
C of Diodotus II. They bear the monogram of A6 (⚭) but with the younger portrait found on C1 bearing monograms ⚭ and ⊖. In fact, photographs suggest
that the reverse die of the first example in C1 was actually recut from the same
die which had produced the second example of C1a: The extensive die-breaks
are identical on these specimens.

SERIES C, GROUP I[35]

OBV: As above.
REV: As above but with control marks ⚭ above the eagle and ⊖ between the feet of Zeus.
EXS: 1) F. Kovacs Stock (1997); 15.81 g.
2) Wahler Collection no. 461, previously; 16.13 g.[36]
3) Ashmolean (Shortt Collection); 13.37g.
4) Persic Gallery Sale 27 no. 86.
5) CNG Sale 39 (1996) no. 851; 16.50 g.
6) AK Exc Hoard 2, coin 8; 16.00 g.
7) ANS 1944.100.74364 (Newell Collection); 16.67 g.[37]
8) BM 1856-11-5-1 (Frere Collection); 16.52 g.
9) F. Kovacs Stock (1997); 15.64g.

This group of nine tetradrachms was struck from six obverse dies but the portraiture is nearly identical across the board. The hair on this younger portrait appears as an uncurled double braid except at the forelock, a feature shared with

35. Bopearachchi 2F and Mitchiner 67d. For a possible drachm in this group, see n.
120.
36. This coin is also Kovacs Sale (1985) no. 82.
37. Previously H. Weber Collection, vol. 3, pt. 2, no. 7852, and Bunbury Collection,
Sotheby Sale (1896) no. 457.

C1a and quite distinct from that in series A. The reverse shows the same alignment of the legend (below the arm of Zeus) as noted in series A, and the monogram ⚒ corresponds to that of A6 and C1a. There is, however, an additional control mark ⊖ between the feet of Zeus. All specimens have a 6:00 die axis (↓).

SERIES C, GROUP 2[38]

OBV: As above.
REV: As above but with control mark N above the eagle.
EXS:
DR 1)   BM (from India); 4.08 g.
DR 2)   BM (Whitehead Collection); 4.04 g.
HD 3)   Private collection.

These two drachms and one hemidrachm, the first such denominations in our inventory, would fit into A7 if not for the portrait. In fact, the evolution of series A (with elder portrait) from ⚒ to N to wreath (groups 6–8) has an exact parallel in this series C (with younger portrait), which moves from ⚒ and ⊖ to N to wreath (groups 1–3).

SERIES C, GROUP 3[39]

OBV: As above.
REV: As above but with wreath (○) above the eagle.
EXS:
DR 1)   BM (Cunningham Collection); 3.89 g.
DR 2)   Persic Gallery Sale 26 no. 67.
3)   Houghton Collection no. 1298; 16.15 g.
4)   AK Hoard 3, coin 18.
5)   AK Hoard 3, coin 19.
6)   Tadjikistan Museum B-H 528; 16.00 g.
7)   Sotheby Sale (1975) no. 36.
8)   AK Exc Hoard 2, coin 9; 15.21 g.
9)   BM 1888-12-8-50 (Cunningham Collection); 16.21 g.
*AV*10)   ANS 1995.51.48 (Fowler Collection); 8.30 g (cut).[40]
*AV*11)   BM 1888-12-8-43 (Cunningham Collection); 8.37 g (cut).

This diverse mintage of drachms, tetradrachms, and gold staters continues the youthful portrait but with the hair now rendered without double braids. These examples are closely die-linked: coins 3–5 were struck from the same pair of dies, coins 8 and 9 share an obverse die, and the staters may also be linked on obverse and reverse. More important, this group is die-linked to D1 in the name of

38. Bopearachchi 3E and Mitchiner 65b and 68b.
39. Bopearachchi 2B and 3A and Mitchiner 67a and 68a.
40. Apparently Hess-Leu Sale 31 (1965) no. 512, previously Naville Sale 5 (1923) no. 2788 and Alexander Grant Collection. The deep cut would distort its original weight.

Diodotus. As with series A, this series ends with a wreath symbol and a small output of gold.[41]

The third and last series in the name of Antiochus is composed of nine groups. This series E bears the youthful portrait of the king, precisely parallel to series C. Unlike either series A or C, however, series E develops the reverse legend *outside* the arm of Zeus, shows much variation in die axis, and always has two or more control marks.

SERIES E, GROUP 1[42]

OBV: Head of younger Diodotus (II) r., wearing diadem. Border of dots.

REV: ΒΑΣΙΛΕΩΣ ΑΝΤΙΟΧΟΥ Zeus standing l., hurling thunderbolt in r. hand, outstretched l. arm draped with aegis; eagle at l. foot of Zeus. Border of dots. Control marks Ⓜ in inner r. field and ♯ in inner l. field.

EXS:

DR 1)   Ashmolean (Shortt Collection); 3.79 g.

DR 2)   Berlin 238/1880; 3.97 g.[43]

HD 3)   Wahler Collection no. 451, previously; 1.82 g.[44]

The first example in this group has an anomaly found on no other coin of series E. It bears the same portrait (in fact die-linked) as the next example and carries the same monograms and "swayback" image of Zeus. It certainly belongs to E1, but it has the reverse legend arranged (albeit awkwardly) *under* the arm of Zeus. Here we have the first issue of the new mint (B), with the die cutters trying to replicate the coinage of the parent mint (A). It was quickly discovered that the old design could not accommodate the additional monograms always present on the coins of the new mint. The monograms in the inner right field necessitated a swayback pose for Zeus and the movement of the word ΒΑΣΙΛΕΩΣ beyond the elbow of the god. This new legend alignment then became one of the distinguishing characteristics of this new mint.

SERIES E, GROUP 2[45]

OBV: As above.

---

41. The additional stater of this type alleged to be in the Fitzwilliam Museum (Cambridge) apparently does not exist; it was mistakenly identified as a Diodotus/Antiochus II coin by R. B. Whitehead, "Notes on the Indo-Greeks," *NC* 20 (1940): 104. The two Diodotus staters from the Tremlett bequest of 1918 both bear the name "Diodotus"; one may be found in the inventory below, series D, group 7, while the other seems to be a fake (appendix C).

42. Bopearachchi 3G and Mitchiner 68c. Bopearachchi lists the first monogram as ♯. This may be correct, but the Berlin piece is not easily read. Mitchiner lists the Shortt specimen with ♯ only. The placement of the monograms varies on these pieces, as noted.

43. The placement of control marks is reversed.

44. Also Sotheby/NFA Sale (1993) no. 908 and now BM 1993-11-6-14.

45. Not represented in either Bopearachchi or Mitchiner.

REV: As above but with control marks ⊓ and Γ in inner r. field and
           ⚠ in inner l. field.
EXS: 1)   R. C. Senior List 4 (1982) no. 46.[46]
HD 2)   Houghton Collection no. 1297; 1.87 g (11:00 axis).

The tetradrachm has an obverse nearly identical to that of the next group;
the hemidrachm very closely resembles the obverse of that in group 1.

SERIES E, GROUP 3[47]

OBV: As above.
REV: As above but with control mark ⊿ in inner l. field and ⚠ in in-
           ner r. field.
EXS: 1)   Kunduz Hoard, coin 7; 16.18 g.
DR 2)   ANS 1995.51.49 (Fowler Collection); 3.77 g (2:00 axis).

SERIES E, GROUP 4[48]

OBV: As above.
REV: As above but with control marks ⚠ and ⏐ ⋀ in inner r. field and
           ⊓ in inner l. field.
EXS: 1)   R. C. Senior (Nov. 1995).[49]

This coin was struck from the same obverse die as the Kunduz Hoard specimen in E3, which itself closely resembles E2.

SERIES E, GROUP 5[50]

OBV: As above.
REV: As above but with control marks ⚠ in inner r. field and N in outer
           r. field.
EXS: 1)   BN 1963 [R3681.26] (LeBerre Collection); 16.40 g (12:00 axis).
DR 2)   BM (Cunningham Collection); 3.89 g (11:00 axis).
DR 3)   F. Kovacs Stock (1997); 4.05 g (5:00 axis).
DR 4)   Houghton Collection no. 1296; 4.08 g (12:00 axis).
DR 5)   BN 1963 [R.3681.28] (LeBerre Collection); 3.79 g (12:00 axis).
HD 6)   BM (Baluchistan); 2.03 g.

This group of mostly low-denomination silver coins continues the portraiture

46. Now in the Hollis Collection.
47. Bopearachchi 2D and 3C and Mitchiner 67b.
48. Not represented in either Bopearachchi or Mitchiner.
49. Now in the Hollis Collection.
50. Bopearachchi 2C, 3B, and 4A and Mitchiner 65c and 69a. I follow the corrected
monogram reading by Bopearachchi, *Monnaies*, p. 148 n. 7; however, I strongly suggest
that our worn hemidrachm, coin 6, bears the same monogram set as the other coins of this
group. The same could be true of ANS 1995.51.266 (Fowler); 1.34 g (6:00 axis), as well
as Sotheby (1958) no. 283 from the Haughton Collection.

of this series, which is parallel to that of series C. The obverse die of the BN tetradrachm (ex. 1) was used to strike the next group in the series.

SERIES E, GROUP 6[51]

OBV: As above.
REV: As above but with monograms Ⱪ in inner l. field and Ⴀ in inner r. field.
EXS: 1) Coin Galleries Sale (1978) no. 270; 15.91 g.

SERIES E, GROUP 7[52]

OBV: As above.
REV: As above but with control marks T Ⴀ in outer r. field, Ⴀ in inner r. field and a wreath (◯) above the eagle.
EXS: 1) Sternberg Sale 29 (1995) no. 264; 16.41 g.

The portrait on this coin closely resembles that of the previous groups. This is the last of six interlocked groups (2–7) bearing the control mark Ⴀ and the first in this series to introduce the wreath symbol found on its remaining issues.

SERIES E, GROUP 8[53]

OBV: As above.
REV: As above with wreath (◯), but with control marks ᛗ T ⊣ in inner r. field.
EXS: 1) Houghton Collection no. 1299; 16.57 g (11:00 axis).

SERIES E, GROUP 9[54]

OBV: As above.
REV: As above, with wreath (◯), but with control marks Γ ᛗ ⊓ in inner r. field.
EXS: 1) Wahler Collection no. 460, previously; 16.31 g (12:00 axis).[55]
DR 2) R. C. Senior Sale List 4 (1982) no. 47.[56]
DR 3) Naville Sale 10 (1925) no. 905; 4.10 g.[57]

These drachms (coins 2 and 3) were struck from the same pair of dies, the obverse of which was used to strike the earliest drachms of series F in the name

51. Not represented in Mitchiner but see Bopearachchi 3D (where the wrong description is listed in terms of denomination and control mark).
52. Not represented in either Bopearachchi or Mitchiner.
53. Not represented in either Bopearachchi or Mitchiner.
54. Not represented in either Bopearachchi or Mitchiner.
55. Also Senior Sale List 1 (1981) no. 11; NFA Sale (1989) no. 746; Sotheby/NFA Sale (1993) no. 908; and now BM 1993-11-6-11.
56. Now in the Hollis Collection.
57. Formerly in the White King Collection.

of Diodotus. Also, the Wahler tetradrachm (coin 1) shares an obverse die with the earliest tetradrachms of series F. It should be noted that series E contains no gold issues. So far, then, series E stands apart from the other series (A and C) in the name of Antiochus in terms of (1) established alignment of the reverse legend *outside* the elbow of Zeus, (2) irregular die axis, (3) lack of gold issues, and (4) profusion of interlocked control mark groups. There is, so far, no known die linkage between these concurrent series A, E, and C. The fabric of these series E coins is irregular, many of them having an appearance well below the standard of other thundering Zeus coins in Antiochus's name.

COINS IN THE NAME OF DIODOTUS

SERIES B, GROUP 1[58]

OBV: Head of elder Diodotus (I) r., wearing diadem. Border of dots.
REV: ΒΑΣΙΛΕΩΣ ΔΙΟΔΟΤΟΥ Zeus striding l., hurling thunderbolt in r. hand; outstretched l. arm draped with aegis; eagle at l. foot of Zeus. Wreath (Ο) above the eagle. Border of dots. No visible control marks.
EXS:
AV 1)   Leu Sale 13 (1975) no. 318; 8.51 g (12:00 axis).
AV 2)   BN (Rollin 1840); 8.56 g.
AV 3)   BN (C. de Bestegui 39); 8.53 g.
AV 4)   Adolph Hess Sale (1955) no. 39.
AV 5)   Robert Jameson Collection, vol. 1, no. 1794; 8.49 g.
       6)   BM 1888-12-8-66 (Cunningham Collection); 16.75 g.[59]
       7)   Wahler Collection no. 452, previously; 15.85 g.
       8)   ANS 1995.51.47 (Fowler Collection); 15.00 g.[60]

This group, impressive in its output of gold, has features that set it apart from all other Diodotid mintages in the precious metals. First of all, the portrait of the king appears idealized, and the sovereign's hair has been rendered in a unique sawtooth pattern from the brow to the nape. The reverse type also shows novel characteristics. The aegis has snakes whose heads rise above the arm of Zeus in a threatening gesture. The stance of Zeus appears with a slight bend at the left knee.

---

58. Not represented in either Bopearachchi or Mitchiner as a distinct group of coins. The border of dots, obverse and reverse, does not show up on the staters but is plainly visible on the tetradrachms. Kovalenko notices the distinctive portraiture (but not reverse elements) and attributes this series (his series 32–34) to Diodotus II: "The Coinage of Diodotus I and Diodotus II," pp. 40–42 and 46.

59. Appeared in the 1992 Fitzwilliam Museum (Cambridge) exhibition "The Crossroads of Asia: Transformation in Image and Symbol in the Art of Ancient Afghanistan and Pakistan," item no. 16 in the catalog of the same title edited by Elizabeth Errington and Joe Cribb (Cambridge: The Ancient India and Iran Trust, 1992). This publication identified the coin as BM 1890-5-1-1 (Chandra Mall and Lakhari Dass). This is probably correct, of course, but I follow my own notes, which suggest a possible mix-up of coin trays (see chap. 2) for BM 1888-12-8-66 and BM 1880-5-1-1. This properly matches the weights.

60. Glendining Sale (Oct. 1987) no. 13.

One coin (example 1) was struck with a 12:00 die axis (↑), an anomaly already noted on some coins of series E in the name of Antiochus. Likewise, this group has the reverse legend outside the arm of Zeus. Coins 1 and 2 share an obverse die that has a slight break visible at the throat of the king. The tetradrachms seem to be a closed set from a single pair of dies. The next group of series B coins carries forward the characteristic obverse and reverse style of the first.

SERIES B, GROUP 2[61]

OBV: As above.
REV: As above but with no wreath or visible control marks.
EXS: 1) Cunningham Collection (1884); 16.35 g.[62]
          2) Munz und Medaillen FPL 294 (1968) no. 1; 16.77 g.
          3) Munz und Medaillen FPL 332 (1972) no.1; 16.43 g.[63]
          4) Persic Gallery Sale 27 no. 87.
          5) Wahler Collection no. 453, previously; 16.34 g.[64]
          6) Kunduz Hoard, coin 8; 15.98 g.
          7) Hamburger Sale (1930) no. 474; 16.73 g.
          8) BM 1860-12-20-5 (Hay Collection); 15.26 g.
          9) Berlin (Fox 1873); 16.64 g.
         10) Malter Sale 66 (1995); 14.72 g.
         11) Renee Kovacs Collection; 16.94 g.
         12) Galerie Antiker Kunst Sale 4 (1987) no. 4; 16.30 g.
         13) Hollis Collection.
*DR*14) F. Kovacs Stock (1997); 3.58 g.

These examples, some badly worn, exhibit two sets of obverse die linkage: coins 2 and 3 and coins 7 and 8. The next group closely resembles this one.

SERIES B, GROUP 3[65]

OBV: As above.
REV: As above but with ⏝ above the eagle.
EXS: 1) Schulman Sale (1963) no. 268.[66]
          2) BM 1874-7-9-2 (Chandra Mall); 16.58 g.

61. Not represented in either Bopearachchi or Mitchiner as part of a distinct group.
62. Cunningham, *CASE*, p. 98. This coin, described as "much rubbed on the reverse" and without a monogram, does not appear to be any of the other tetradrachms listed in this inventory. Cunningham includes a drawing of this coin's obverse (plate 1, no. 2) which renders the king's hair as characteristic for group B.
63. Formerly Hess-Leu Sale 45 (1970) no. 392.
64. Later, NFA Sale (1989) no. 747.
65. Bopearachchi 6E and Mitchiner 71b.
66. Remarkably similar to example 2: both were struck in exactly the same way on the flan (note the head and arm of Zeus) and have exactly the same shape. Yet they cannot be the same coin, since the BM specimen, still in the museum, could obviously not have

3) ANS 1944.100.74366 (Newell Collection); 15.32 g.[67]
4) AK Hoard 3, coin 25.
5) Rahman Collection no. 96; 16.85 g.

This group was struck from no more than two obverse dies and brings to a close the uniquely styled coins of series B. The remaining issues in the name of Diodotus all bear the younger portrait.

SERIES D, GROUP 1[68]

OBV: Head of younger Diodotus (II) r., wearing diadem. Border of dots.

REV: ΒΑΣΙΛΕΩΣ ΔΙΟΔΟΤΟΥ Zeus striding l., hurling thunderbolt in r. hand; outstretched l. arm draped with aegis; eagle at l. foot of Zeus. Wreath (◯) above the eagle and control mark Ρ in inner r. field. Border of dots.

EX: 1)   Sotheby/NFA Sale (1993) no. 908; 16.66 g.[69]

The portrait on this coin strongly resembles that of series C and E in the name of Antiochus. In this case, as in series C, the reverse legend has been aligned under the arm of Zeus. This coin is die-linked to the last tetradrachms in series C, which establishes the connection between coins of this mint struck in the name of Antiochus and then in the name of Diodotus.[70]

SERIES D, GROUP 2[71]

OBV: As above.

REV: As above, with wreath (◯) above the eagle, but with control mark Ρ or Τ in inner r. field.

EX:

DR 1)   Wahler Collection no. 450, previously; 4.06 g.[72]

---

appeared in a 1963 auction. Given the less distinct "striking" of this example, it is possible that it is a cast forgery of the BM tetradrachm.

67. Previously in the collection of R. B. Whitehead.

68. Not represented in either Bopearachchi or Mitchiner.

69. Published in *NFA Journal* (Summer 1988) lot 81 and NFA Winter Bid Sale (1987) no. 494; now BM 1993-11-6-12.

70. This die linkage is mentioned in *NFA Journal* (Summer 1988) lot 81, but its significance has not before been recognized.

71. Not represented in either Bopearachchi or Mitchiner. The reading of the control mark is not certain; it could be a variety of my D1. For caution's sake, however, I list it separately as perhaps tau plus rho or simply tau. If not actually part of group 1 it is undoubtedly closely associated with it.

72. Also Munz und Medaillen Sale (1974) no. 13; NFA Sale (1989) no. 749; and NFA/Sotheby Sale (1993) no. 907; now BM 1993-11-6-15. Kovalenko asserts ("The Coinage of Diodotus I and Diodotus II," p. 34) that this coin shares an obverse die with coin 4 of my E5 struck in the name of Antiochus. The dies appear to me quite distinguishable in their treatments of the hair and diadem of the king.

SERIES D, GROUP 3[73]

OBV: As above.
REV: As above, with wreath (Ο) above eagle, but with control mark Σ
         in inner r. field.
EXS: 1) CNG Sale 39 (1996) no. 852; 16.50 g.
      2) F. Kovacs Stock (1997); 16.29 g.

SERIES D, GROUP 4[74]

OBV: As above.
REV: As above, with wreath (Ο) above eagle, but with control mark
         N in inner r. field.
EX: 1) Rahman Collection no. 98; 16.48 g.

SÉRIES D, GROUP 5[75]

OBV: As above.
REV: As above, with wreath (Ο) above eagle, but with control mark
         A between the feet of Zeus.
EX: 1) Rahman Collection no. 97; 16.60 g.

SERIES D, GROUP 6[76]

OBV: As above.
REV: As above, with wreath Ο above the eagle, but with control mark
         B in inner r. field.
EXS: 1) Punjab Museum, Lahore; 16.52 g.[77]
      2) Lucien de Hirsch Collection no. 1775.
      3) H. P. Poddar Collection.[78]
DR 4) Punjab Museum, Lahore; 3.7 g.[79]

After these small groups of tetradrachms and drachms with wreath and control marks P , P or T, N, Σ, A, and B , series D continues without the let-
tered control marks. A massive striking of gold staters, plus some tetradrachms
and drachms, follows in group 7.

73. Not represented in either Bopearachchi or Mitchiner.
74. Not represented in either Bopearachchi or Mitchiner.
75. Not represented in either Bopearachchi or Mitchiner.
76. Not in Mitchiner but see Bopearachchi 6C.
77. *PMC*, no. 2 (from the Bleazby Collection). Also Schulman (1904) no. 4.
78. No photograph of this coin is available, but Lahiri describes it as "one fine coin
with some portions chipped off": *Corpus*, p. 114 (coin 6.4). This sufficiently distinguishes
this example from the others in our inventory.
79. *PMC*, p. 10, describes a drachm of the same type as the tetradrachm (example 1)
"but rubbed" and "indistinct."

SERIES D, GROUP 7[80]

OBV: As above.
REV: As above, with wreath Ỗ above the eagle, but no control marks.
EXS:
AV   1)   Vinchon Sale (1969) no. 144; 8.44 g.[81]
AV   2)   Berlin 172/1873; 8.36 g (cut).
AV   3)   Berlin (Loebbecke 1906); 8.36 g (cut).
AV   4)   Hess-Leu Sale 45 (1970) no. 391; 8.36 g (cut).[82]
AV   5)   Kumar Collection (cut).
AV   6)   Ashmolean (Shortt Collection); 8.32 g (cut).[83]
AV   7)   Sotheby Sale (1897) no. 405 (Montagu Collection); 8.30 g (cut).
AV   8)   BM 1874-7-9-1 (Chandra Mall); 8.33 g (cut).
AV   9)   Hirsch Sale 21 (1908) no. 4410; 8.27 g (cut).
AV   10) Vinchon Sale (1966) no. 232; (cut).
AV   11) Hurter Sale (1930) no. 473; 8.31 g (cut).
AV   12) BN 1923 (Lahore); 8.30 g (cut).[84]
AV   13) CNG Sale 35 (1995) no. 436; 8.18 g (cut).
AV   14) Fitzwilliam Museum (Tremlett Collection); 8.33 g.
AV   15) SNG Copenhagen no. 251; 8.35 g.
AV   16) Indian Museum, Calcutta, coin 1; 8.42 g.
AV   17) Ashmolean; 8.39 g.
AV   18) Philipson Sale (1909) no. 3133; 8.33 g.
AV   19) Vinchon Sale (1956) no. 658 (Hindamian Collection).[85]
AV   20) Feuardent Sale (1919) no. 420 (Collignon Collection).
AV   21) ANS 1980.125.1 (Berry Collection); 8.27 g.
AV   22) Leu Sale 18 (1977) no. 263; 8.27 g.[86]
AV   23) NFA Sale 5 (1978) no. 225; 8.29 g.[87]
       24) Schweizerische Kreditanstalt Sale 2 (1984) no. 301; 16.46 g.
       25) Munzhd Basel Sale 4 (1935) no. 912; 15.36 g.
       26) ANS 1995.51.44 (Fowler Collection); 16.09 g.[88]
       27) ESM, plate 53.19.
       28) AK Exc Hoard 2, coin 11; 15.82 g.
       29) AK Exc Hoard 2, coin 10; 15.89 g.

80. Not represented as a group by either Bopearachchi or Mitchiner.
81. The lettering on this coin invites some caution about its authenticity.
82. Also Malter Sale (1969) no. 1; Schulman Sale (1963) no. 32; and Hamburger Sale (1910) no. 291.
83. Previously Glendining Sale (1961) no. 2739 (Lockett Collection).
84. Mistakenly identified as "Rollin 1840" in Bopearachchi's catalog (series 5, coin 11); see chap. 4. The following two coins (13 and 14) were struck from the same obverse and reverse dies as this BN specimen.
85. Now apparently BM 1987-6-49-65.
86. Also Munz und Medaillen Sale 19 (1959) no. 566.
87. Previously Superior Sale (1975) no. 3043.
88. Also Coin Galleries Sale (1974) no. 354.

30) ANS 1995.51.45 (Fowler Collection); 16.17 g.
31) Wahler Collection no. 458, previously; 16.05 g.
32) Hollis Collection.
33) AK Hoard 3, coin 27.
34) AK Hoard 3, coin 26.
35) BM 1880-5-1-1 (Chandra Mall); 16.66 g.
36) ANS 1970.154.2; 16.59 g.[89]
37) F. Kovacs Stock (1996); 16.12 g.
38) Rahman Collection no. 95; 16.15 g.
39) *Coin Hoards* 8, hoard 471.[90]
40) F. Kovacs Stock (1997); 16.65 g.
41) F. Kovacs Stock (1997); 16.33 g.
42) F. Kovacs Stock (1997); 16.49 g.
43) F. Kovacs Stock (1997); 16.20 g.
44) F. Kovacs Stock (1998); 16.41 g.
45) F. Kovacs Stock (1998); 16.38 g.
*DR*46) Ashmolean; 3.94 g.
*DR*47) Shortt Collection.

This huge group of twenty-three staters, twenty-two tetradrachms, and two drachms constitutes the largest single emission of coins in the name of Diodotus. In fact, there are many more known examples of the gold staters, but the additional coins are probably false. There are at least thirteen of these forged staters, all die-linked to the specimens rejected by Jenkins.[91]

Of the twenty-three examples of genuine staters listed here, twelve have been cut to various extents across the portrait of the king. Although ancient states sometimes defaced counterfeit coins and removed them from circulation, this does not seem to be the situation with these staters.[92] The cuts do not deface the entire coin but rather are made in a precise way to remove a fraction of the gold from the thickest portion of the coin—the high-relief head of the king. The likeliest explanation is that these coins were originally struck on a high weight standard that, over time, was reduced. Among the *uncut* examples, in fact, we do find some coins weighing near the normal Attic standard of 8.48 g, but most weigh nearer 8.30 g. As these lower-weight coins entered circulation, the older and heavier pieces would have been recalled and reminted. Those holding some of these older coins might themselves have cut down the pieces to the new weight standard, thus acquiring a personal bonus of gold clippings. We may note how precisely the cut staters fit the sequence of decreasing weight that is evident for the uncut coins.

This fact not only helps to arrange the staters in proper order but indicates

---

89. From Munz und Medaillen, 1970.

90. Found in Tartous, Syria, in 1987 along with some 199 other tetradrachms buried ca. 120 B.C.

91. See chap. 4, n. 8. For a list of some of these forgeries, consult appendix C.

92. See, e.g., the Athenian law regulating currency in the agora: R. S. Stroud, "An Athenian Law on Silver Coinage," *Hesperia* 43 (1974): 157–188.

two things of importance for the Bactrian economy. First, some crisis probably precipitated this revision of the gold mintage (e.g., a shortage of gold reserves). Second, the trouble taken to cut the heavier coins in circulation suggests to us that the staters were accepted in commerce on face value rather than as bullion. If each coin had been weighed in the balance during bartering there would have been no need to adjust the heavier pieces. This is an indication that the economy was becoming truly monetized by this point in Bactrian history. Of course, the gold clippings could at the same time have been saved and used as bullion. As expected, some level of barter was maintained even as the advantages of mone-tization were more widely appreciated in the East.

SERIES D, GROUP 8[93]

OBV: As above.
REV: As above but with control mark ᛗ in place of the wreath above
         the eagle.[94]
EXS:
DR 1) ANS 1995.51.43 (Fowler Collection); 3.97 g.
DR 2) R. C. Senior Sale List 4 (1982) no. 48.[95]
DR 3) ANS 1995.51.293; 4.06 g.[96]
DR 4) Persic Gallery Sale 32 no. 47; 3.70 g.
     5) Bukhara Hoard, coin 5; 16.5 g.[97]
     6) F. Kovacs Stock (1997); 16.19 g.

This group concludes the mintage of series D. Very much like this series, the next series (F) evolves from groups bearing both wreath and control mark(s) to wreath alone (with gold issues) and finally the monogram ᛗ. The same por-traiture is evident on both series. The key differences include the greater num-ber of control marks on series F (as with series E), the alignment of the reverse legend *outside* the arm of Zeus on series F (as with series E), and the inconsis-tent die axis (again, as with series E). This strongly suggests that series D and F are the simultaneous issues of different mints. This view is strengthened by the parallel die linkage of series C to D and series E to F. There is apparently no die linkage between these mints, although the last specimen in D8 closely resembles the obverses of F7.

93. In part, Bopearachchi 7E and Mitchiner 75b.
94. A drachm in the National Museum of Georgia at Tbilisi (inv. 498, Alex Ivanov, 1933), which I have not seen, is described as having both the monogram ᛗ *and* the wreath: Bernard, *AK* 4, p. 149. This lone specimen may represent a bridge between series D groups 7 and 8. There is also a drachm, BM 1888-5-3-1 (4.10 g), that has a control mark resembling the crescent on B3 (cf. Bopearachchi 7D). The mark could, however, perhaps be read as the ᛗ of D8. Clearly, the BM drachm belongs somewhere in or near this mintage but remains unassigned for the moment.
95. Now in the Hollis Collection.
96. Previously Persic Gallery Sale 24 no. 110.
97. Rtveladze, "La circulation monétaire au nord de l'Oxus."

SERIES F, GROUP 1[98]

OBV: Head of younger Diodotus (II) r., wearing diadem.
REV: ΒΑΣΙΛΕΩΣ ΔΙΟΔΟΤΟΥ Zeus striding l., hurling thunderbolt in r. hand; outstretched l. arm draped with aegis; eagle at l. foot of Zeus. Wreath (◯) above the eagle, control marks Γ ⋈Γ in inner r. field.
EXS:
DR 1) J. de Bartholomaei (1843); 4.21 g.[99]
DR 2) Berlin (Loebbecke 1906); 3.58 g.[100]

These two drachms in the name of Diodotus carry over from series E the same portraiture, lettering style, and essentially the same monogram set. The progression is clear and unbroken at this critical juncture. Actual die linkage can be seen in these worn drachms of F1; the following group is die-linked to E9, as most certainly are the tetradrachms of F3.

SERIES F, GROUP 2[101]

OBV: As above.
REV: As above, with wreath (◯) above the eagle, but with control marks Γ and ⋈ in inner r. field.
EXS:
DR 1) BM 1888-12-8-68 (Cunningham Collection); 4.0 g (drilled) (9:00 axis).
DR 2) ANS 1978.45.1 (Spengler Collection); 3.96 g (12:00 axis).[102]
DR 3) Ashmolean; 3.63 g (11:00 axis).

SERIES F, GROUP 3[103]

OBV: As above.
REV: As above, with wreath (◯) above eagle, but with sole monogram ⋈ in inner r. field. Border of dots.
EXS: 1) Sternberg Sale 29 (Oct. 1995) no. 265; 16.78 g (12:00 axis).
2) F. Kovacs Stock (1997), 16.32 g (12:00 axis).
3) AK Exc Hoard 2, coin 12; 15.77 g (12:00 axis).
4) Munz und Medaillen Sale (1973) no. 1; 16.50 g.

98. Bopearachchi 7C; not represented in Mitchiner.
99. The first Diodotus drachm ever to be published and only the third Diodotus coin known in its day (see chap. 4).
100. Bopearachchi describes this coin as "inédite et unique": *Monnaies,* p. 150 n. 19. Obviously, this is wrong by a century and a half (see n. 99).
101. Bopearachchi's 7F records the second monogram incorrectly for this BM specimen; not represented in Mitchiner.
102. Assigned to this group with some confidence even though the monogram can only partly be detected. There may also be a hemidrachm in the Hollis Collection, listed below as "uncertain" coin 19.
103. Bopearachchi 6D, but his reference to specimens in AK Hoard 3 is an error.

The first two tetradrachms here were struck from the same obverse die as coin 1 of E9. The excavation coin (example 3) seems to be die-linked as well, but the photographs are not distinct enough to remove all doubt. The progression is nevertheless adequately proven from the last group of series E to the earliest groups of series F.

SERIES F, GROUP 4[104]

OBV: As above. Border of dots.
REV: As above, with wreath (Ɔ) above the eagle, but with control marks ⵍ in inner r. field and ⵍ in outer r. field.
EX: 1) R. C. Senior (Nov. 1995).[105]

SERIES F, GROUP 5[106]

OBV: As above.
REV: As above, with wreath (Ɔ), but eagle not visible; monograms ⵍ ⵍ ⵍ (?).
EXS:
DR 1) Munz und Medaillen Sale 37 (1968) no. 280; 4.07 g.
DR 2) Wahler Collection,, previously; 3.52 g (5:00 axis).[107]
DR 3) Hermitage Collection 13/10; 4.09 g.
DR 4) ANS 1993.29.8 (Fowler Collection); 4.07 g.

All four of these drachms were struck from the same obverse die.

SERIES F, GROUP 6[108]

OBV: As above.
REV: As above, with wreath (Ɔ) above eagle, but no control marks.

---

104. Not represented in Bopearachchi or Mitchiner.
105. Now in the Hollis Collection.
106. Not represented in either Bopearachchi or Mitchiner. There may also be a hemidrachm in this group: a coin described to me (personal communication from A. Hollis) as "↑↑ not clear in whose name. To r. ⵍ and perhaps M." I have not had an opportunity to see the specimen, so I do not assign it yet to this series. Kovalenko does not list all three monograms and condemns the two specimens he knows as fakes ("The Coinage of Diodotus I and Diodotus II," pp. 32–33). Coins 1 and 4 listed here are not cast copies, as their appearance proves. For coins 2 and 3 see the following note.
107. From Spink stock (1977); also Sotheby/NFA Sale (1993) no. 908. It was once in the famous collection of A. Cunningham: see CASE, p. 99 and plate 1, fig. 4. It is now BM 1993-11-6-13, alleged by Kovalenko to be a forgery (see n. 106). This cannot be certain. The Ashmolean example is demonstrably a cast forgery, as is either this BM drachm or the next one from the Hermitage. These coins are identical in every respect. Since the genuine prototype cannot be singled out, both possibilities are listed here.
108. Bopearachchi 5A, 6B, and 7B and Mitchiner 73a. We must exclude, of course, the coins with ΒΑΣΙΛΕΩΣ arranged below Zeus's elbow, a distinction not made in the catalogs by Bopearachchi and Mitchiner.

EXS:
AV 1) ANS 1977.158.113 (R. J. Kelley 1977); 8.54 g (cut).[109]
AV 2) ANS 1944.100.74365 (Newell Collection); 8.44 g (cut).[110]
AV 3) BM 1879-4-1-5 (Chandra Mall); 8.46 g.
AV 4) ANS 1980.109.108 (A. J. Fecht 1980); 8.45 g.[111]
AV 5) Harlan Berk Sale (1995) no. 50; 8.45 g.
AV 6) Leu Sale 28 (1981) no. 208; 8.39 g.[112]
AV 7) Naville Sale 7/Bement Collection (1924) no. 1785; 8.31 g.[113]
AV 8) Lucien de Hirsch Collection no. 1774.
       9) AK Hoard 3, coin 28.
DR 10) CNG Sale 37 (1996) no. 797; 4.00 g.[114]
DR 11) Rahman Collection no. 93; 3.95 g.[115]
DR 12) F. Kovacs Stock (1997); 4.03 g (12:00 axis).

The eight staters in this group manifest the same pattern of weight reduction
on wreath-only coins already noted for D7. We find very heavy coins cut to a
smaller standard and then uncut specimens that have been dropped down to a
norm of some 8.30 g. These staters are die-linked on obverse (coins 2, 3, 4, 5)
and perhaps reverse (coins 6 and 7).

SERIES F, GROUP 7[116]

OBV: As above.
REV: As above, but without wreath; control mark Ⲙ above the eagle.
EXS: 1) Wahler Collection no. 459, previously; 15.89 g.[117]
         2) F. Kovacs Stock (1996); 16.35 g.
         3) AK Exc Hoard 2, coin 13; 15.48 g.[118]
         4) BN K2801; 16.60 g.
         5) Coin Galleries Sale (1974) no. 355; 16.30 g.
         6) BN 1963 [R.3681.27] (LeBerre Collection); 16.11 g.
         7) BN 1973.188.22 (Kieffer Collection); 16.41 g.

109. Ratto Sale (1927) no. 2819 and later Munz and Medaillen Sale (1953).
110. Naville Sale I (1921) no. 3141; Naville Sale V (1923) no. 2889; and reportedly
Hirsch Sale IV (1927) 8.E.
111. Ratto Sale (1912) no. 1150.
112. Later appears as Monnaies Antiques (1993) no. 149.
113. Seems to be Hirsch Sale (1904) no. 467 and Schulman/White King Collection
(1904) no. 954.
114. Lot no. 796 in the same catalog, a drachm weighing 4.40 g, may also belong in
this group, but the wreath is difficult to see on the reverse.
115. Incorrectly listed by Bopearachchi and Rahman, *Pre-Kushana Coins,* as an issue
in the name of Antiochus.
116. In part Bopearachchi 6F and 7D and Mitchiner 75b.
117. Also NFA Sale II (1976) no. 308 and subsequently NFA Sale (1989) no. 748. The
reverse appears to be from a recut die or, more likely, double-struck. The same is true of
the following, die-linked specimen.
118. I agree with Bopearachchi's reading of the control mark on this piece: *Monnaies,*
p. 150 n. 17.

8) Schlesinger Sale 13/Hermitage (1935) no. 1520; 16.4 g.
9) Sotheby Sale (1970) no. 250; 16.41 g.[119]
10) BM 1922-4-24-100 (Whitehead Collection); 16.25 g.
11) CNG Sale 37 (1996) no. 795; 15.97 g.
12) Munz Zentrum Sale 58 no. 2593; 16.33 g.
13) F. Kovacs Stock (1997); 16.01 g.
14) F. Kovacs Stock (1997); 16.50 g.
15) F. Kovacs Stock (1997); 15.78 g.
16) F. Kovacs Stock (1997); 15.58 g.
DR 17) Shortt Collection.
DR 18) BM 1888-12-8-69 (Cunningham Collection); 4.04 g.
DR 19) BM 1869-1-2-1 (Edwards Collection); 4.04 g.
DR 20) Ashmolean; 4.09 g.

These sixteen tetradrachms and four drachms[120] show a maturing but still relatively young portrait of the king that exactly parallels D8. The tetradrachms
here are closely die-linked. Coins 1 and 2 and 3–4 have the same obverse dies;
coins 3 and 4 have the same reverse die as well. Coins 5–8 share an obverse die,
while the reverses of 6 and 7 are also linked.

SERIES F, GROUP 8[121]

OBV: As above.
REV: As above, but with monograms ꡡ ⊐ in inner r. field.
EXS: 1) Berlin (Loebbecke 1908); 16.48 g.[122]
        2) Persic Gallery Sale 25 no. 116.
        3) F. Kovacs Stock (1997); 16.44 g.[123]
        4) F. Kovacs Stock (1997); 15.74 g.
DR 5) Hollis Collection.
DR 6) Persic Gallery Sale 28 no. 65.[124]

The coins of this last group continue on the tetradrachms the portraiture of
group 7 but with signs of degenerating quality. The obverse of coin 3 may have
been reworked, and its reverse exhibits an unusually long and deep die break
running from the edge at 6:00 all the way up to Zeus's shoulder. The drachms
have crude obverses, perhaps overstrikes. These are signs of some disturbance
or strain within the operations of the royal mint.

This catalog has for the first time presented a very distinct picture of six se-

119. Allotte de la Füye (Paris, 1925) no. 1581.
120. An additional specimen of each may exist, but these might also be coins already
listed: a tetradrachm of Gibbs/Wigan recorded by Cunningham, *CASE*, p. 98, and a drachm
from the Haughton Collection auctioned by Sotheby (1958) no. 282.
121. Bopearachchi 6G and Mitchiner 74b.
122. Once belonged to the Sim Collection, according to Cunningham, *CASE*, p. 98.
123. The second control mark on this tetradrachm, as on the following drachms, has
been placed in the outer right field.
124. Also Persic Gallery Sale 24 no. 111.

ries of thundering Zeus coins, three each in the name of Antiochus and Diodotus. In addition to more than 260 gold and silver specimens arranged within these series, there are coins that I have not been able to assign to their proper places within this system. In some cases the coin is too worn to identify; in others I have not yet been able to obtain enough data (full description, photograph, or cast) to attribute the coin with confidence. For the sake of completeness, I note the existence (and possible series attribution) of these additional specimens.

UNCERTAIN ATTRIBUTIONS

      1) R. C. Senior Sale 4 (1982) no. 45 (A 6?).
      2) Lucien de Hirsch Collection no. 1649.
      3) SNC (1974) no. 2542; 16.03 g. (A?).
      4) Rahman Collection no. 1008 (A?).[125]
      5) Ashmolean Museum, 16.00 g (B, group ?).
DR 6) CNG Sale 38 (1996) no. 483; 4.07 g (C1?).[126]
DR 7) Tbilisi Museum no. 498 (Ivanov Collection); 3.94 g (D?).
DR 8) Indian Museum, Calcutta; 3.37 g (D?).
DR 9) BM 1888-12-8-69 (Cunningham Collection); 4.10 g (D?).
HD 10) ANS 1995.51.266 (Fowler Collection) = R. C. Senior 1991; 1.34 g (E?).
HD 11) Sotheby (1958) no. 283 (Haughton Collection) (E?).
DR 12) Ashmolean Museum (F? cast forgery?).
      13) Kabala Hoard, coin 141; 16.40 g (E?).
DR 14) BM; 4.02 g (E?).
DR 15) Pushkin Museum, Roz 1300; 3.35 g (E?).[127]
DR 16) Rahman Collection no. 94; 3.90 g (2:00 axis)(E5?).[128]
      17) Rahman Collection no. 92; 15.95 g (2:00 axis) (E7?).[129]
DR 18) BM 1888-12-8-67; 3.65 g (F?).
HD 19) Hollis Collection (F?).
*DR 20) Hollis Collection (F?).
HD 21) Ashmolean Museum; 1.69 g (F?).

125. From the second Mir Zakah hoard, this tetradrachm has been attributed the weight of "8.90 g" in the recent publication of this impressive private collection. See n. 31.

126. If indeed a second monogram exists between Zeus's feet, this coin would be the first drachm issued by Diodotus II at this mint; otherwise, it may be attributed to C1a.

127. This poorly preserved specimen comes from the collection of V. Rosanov, later moved in 1924 from the Oriental Institute to the Pushkin State Museum of Fine Arts. One or more of its three (?) monograms is uncertain, and its authenticity has been questioned. The coin is very carefully described in N. Smirnova, "Bactrian Coins in the Pushkin State Museum of Fine Arts," *Ancient Civilizations* 2 (1995): 335–338, 345.

128. Bopearachchi and Rahman, *Pre-Kushana Coins*, list this as an "unreported" monogram variety, but the coin seems to fit into series E, group 5, in all respects except that the second control mark lies off-flan to the right.

129. Said to be from Ai Khanoum, may belong to E7; if not, it constitutes a separate group between 7 and 8.

DR 22) Sotheby Sale (1958) no. 283; 3.91 g (F?).
DR 23) CNG Sale 37 (1996) no. 796; 4.40 g (F?).
    24)   Ashmolean Museum; 15.03 g (E or F?).
    25)   Hermitage Collection 7/11; 15.85 g (cut) (A?).[130]
    26)   Hermitage Collection 6/3; 16.3 g (A8?).
    27)   Hermitage Collection 10/7; 16.48 g (F?).
    28)   Hermitage Collection 5/2; 16.55 g.
    29)   Hermitage Collection 8/5; 13.95 g.
    30)   Hermitage Collection 7/a; 16.85 g.
    31)   Hermitage Collection 11/8; 16.42 g.
    32)   Hermitage Collection 12/g; 13.87 g.

130. I add some worn and indistinct tetradrachms I saw in St. Petersburg (Russia), some of which were mounted for an exhibition in the Central Asia Department so that, unfortunately, the reverse sides could not be examined.

A Catalog of Diodotid Coinage in Bronze

Following the conventions used in appendix A, this inventory of Diodotid bronze issues presents series G (Hermes types in the name of Antiochus), series H (Hermes types in the name of Diodotus), and series I (Zeus types in the name of Diodotus). To the abbreviations listed for appendix A may be added the following: DBL (double), SGL (single), HLF (half), and QTR (quarter). Where known, the diameter is also listed.

SERIES G, GROUP I[1]

OBV: Head of Hermes r., wearing petasos. Circle of dots.
REV: ΒΑΣΙΛΕΩΣ ΑΝΤΙΟΧΟΥ Crossed caducei.
EXS:
*DBL*1) BM; 7.24 g.
    2) Houghton Collection no. 1293; 7.33 g (12:00 axis).
    3) CNG Sale 37 (1996) no. 629 (Lindgren Collection); 9.05 g.
    4) Ashmolean; 7.85 g.
*SGL*5) ANS 1944.100.74361 (Newell Collection); 2.92 g.

SERIES G, GROUP 2[2]

OBV: As above.
REV: As above but with a single caduceus; control mark ⬙ in outer l. field.
EX: *DBL*1) BM; 6.50 g.

---

1. Mitchiner 76a and 77a; not represented in Bopearachchi.
2. Mitchiner 78a but wrongly described as bearing the name of Diodotus rather than Antiochus; corrected by Bopearachchi, *Monnaies*, p. 45 n. 2, but not considered by him a Diodotid issue.

SERIES G, GROUP 3[3]

OBV: As above, wearing cloak.
REV: As above but with control mark ⊖ in inner l. field and grape cluster in inner r. field.
EX:*DBL*1) B. Kritt; 7.11 g/21 mm.

SERIES G, GROUP 4[4]

OBV: As above.
REV: As above, but with a wreath (◯) in inner r. field and control mark ⊘ in inner I. field.
EX:*DBL*1) Jerusalem 354 (Spaer Collection); 7.83 g/20 mm.

This group, which adds a wreath symbol in place of the grape cluster, brings to a close the bronze issues in the name of Antiochus. The remaining two series bear the name "Diodotus," the next carrying over the obverse type of Hermes.

SERIES H, GROUP 1[5]

OBV: As above.
REV: ΒΑΣΙΛΕΩΣ ΔΙΟΔΟΤΟΥ Helmeted Athena standing front with l. leg bent, holding a spear in r. hand and a grounded shield with her l. Circle of dots. No visible control marks.
EXS:
*DBL*1)   Sternberg Sale 29 (1995) no. 267; 9.93 g/22 mm.
     2)   Herat Museum no. 4; 8.1 g/22.5 mm.[6]

3. Not represented in either Bopearachchi or Mitchiner.
4. Not represented in either Bopearachchi or Mitchiner.
5. Bopearachchi 12, 13, 14 (but lists no quarters) and Mitchiner 79, 80, 81. The obverse, clearly the same as that on the earlier Hermaic bronzes of series G, has been variously identified over the years. Some have mistaken the bust for that of Diodotus himself, wearing a *kausia*: PMC, p. 10; Lahiri, *Corpus*, p. 114; and D. W. MacDowall and M. Ibrahim, "Pre-Islamic Coins in Herat Museum," *Afghan Studies* 2 (1979): 46. Mitchiner's type 81 is alleged to be a separate issue showing Hermes (not the king) diademed, but there is no sign on any of these coins of the dangling ends of a diadem, even on the best-preserved specimens. Perhaps we have here the strap that, along with the string tied under the chin, holds the hat in place. Such ties may be seen elsewhere in Greek art, as on the petasos flying through the air on the famous Pella mosaic of a stag hunt by Gnosis or the petasos worn by the horseman on an Attic Red Figure kylix signed by Euphronios and now in the Munich Antikensammlungen (inv. 2620). E. V. Zejmal describes the head on these Diodotid bronzes as Herakles (rather than Hermes) in his notice of finds at Takht-i Sangin: "Problèmes de circulation monétaire dans la Bactriane hellénistique," p. 277 n. 4, item A, in J.-C. Gardin, ed., *L'archéologie de la Bactriane ancienne* (Paris: CNRS, 1985). Some busts, as on G3 and 4, are cloaked.
6. See MacDowall and Ibrahim, "Pre-Islamic Coins," p. 46. The authors attribute "this rare type" to a mint in Aria, but this surmise is based on their knowledge of but nine specimens in all denominations. This coin was struck from the same obverse die as example 3 below.

3) Tadjikistan Museum H-431/97; 7.16 g/23.7 mm[7]
4) Tadjikistan Museum КП 1091/2032; 8.48 g/21.5 mm.
5) ANS 1995.51.42 (Fowler Collection); 7.53 g.
6) AK TF 9; 6.88 g.
7) Persic Gallery Sale 28 no. 66; 6.9 g.
8) BM 1890-5-2-1 (Chandra Mall); 6.80 g.
9) Persic Gallery Sale 35 no. 39; 7.7 g.
10) ANS 1979.45.2 (Spengler Collection); 8.20 g.
11) BM 1888-12-8-7; 6.47 g.[8]
12) BN 1974.410 (LeBerre Collection); 6.93 g.
13) Persic Gallery Sale 34 no. 28; 7.4 g.
14) ANS 1944.100.74368 (Newell Collection); 6.76 g.[9]
15) AK TF 48; 5.59 g/20 mm.
16) ANS 1995.51.41 (Fowler Collection); 6.93 g.[10]
17) Punjab Museum no. 4; 10.95 g/22 mm.
18) AK 91(1); 6.21 g/22 mm.[11]
19) Punjab Museum no. 5 (Bleazby Collection).[12]
20) Takht-i Sangin Exc.
21) Herat Museum no. 5; 6.9 g/23 mm.
22) ANS 1995.51.286 (Fowler Collection); 9.17 g.
23) Rahman Collection no. 100; 10.00 g/22 mm.
24) Gyar-Kala 1992 (Volchev Collection); 4.59 g/20 mm.[13]
25) Gyar-Kala 1953 inv. 1018; 7.10 g/23 mm.
26) Ashmolean; 6.77 g.
27) Ashmolean; 4.38 g.
28) F. Kovacs Stock (1997).
SGL 29) ANS 1979.45.3 (Spengler Collection); 3.63 g.
30) ANS 1986.32.3 (Spengler Collection); 3.50 g.
31) AK 92 (198); 3.48 g/17 mm.
32) AK 93 (282); 3.47 g/17 mm.
33) ANS 1979.45.4 (Spengler Collection); 3.00 g.
34) CNG Sale 37 (1996) no. 798; 3.02 g.
*HLF*35) ANS 1974.145.2; 1.76 g.[14]

7. This coin and the next are from excavations at Takht-i Sangin (1978 and 1981 respectively). The weight of example 3 has been listed alternatively as 7.26 g. It may have a thunderbolt stamped on the reverse as a countermark (cf. n. 11).
8. This specimen has no omicron visible near the arm of Athena.
9. Schulman Sale (1904) no. 7.
10. R. J. Myers Sale (1974) no. 215.
11. This specimen was excavated in the "temple à niches indentées" and clearly bears an important countermark—the thunderbolt of Zeus inside an oval—across the spear of Athena. See plate 23.
12. Examples 19–21 are not illustrated in published sources.
13. This specimen and the next are reported in N. Smirnova, "On Finds of Hellenistic Coins in Turkmenistan," Ancient Civilizations 3 (1996): 279.
14. Acquired from Bank Leu in 1974; this coin shares an obverse die with example 36 below.

36) Hollis Collection.[15]
37) Spink; 1.82 g.[16]
38) AK TF 47; 0.96 g/13 mm.
39) AK 94 (23); 2.29 g/14 mm.
40) Persic Gallery Sale 24 no. 113; 1.7 g.
41) Persic Gallery Sale 25 no. 117; 1.7 g.[17]
42) AK 95 (162); 1.89 g/12 mm.
43) AK 98 (273); 1.40 g/12 mm.
44) AK 97 (14); 1.43 g/13 mm.
45) ANS 1993.29.10 (Senior); 1.88 g.
46) ANS 1986.32.4 (Spengler Collection); 1.85 g.
47) ANS 1995.51.40 (Fowler Collection); 2.27 g.
48) AK 96 (246); 1.74 g/15 mm.
49) Tadjikistan Museum КП 1091/4248; 1.44 g/12.8 mm.
50) ANS 1985.19.9 (Spengler Collection); 1.53 g.
51) AK TF 42; 1.34 g (broken)/12 mm.
52) Senior Collection.[18]
53) Ashmolean; 1.72 g.
54) Persic Gallery Sale 38 no. 30; 2.0 g.
*QTR*55) Tadjikistan Museum КП 1091/4510; 0.76 g/10.1 mm.

Next we turn to the Diodotid bronzes that carry the obverse type of bearded Zeus. So far, there are none that are securely attributable to a Diodotus minted in the name of Antiochus.[19] Thus, all of series I, as we now know it, was issued by Diodotus II in his own name.

SERIES I, GROUP I[20]

OBV: Head of bearded Zeus r., laureate. Border of dots.
REV: ΒΑΣΙΛΕΩΣ ΔΙΟΔΟΤΟΥ Artemis striding to r., clad in chiton and boots, quiver strung over r. shoulder, and holding a long torch with both hands. Dog leaping to r. at her feet. Border of dots.

15. Mitchiner type 80.a.1.
16. Mitchiner type 80.a.2.
17. This coin weighs and looks much the same as example 40 above, but the photographs reveal sufficient differences to identify these as two distinct specimens.
18. Mitchiner type 80.a.4 and, it seems, type 80.a.3. Mitchiner lists these as two different coins, both in private hands, but the photographs suggest that they are identical down to shape, indentations, position on the flan, etc.
19. As in the case of the stag/caduceus coin discussed in chapter 6, there exists a bronze coin, struck in the name of Antiochus, with Zeus on the obverse and a thunderbolt on the reverse. This coin, too, was first assigned by Bernard to the reign of Antiochus I and later reattributed to Antiochus II. It *may* have been issued during the hegemony of Diodotus I, but this is very uncertain.
20. Bopearachchi 10 and Mitchiner 82.a. Mitchiner does not distinguish between reverses with and without Artemis's dog, and he describes Zeus as diademed rather than laureate.

EXS:
DBL 1) BM 1881-12-5-7; 9.00 g/21 mm.[21]
        2) Persic Gallery Sale 35 no. 40; 7.0 g/24 mm.
        3) ANS 1991.11.1 (Spengler Collection); 6.67 g/21 mm.
        4) Persic Gallery Sale 34 no. 27; 22 mm.
        5) BN Y20009 (Hackin Collection); 7.30 g/20 mm.
        6) Sternberg Sale 29 (1995) no. 266; 7.38 g/21 mm.

These six coins form a distinctive group in several important respects. First they show a hunting dog bounding beside the goddess. This feature disappears from subsequent groups of series I. The first four examples seem all to be struck from the same reverse die. The obverses are more difficult to judge, but the first five do share an idiosyncratic rendering of Zeus's hair with waves or curls across the crown of the head.

SERIES I, GROUP 2[22]

OBV: As above.
REV: As above, but without the dog; a star in outer r. field.
EXS:
DBL 1)   Persic Gallery Sale 33 no. 55; 7.6 g.
        2)   ANS 1993.29.9 (Fowler Collection); 8.16 g.
        3)   BN 1970/601 (LeBerre Collection); 9.81 g.
        4)   Persic Gallery Sale 27 no. 88.
        5)   BM 1888-12-8-70 (Cunningham Collection); 8.03 g.
        6)   BM 1922-4-24-2886 (Whitehead); 6.17 g.
        7)   BM 1867-6-5-5 (S. Dass); 7.72 g.[23]
        8)   Fitzwilliam Museum 9684 (McClean); 10.6 gm.
        9)   AK 83 (135); 6.6 g/21 mm.[24]
       10)   AK 81 (97); 6.91 g/20 mm.
       11)   R. J. Myers Sale (1974) no. 214.[25]
       12)   Schulman Sale (1938) no. 1427.
       13)   ANS 1944.100.74367 (Newell); 6.51 g.[26]
       14)   AK TF 25; 5.78 g/20 mm.
       15)   AK 86 (164); 5.64 g (cut)/19 mm.
       16)   AK 82 (92); 6.84 g/21 mm.
       17)   AK 80 (124); 7.89 g/21 mm.
       18)   AK 84 (34); 6.42 g/21 mm.

21. This specimen has a die axis slightly closer to 7:00 rather than the usual 6:00.
22. Bopearachchi 8 and 9 and Mitchiner 82, but, again, Mitchiner takes no notice of the star on these bronze issues.
23. The die axis for this coin is 5:00 rather than 6:00.
24. Bernard, AK 4, p. 55, notes the variant posture of Artemis on this specimen.
25. This coin and the next are presumably doubles on the basis of their size; their weights are not recorded in the auction catalogs.
26. The star on this coin and on the remaining doubles cannot be positively identified on the edge of the flan because of the circumstances of striking and wear.

19) ANS 1976.215.1 (Houghton); 6.99 g.
20) Hollis Collection.[27]
21) AK 79 (200); 8.2 g/20 mm.
22) AK 85 (15); 6.23 g/22 mm.
23) AK 78 (37); 9.13 g/21 mm.
24) AK 88 (78); 5.31 g/21 mm.
25) AK 87 (131); 5.34 g/21 mm.
26) Rahman Collection no. 99; 7.75 g/21 mm.
27) Gyar-Kala 1954 inv. 329; 5.33 g/20 mm.[28]
28) Gyar-Kala 1994 inv. 5000; 5.22 g/20.5 mm.
29) Ashmolean; 9.27 g.
30) Ashmolean; 8.24 g.
31) Ashmolean; 6.71 g.
*SGL*32) AK 89 (122); 3.2 g/16 mm.
33) Ashmolean (Shortt Collection); 3.33 g.
34) Persic Gallery stock.
35) AK 90 (187); 2.89 g/16 mm.
36) ANS 1979.45.5 (Spengler); 3.88 g.[29]
37) BN 1985.1044; 3.14 g/16 mm.
38) ANS 1993.30.1 (Fowler Collection); 3.40 g.

This large group exhibits no certain die linkage.[30] Nearly half of these coins were excavated at Ai Khanoum, and none have so far been recorded from Takht-i Sangin or the Tadjikistan Museum.[31] The star detectable on about half of these examples could perhaps represent the mythical Orion, who was slain by Artemis and transformed into the well-known constellation.[32]

SERIES I, GROUP 3[33]

OBV: Head of a king to r. , wearing diadem.
REV: As above, but the star is either missing or possibly placed in inner r. field beneath l. arm of Artemis.
EX: *DBL*1) Berlin 411/1925; 4.71 g.

There are as yet no known examples of halves in series I, but a fair sampling of related quarters has now been published since the first were identified in 1977. They clearly employ standard "abbreviations" for the Zeus/Artemis type of se-

27. Mitchiner type 82.a.5.
28. This specimen and the next are reported in Smirnova, "On Finds of Hellenistic Coins in Turkmenistan," p. 279.
29. Only on this single is the star plainly visible.
30. A number of additional specimens are not listed here because of insufficient information, e.g., Sotheby Sale (1958) no. 284.
31. A specimen of unknown denomination is illustrated in G. A. Pugachenkova and E. V. Rtveladze, *Northern Bactria-Tocharistan* (in Russian) (Tashkent, 1990), p. 43, no. 2, from Termez.
32. For further discussion of this coin-type, see chap. 6.
33. Bopearachchi, *Monnaies,* pp. 42, 151–152; unknown to Mitchiner.

ries I in order to fit the requisite flan. Especially given the wide space needed for the running Artemis reverse, the divine attributes of eagle and quiver make do on this denomination. This eagle, in fact, is surely the same as found at Zeus's feet on the precious-metal coinage; the very same pose is depicted. Likewise, the quiver is the same as seen strapped to Artemis's shoulder on the larger bronzes.

SERIES I, GROUP 4[34]

OBV: Eagle standing to l. with wings outstretched. Border of dots.
REV: ΒΑΣΙΛΕΩΣ ΔΙΟΔΟΤΟΥ Quiver, tubular with pointed top, stand-
            ing upright with dangling straps.
EXS:
QTR 1) ANS 1974.145.3; 1.05 g.[35]
       2) ANS 1985.19.14 (Spengler); 0.99 g.
       3) Sternberg Sale 29 (1995) no. 268; 0.96 g/10 mm.
       4) ANS 1986.32.2 (Spengler); 0.84 g.
       5) ANS 1995.51.313 (Fowler); 0.90 g.
       6) Persic Gallery Sale 34 no. 29; 1.0 g.
       7) AK 100 (191); 0.64 g/12 mm.
       8) AK 102 (156); 0.54 g (broken)/10 mm.
       9) AK 101 (108); 0.59 g (broken)/11 mm.
      10) Persic Gallery Sale 27 no. 89; 1.1 g.
      11) Persic Gallery Sale 24 no. 114; 0.08 g.
      12) Persic Gallery Sale 36 no. 42; 0.04 g/9 mm.[36]
      13) Ashmolean; 0.97 g.

SERIES I, GROUP 5[37]

OBV: As above.
REV: As above but with a bow alongside the quiver.[38]
EXS:
QTR 1) AK 103 (5); 0.31 g/8 mm.
       2) BM; 0.79 g/10 mm.
       3) BM; 0.83 g/11 mm.

SERIES I, GROUP 6[39]

34. Bopearachchi 15; not represented in Mitchiner. On the style of the quiver, see chap. 6, n. 49.
35. One of the first examples known, from Bank Leu (April 1974); published by Hyla Troxell, "Greek Accessions: Asia Minor to India," *ANSMN* 22 (1977): 25. See also I 7.
36. This tiny coin raises the possibility of a domination below the quarter.
37. Not represented in either Bopearachchi or Mitchiner.
38. This feature has been noted by Bernard, *AK* 4, p. 57, although available photographs make the bow very difficult to discern. Details on the next two coins, both in the BM, are given by Bernard.
39. Not represented in either Bopearachchi or Mitchiner.

OBV: As above but the eagle now stands to r.
REV: Uncertain.[40]
EX: *QTR*1) AK 99(6); 0.75 g/9 mm.

SERIES I, GROUP 7[41]

OBV: As above but with inscription: ΒΑΣΙΛΕΩΣ ΔΙΟΔΟΤΟΥ.
REV: Uncertain; circle of dots.[42]
EX: *QTR*1) ANS 1976.215.2 (Houghton); 1.12 g (12:00 axis).

This unique specimen, like the one previous, raises many questions. Why has
the eagle been turned? Why is the eagle now flanked by the coin's inscription?
Does this, together with the circle of dots on the other side, mean that the eagle
is now on the reverse and the quiver (?) on the obverse? If not a quiver, what is
this curious object, and why should it replace the usual type? Why is this last
coin struck on the "wrong" axis?

40. As listed by Bernard, *AK* 4, p. 57, the reverse is likely the usual quiver (without
bow) and inscription as on I 4. However, his photograph gives a *reverse* of eagle to left
(plate 5), which is probably a printer's error.
41. Not represented in either Bopearachchi or Mitchiner.
42. Generally, the type has been referred to as a quiver (cf. Troxell, "Greek Accessions,"
and Bernard, *AK* 4, p. 57), but its appearance seems quite unlike that on our other series
I coins. A strong, stepped base is evident, suggesting a stone pillar or altar. Bernard mentions a *cippus* (tombstone), which is a good match for this curious object.

Some Diodotid Gold Forgeries

The following coins, probably modern forgeries, have been omitted from the catalogs of appendix A. The market value of Bactrian coins, particularly the gold specimens, has inspired a centuries-old trade in high-quality fakes. These are often difficult to spot except through die linkage. Naturally, scholars will disagree on many cases; there is a subjective factor at play, especially when coins cannot always be examined directly. Preferring to err on the side of caution, I include in this list many excellent specimens that may someday be proven genuine. For the present, however, the inventory of probable gold forgeries includes:

COINS IN THE NAME OF ANTIOCHUS

BM 1888-12-8-44 (Cunningham); 8.29 g.
Schlesinger Sale 13 (1935) no. 1430; 8.2 g.
BM 1929-12-2-2 (Rogers); 8.30 g.

COINS IN THE NAME OF DIODOTUS

Sotheby Sale (1958) no. 280 (Haughton); 8.35 g.
State Museum, Lucknow no. 7300.
ANS (Newell); 8.38 g.
ANS 1995.51.46 (Leu 1986, Spink 1986); 8.28 g.
BM 1888-12-8-64 (Cunningham); 8.37 g.
Danish National Museum, SNG no. 251.
Boston MFA (Warren); 8.78 g.
BN (Armand-Valton 541); 8.35 g.
Fitzwilliam Museum (Tremlett); 8.32 g.
Boston MFA (Sotheby 1993, NFA 1980); 8.42 g.
NFA Sale 2 (1976) no. 307; 8.39 g.
Punjab Museum, Lahore, no. 1; 8.42 g.

Ball Sale 6 (1932); 8.6 g.
BM 1888-12-8-63 (Cunningham); 8.28 g.
Boston MFA no. 1312 (Sotheby 1896); 8.26 g.
BN (Valton 542); 8.57 g.
Maj. Hay (1862); 8.58 g.
BM 1868-12-43-1 (Cunningham).

APPENDIX D

A Selection of
Ancient Texts

The written sources for Bactrian history have not generally survived the intervening ages. The extant inscriptional evidence (discussed mainly in chaps. 2 and 3) and the literary texts (discussed mainly in chap. 3) tend to be fragmentary, widely scattered, and sometimes difficult for even the expert to find. For the convenience of the general reader, English translations of the main texts are assembled here as an accompaniment to the numismatic evidence collected in appendices A, B, and C.

INSCRIPTIONS

Fragmentary inscriptions, graffiti, and papyri have been discovered in such diverse places as Ai Khanoum, Dalverzin, Emshi-Tepe, Kampyr-Tepe, Kara-Kamara, Afrasiab, Tepe Nimlik, Qala-i Sam, and Bir-Kot.[1] Many of these cannot be read because only a few letters or words survive. Others have been disputed or dismissed by experts.[2] The relevant coin inscriptions have been treated fully in the text. Of the remaining documents, the following (listed in approximate chronological order) contribute most to our understanding of the period of Greek rule in Bactria.

1. Babylon, excerpt from cuneiform tablet (BM 92689) dated 276–274 B.C.:

"In that year the king [Antiochus I] left his court, queen, and crown prince in Sapardu [Sardis] to keep a strong guard. He went to the

---

1. A convenient survey may be found in Rapin, *AK* 8, pp. 387–392. See also F. R. Allchin and N. Hammond, eds., *The Archaeology of Afghanistan* (London: Academic Press, 1978), pp. 191–201 (Achaemenid and Greek periods), and 235–245 (Kushan and later); Burstein, *Hellenistic Age*, pp. 67–68 and 71–72 (translations and notes).

2. For example, the interlinear Sanskrit inscriptions reported by S. Paranavitana, *The Greeks and the Mauryas* (Colombo: Lake House Investments Ltd., 1971).

province of Ebirnari [Syria] and marched against the Egyptian army [of Ptolemy II], which was camped in Ebirnari. The Egyptians fled before him. On the twenty-fourth of Adar the satrap of Akkad dispatched a great amount of silver, textiles, furniture, and other gear from Babylon and Seleucia, the royal city, and twenty elephants that the satrap of Bactria had sent to the king, to Ebirnari for the king."[3]

2. Kandahar, Greek epigram on statue base dated 300–250 B.C.:
   "Of the wild beast . . . set up this in the sacred precinct, the son of Aristonax Alex . . . among his fellow-citizens and of my savior . . ." [4]

3. Ai Khanoum, on Greek funerary urns dated 300–250 B.C.:
   "The remains of a little boy and little girl, of Lysanias and Isidora, and of Cosmas."[5]

4. Ai Khanoum, Greek preamble and maxims dated 300–250 B.C.:
   "These wise sayings of earlier men, the words of well-known men, are enshrined in the holy Pytho [at Delphi]. There Klearchos copied them faithfully, and set them up here in the sanctuary of Kineas, blazing from afar.

   As a child, be well-behaved.
   As a youth, be self-controlled.
   As an adult, be just.
   As an elder, be wise.
   As one dying, be without pain."[6]

5: Kandahar, bilingual (Greek/Aramaic) Asokan edict dated 258 B.C.:
   "Ten years having passed, King Piodasses [Asoka] revealed piety [Dharma] to men. Thenceforth he made men more pious and made all things prosper throughout the entire land. The king abstained from [eating] living creatures, and [following his example] other men did likewise, and all who were hunters or fishermen have ceased their work. Those lacking self-control have, as far as possible, overcome their weakness and, unlike before, have become obedient to their father, mother,

---

3. Adapted from Sidney Smith, ed., *Babylonian Historical Texts* (London: Methuen, 1924) pp. 150–159; see also Sherwin-White and Kuhrt, *Samarkhand to Sardis*, pp. 46–47.
4. P. M. Fraser, "The Son of Aristonax at Kandahar," *Afghan Studies* 2 (1979): 9–21. An alternative reading of the text has been proposed: A. N. Oikonomides, "The Temenos of Alexander the Great at Alexandria in Arachosia (Old Khandahar)," *ZPE* 56 (1984): 145–147.
5. P. Bernard, "Campagne de fouilles à Ai Khanoum (Afghanistan)," *CRAI* (1972): 605–632, esp. 618–619. Other very fragmentary funerary inscriptions include one in verse and another mentioning "kings."
6. L. Robert, "De Delphes à l'Oxus," *CRAI* (1968): 416–457. The list of maxims at Ai Khanoum is, unfortunately, incomplete; only the last 5 (of 147) survive on the monument. For an interesting comparison of this document with the following one, see V. -P. Yailenko, "Les maximes delphiques d'Ai Khanoum et la formation de la doctrine du *Dhamma* d'Asoka," *DHA* 16 (1990): 239–256.

and elders. By doing these things, they will live more profitably in the future."[7]

6. Adulis, Greek account of the Third Syrian War dated 246–222 B.C.:

"The Great King Ptolemy [III], son of King Ptolemy [II] and Queen Arsinoë the Brother-Sister gods, children of King Ptolemy [I] and Queen Berenike the Savior gods, descended through his father from Zeus's son Herakles and through his mother from Zeus's son Dionysus, inherited from his father kingship over Egypt, Libya, Syria, Phoenicia, Cyprus, Lycia, Caria, and the Cyclades Islands. He invaded Asia with his infantry, cavalry, fleet, and elephants from Trogodytike and Ethiopia, which his father and he were the first to hunt, capture, and train for war. Having conquered all lands west of the Euphrates and of Cilicia, Pamphylia, Ionia, the Hellespont, Thrace, and overcome all forces in these places including the Indian elephants and subjected all rulers of these areas to his will, he crossed the Euphrates River and subdued Mesopotamia, Babylonia, Susiana, Persis, Media, and everything else as far as Bactria. He sought out all sacred objects plundered from Egypt by the Persians and returned these, together with treasures from the conquered lands, to Egypt. He led his forces . . . "[8]

7. Provenance uncertain, Greek parchment tax receipt dated ca. 180–160 B.C.:

"During the reign of Antimachus the God and Eumenes and Antimachus . . . the fourth year, month of Olous, in Asangorna, the guardian of the law being . . . The tax collector Menodotus, in the presence of . . . who was also sent out by Demonax the former . . . , and of Simus who was . . . by the agency of Diodorus, controller of revenues, acknowledges receipt from . . . the son of Dataes from the priests . . . the dues relating to the purchase."[9]

8. Delos, Greek dedication of Hyspasines dated 179 B.C.:

"The upper part of a lion on a plinth, the dedication of Hyspasines, son of Mithroaxos, a Bactrian."[10]

---

7. See Burstein, *Hellenistic Age,* pp. 67–68, for a full bibliography. Other Asokan inscriptions (including rock edict 13, which mentions the Buddhist missionaries sent to the West) are translated in Romila Thapar, *Asoka and the Decline of the Mauryas,* 2d ed. (Oxford: Oxford University Press, 1973).

8. *OGIS* 54. The actual inscription is lost, but the traveler Cosmas Indicopleustes made a copy in the sixth century A.D. See Burstein, *Hellenistic Age,* pp. 125–126, and Austin, *Hellenistic World,* p. 365.

9. J. R. Rea, R. C. Senior, and A. S. Hollis, "A Tax Receipt from Hellenistic Bactria," *ZPE* 104 (1994): 261–280. The location of the city of Asangorna remains uncertain.

10. Félix Durrbach, *Inscriptions de Délos* (Paris: Librairie Ancienne Honoré Champion, 1929), no. 442 B, l. 109 and 443 Bb, l. 33; cf. F. Durrbach and P. Roussel, *Inscriptions de Délos* (Paris: Champion, 1935), no. 1432 Aa II, ll.26–27, where the temple inventory describes the ex-voto dedication as a relief carving of a Hyrcanian dog. See Plutarch *Moralia* 499D (below); cf. Cicero *Tusculan Disputations* 1.45.108; and Strabo 11.11.3 (below).

9. Ai Khanoum, Greek gymnasium dedication dated ca. 200–150 B.C.:

"Triballos and Strato, sons of Strato, to Hermes and Herakles."[11]

10. Takht-i Sangin, Greek altar dedication dated ca. mid-second century B.C.:

"Atrosokes dedicated this ex-voto to the Oxus."[12]

11. Ai Khanoum, Greek treasury records dated ca. 150 B.C.:

"Year 24, month . . . container of olive oil, partially empty . . . "

"Under the direction of Zeno, there have been counted five hundred drachms through the agency of Oxyboakes and Oxybazos. Oxyboakes sealed the jar."

"Under the direction of Philiskos, ten thousand Taxilan (?) *karshapana* coins through the agency of Aryandes and Straton . . . "

"Through the agency of Cosmas, silver of good quality, validated by Nikeratos and sealed by Nikeratos himself."[13]

12. Reh (India), Brahmi pillar inscription dated ca. 150 B.C.:

"Of the king of kings, Great Savior, Just, Victorious, and Invincible, Menander . . . "[14]

13. Bajaur (Pakistan), Kharoshthi casket inscription dated ca. 150 B.C.:

"In the reign of King Menander, on the fourteenth day of Karttika . . ."
[15]

14. Besnegar (India), Brahmi pillar dedication dated to the late second century B.C.:

"This Garuda pillar of Vasudeva, the god of gods, was commissioned

11. Veuve, *AK* 6, pp. 28, 111–112 (with P. Bernard's comments on the date).

12. B. A. Litvinsky and I. Pichikyan, "Découvertes dans un sanctuaire du dieu Oxus de la Bactriane septentrionale," *RA* (1981–82): 195–216; B. A. Litvinsky, Y. G. Vino-gradov, and I. Pichikyan, "The Votive Offering of Atrosokes, from the Temple of Oxus in Northern Bactria" (in Russian, English summary), *VDI* (1985): 84–110. The Iranian name "Atrosokes" is taken to mean "possessing the power of divine fire."

13. These examples of bureaucratic inscriptions inked onto jars in the royal treasury are drawn from Claude Rapin, "Les inscriptions économiques de la trésorerie hellénistique d'Ai Khanoum (Afghanistan)," *BCH* 107 (1983): 315–372; cf. Rapin, "Les textes lit-téraires grecs de la trésorerie d'Ai Khanoum," *BCH* 111 (1987): 225–266, for the literary (philosophical) texts associated with the treasury library.

14. G. R. Sharma, *Reh Inscription of Menander and the Indo-Greek Invasion of the Ganga Valley* (Allahabad: Abinash, 1980). The reading of Menander's name is question-able, making it possible that this inscription belongs to a later, even post-Greek period.

15. N. G. Majumdar, "The Bajaur Casket of the Reign of Menander," *Epigraphia In-dica* 24 (1937): 1–8. The following words regarding Buddhist relics are incomplete, and a second, much later inscription notes the reconsecration of the casket. See Narain, *IG*, pp. 79–80.

by Heliodoros, son of Dion from Taxila, a worshiper of Vishnu who came as the Greek ambassador from the court of Antalcidas, the Great King, to Bhagabhadra, Son of Kosi, the Savior, who was then in the fourteenth year of his prosperous reign.

Three timeless precepts, when practiced, lead to heaven: Self-control, Charity, and Conscientiousness."[16]

LITERARY SOURCES

Translations of the main references in Greek and Latin literature are provided here for the period of Greek rule in Bactria. The sources associated with Alexander the Great's campaigns have been treated elsewhere (Holt, *Alexander and Bactria*). As a matter of economy, long texts that do not bear directly upon the period under study have been omitted. These include the *Milindapañha* ("The Questions of Milinda," referring to Menander) and the Chinese extracts from Chang-k'ien's report on post-Greek Bactria.[17] For the reader's convenience in looking up passages, texts have been arranged in alphabetical order by name of the author.

AELIAN *ON ANIMALS* 15.8:

"There is a city (named Perimoula) that was ruled by a man of royal blood named Soras, at the time when Eucratides ruled Bactria."

AMMIANUS MARCELLINUS *HISTORY* 23.6.2–3:

"The kingdom of Parthia took its name from the Parthian Arsaces after the fates took away Alexander the Great from Babylon. A man of obscure origins, Arsaces was in his youth a brigand leader whose character improved until he achieved great things. After many glorious and brave deeds, and having overcome Seleucus Nikator [rather, Callinicus], . . . Arsaces expelled the Macedonian garrisons and settled into a peaceful life as a temperate, mild leader."

ANONYMOUS, *PERIPLUS MARIS ERYTHRAEI* (CIRCUMNAVIGATION OF THE RED SEA) 47:

"Beyond Barygaza [modern Broach] there are many inland peoples . . . and above these [to the north] are the very warlike Bactrians, who have their own kingdom. . . . Even now in Barygaza old drachms stamped with inscriptions in Greek lettering come to hand, the coins of Apollodotus and Menander, who were kings after Alexander."[18]

---

16. D. C. Sircar, ed., *Select Inscriptions Bearing on Indian History and Civilization*, 2d ed. (Calcutta: University of Calcutta, 1965), vol. 1, no. 2; cf. Burstein, *Hellenistic Age*, p. 72.

17. For an excellent guide to these Chinese and Indian sources, consult M. Kordosis, "China and the Greek World: An Introduction to Greek-Chinese Studies with Special Reference to the Chinese Sources," *Historikogeographika* 4 (1994): 253–304.

18. On this passage, see *GBI*, pp. 149, 527.

APPIAN *SYRIAN WARS* 65:

"After the death of Seleucus [I], son succeeded father as ruler of Syria in the following line of succession: first was Antiochus [I], the one who loved his stepmother and was given the surname Soter because he drove out the Gauls invading Asia from Europe; second came another Antiochus [II], born of their marriage and first surnamed Theos by the Milesians because he destroyed their tyrant Timarchos. This Antiochus Theos was poisoned by one of his wives. He had two, Laodice and Berenike, the first from love and the second, a daughter of Ptolemy [II] Philadelphus, by diplomatic arrangement. Laodice killed him and later also Berenike and Berenike's newborn child. To avenge these deeds, Ptolemy [III], son of Philadelphus, killed Laodice, invaded Syria, and advanced to Babylon. And the Parthians at this time began their revolt because of the turmoil in the Seleucid empire."

ARRIAN *PARTHIKA* (FGrH F30A-PHOTIUS):

"The brothers Arsaces and Tiridates . . . overthrew Pherecles, the satrap of Parthia appointed by Antiochus Theos. . . . "

ARRIAN *PARTHIKA* (FGrH F31-SYNCELLUS):

"When Antiochus, the one called Callinicus and also Seleucus [meaning Antiochus II or Seleucus II?], was king . . . a certain Arsaces and Tiridates, Persian brothers, were satraps of Bactria, and the Macedonian Agathocles was *eparch* of Persica. This Agathocles loved Tiridates . . . and tried to seduce him but failed and was killed by Tiridates and his brother Arsaces, who became king. . . ."

ATHENAEUS *DEIPNOSOPHISTAE* 15.636A:

"And I [the tragic poet Diogenes] hear that the maidens of Lydia and Bactria who dwell alongside the Halys River worship Artemis the Tmolian goddess."[19]

ATHENAEUS *DEIPNOSOPHISTAE* 15.652F:

"Hegesander says that Amitrochates [Bindusura], the king of the Indians, wrote to Antiochus [I] requiring him to send a sweet, some figs, and a marketplace sophist. To this request Antiochus responded, 'We send off to you the figs and sweet, but among the Greeks a sophist cannot legally be sold.'"[20]

HERODIAN *HISTORY OF ROME AFTER MARCUS AURELIUS* 6.2.7:

"After Darius [III] lost his empire to Alexander [III] of Macedonia, the lands

19. The manuscript could be corrupt in its reference to Bactria.
20. Hegesander of Delphi, the source for this passage, wrote in the second century B.C. a (lost) collection of anecdotes about Hellenistic kings and court life.

of the East and all Asia were divided and ruled by the successors of Alexander. But when they set upon each other and the power of the Macedonians weakened with constant warfare, it is said that the Parthian Arsaces was first to push the barbarians into revolt from the Macedonians. So, having been granted the diadem by the willing Parthians and surrounding barbarians, he ruled as king."

JUSTIN *EPITOME OF POMPEIUS TROGUS* 41.4.1–20:

"After the death of Alexander the Great, when the kingdoms of the East were being divided among his successors, the governance of Parthia was given to Stasanor, a foreign ally, because no Macedonian cared to accept it. Afterward, when the Macedonians were involved in war among themselves, the Parthians and other peoples of Upper Asia [the satrapies east of Mesopotamia] followed Eumenes, a Greek, whose defeat transferred them to Antigonus's authority. Next the Parthians were under the power of Seleucus [I] Nikator and thereafter Antiochus [I] and his successors. From the great-grandson Seleucus [II] the Parthians were the first to defect at the time of the First Punic War, when L. Manlius Vulso and M. Atilius Regulus were consuls of Rome. The discord of the two royal brothers Seleucus [II] and Antiochus (Hierax) gave the Parthians impunity for their revolt, because, while each brother tried to snatch the empire for himself, they failed to pursue the defectors. At that same period of time, Theodotus [a variant spelling of "Diodotus"], the governor of the thousand cities of Bactria, also rebelled and ordered that he be called king; all the eastern peoples followed his example and defected from the Macedonians.

"There was at this time one Arsaces, a man of uncertain origins but certainly of proven bravery. This man, accustomed to live by brigandage and plunder, and having heard that Seleucus [II] was defeated by the Gauls [at the Battle of Ancyra in 240–239 B.C.], was thus freed from fear of the king. He invaded Parthia with a band of robbers, caught their governor Andragoras by surprise, removed him from power, and took over. Not much later, Arsaces also seized Hyrcania, and thus endowed with power over two states he prepared a large army out of fear of Seleucus [II] and Theodotus [I], king of Bactria. But when Theodotus [I] soon died, Arsaces was relieved of dread and made peace and a treaty with the like-named son, Theodotus [II]. Not long afterward, when King Seleucus [II] came to punish the rebels, Arsaces was victorious in battle. That day the Parthians henceforth observed as the solemn beginning of their freedom."

PLUTARCH *MORALIA* 499D:

"Whenever they meet with a happy end, the dead of the Hyrcanians are devoured by dogs and the Bactrians by birds, according to custom."

PLUTARCH *MORALIA* 821D:

"After a man named Menander had reigned well as king in Bactria and then died in camp, the cities observed the other usual funeral rites, but they quarreled over his actual remains and with difficulty agreed to divide up his ashes into equal shares and to set up monuments [Buddhist stupas?] of the man beside all the cities."

POLYBIUS *HISTORIES* 10.49:

"When he received word that Euthydemus was near Tapuria with his military forces, and that ten thousand [Bactrian] cavalrymen were stationed in front to guard the ford at the Arius River, Antiochus [III] chose to abandon the siege [place unknown] and face this situation. Since the river was a march of three days away, he traveled at a measured pace for two days and then commanded the rest to set off at daybreak after breakfast while he himself advanced at a fast pace overnight with the cavalry and light infantry, together with ten thousand peltasts. For Antiochus had learned that while the enemy cavalry lay in wait during the day by the edge of the river, at night they pulled back to a city not less than twenty stades [about two and a half miles] away. Because the plain was easy to cross on horseback, Antiochus completed the march by night and at daybreak crossed the river with most of his own forces.

"The cavalry of the Bactrians, when alerted by their scouts, sallied forth and engaged the enemy. Antiochus considered it vital to withstand the first charge of the enemy, so he summoned two thousand cavalrymen accustomed to facing danger around him [the royal squadron?]; the rest he ordered to deploy by squads and troops and there to hold each of their usual positions. He himself with the aforementioned cavalry met and engaged the first of the Bactrians to charge. Antiochus seems in this particular engagement to have fought the most conspicuously of those with him. Accordingly, although many were killed on both sides, the king's forces defeated the first cavalry charge. . . .

"At a critical moment, Panaetolus [a mercenary captain] issued commands to join Antiochus and those battling beside him. He compelled the oncoming Bactrians to change course and flee headlong in disarray. Those being pressed upon by Panaetolus did not halt until they had reached Euthydemus, though most had already been killed. The [Seleucid] king's cavalry, having killed many, on the one hand, and taken many alive, on the other, retired and camped beside the river. In this particular battle, Antiochus's horse was wounded and killed, and the king himself was struck through the mouth and lost some of his teeth. On the whole, he acquired on that occasion his greatest reputation for valor. Because of this battle, Euthydemus was caught off guard and retreated with his forces into the Bactrian city of Zariaspa."

POLYBIUS *HISTORIES* 11.34:

"For Euthydemus [like Teleas the envoy] was himself a Magnesian and, defending himself to Teleas, alleged that it was unjust for Antiochus to demand his removal from power, since he himself had not rebelled against the king. Rather, when others had revolted, he had destroyed their descendants and thus gained possession of the Bactrian throne. After further discussing this matter along these same lines, he begged Teleas to mediate peace in a kindly manner, exhorting Antiochus not to begrudge him his royal name and state. For if Antiochus did not make these concessions, neither of them would be safe: not far away were great numbers of nomads who not only posed a danger to them both but also threatened to barbarize the whole area if they attacked. After saying these things, Euthydemus sent Teleas to Antiochus.

"The [Seleucid] king had long been looking for a way out of the situation, so hearing these things from Teleas he readily accepted peace for the aforementioned reasons. After Teleas had shuttled between them many times, Euthydemus finally dispatched his son Demetrius to confirm the agreements. Antiochus gladly received him and judged the young man to be worthy of royal rank because of his appearance, dignified bearing, and conversation. First, Antiochus promised to give him one of his own daughters in marriage. Second, he conceded to his father [Euthydemus] the title of king. Concerning the rest of the terms, he made a written treaty and sworn alliance. Then, after lavishly provisioning his army, he marched away, adding Euthydemus's elephants to his own.

"Crossing the Caucasus Mountains and descending into India, he renewed the treaty of friendship with Sophagasenus, King of the Indians, and seized more elephants so that there were now 150 altogether. Moreover, he provisioned his army again. Then he himself marched off with his army, leaving behind Androsthenes of Cyzicus to recover the treasure promised to Antiochus by the Indian king. . . . Such, therefore, was the outcome of this campaign into the upper satrapies, through which Antiochus made subject to his authority not only the eastern satraps but also the coastal cities and the dynasts this side of the Taurus Mountains. In short, he secured his kingdom, astounding all of his subjects with his courage and diligence. Because of this expedition, he appeared worthy of his royal office not only to those in Asia but also to those in Europe."

STRABO *GEOGRAPHY* 11.9.2:

"Revolutionary movements arose outside the Taurus because the [Seleucid] kings of Syria and Media who possessed these territories were busy fighting [against others/against each other].

"The first to rebel had been entrusted with governing Bactria, namely, those around Euthydemus, and then [the satraps] of all the neighboring regions. Thereafter Arsaces, a Scythian leading some of the Dahae (the nomads called the Aparni who lived along the Oxus) invaded Parthia and conquered it. In the beginning, Arsaces was weak because both he and his successors were continuously at war against those being deprived of their land; later, however, the ones always taking the land from their neighbors through military success became so powerful that they finally gained authority over everything inside [east of] the Euphrates. They also annexed part of Bactria, having overpowered the Scythians and still earlier those around Eucratides. At present, they rule so much territory and so many peoples that they have become, in a way, rivals of the Romans. . . ."

STRABO *GEOGRAPHY* 11.9.3:

"They say that the Aparnian Dahae were emigrants from those Dahae called Xandii or Parii, above Lake Maeotis, but it is not altogether agreed that the Dahae are some of the Scythians from above Maeotis. But to resume, they say that Arsaces was a descendant of these people, while others claim that he was a Bactrian who fled the growing power of those around Diodotus and caused the Parthian defection. But since I have recorded many things about the ways of the Parthians in the sixth book of my *Historical Sketches* and the second book of my *History After Polybius,* I shall omit them here. . . ."[21]

STRABO *GEOGRAPHY* 11.11.1:

"Part of Bactria lies beside Aria toward the north, but most of it lies above and to the east of Aria. It is large and all-productive except for oil. Because of the excellence of the land, the Greeks who rebelled there grew so powerful that they conquered both Ariana and India as well, according to Apollodorus of Artemita. And so they subdued more peoples than Alexander, especially Menander if indeed he crossed the Hypanis River toward the east and advanced as far as the Imaus, for some were subdued by Menander himself, and some by Demetrius the son of Euthydemus, the king of Bactria. They took over not only Patalene but also the rest of the coast, which is called the kingdom of Saraostos and Sigerdis. In sum, Apollodorus says that Bactria is the jewel of all Ariana; moreover, they extended their empire as far as the Seres and Phryni."

STRABO *GEOGRAPHY* 11.11.2:

"The cities of Bactria were Bactra, which they also call Zariaspa and through which flows a river of the same name that empties into the Oxus, also Darapsa, and others more. Among these was Eucratidia, named after its ruler. The Greeks who took possession of the region divided it into satrapies, of which the Parthians took Touriva [Tapuria?] and Aspionus from Eucratides; they [the Greeks] also controlled Sogdiana, which lies above and to the east of Bactria between the Oxus River—demarcating Bactrians from Sogdians—and the Jaxartes River, likewise separating the Sogdians from the nomads."

STRABO *GEOGRAPHY* 11.11.3:

"Accordingly, in ancient times not much distinguished the lives and customs of the Sogdians and Bactrians from those of the nomads, although the Bactrians were slightly more civilized. Yet, Onesicritus and his followers say not the best things about any of them, namely, that those who have been worn out by age or illness are thrown alive to dogs maintained just for this purpose. He writes that

21. "Lake Maeotis" may here refer either to the Sea of Azov or to the Aral Sea.

these dogs are called 'entombers' in the local language and that, while it looks spotless outside the walls of the Bactrian metropolis, the inside is littered with human bones. He says also that Alexander put an end to this custom. . . ."

STRABO *GEOGRAPHY* 15.1.3:

"Not many who have written about India in much earlier times or who sail there now report anything that is accurate. Apollodorus, at any rate, the author of the *Parthika,* when referring to the Greeks who broke Bactria free from the Syrian kings descended from Seleucus [1] Nikator, says, on the one hand, that they grew in power and attacked India as well, but, on the other hand, he discloses nothing new and even disputes what is known by reporting that they conquered more of India than the Macedonians [with Alexander]. He actually says that Eucratides ruled a thousand cities. . . ."

Glossary

AEGIS   a protective goatskin bearing the face of Medusa and bordered with snakes, made for Zeus by the god Hephaestus. Shaken by Zeus, the aegis thunders and, along with his lightning bolts, scatters enemies in fear.

AMPHORA   (pl. amphorae) a pottery vessel with double handles and narrow neck used for storage or transport.

ANABASIS   a march upland from the coast, normally referring to an expedition into the interior of the old Persian Empire as in the cases of Alexander the Great and Antiochus the Great.

ANIKETOS   a royal epithet, meaning "Invincible" in Greek.

ATTIC STANDARD   the established system of weights used by Classical Athens and, later, many Hellenistic states.

BRAHMI   an early Indian script found on some Indo-Greek coins.

CADUCEUS   a herald's staff, the attribute of Hermes the messenger-god.

CALLINICUS   a royal epithet, meaning "Glorious Victory" in Greek.

CHITON   a Greek tunic.

COIN-TYPE   or simply type, the principal design on the face of a coin, such as a deity or emblem.

CONTROL MARK   see Monogram.

COUNTERMARK   a punched marking, usually a special symbol, applied to a coin already in use, normally to revalue or revalidate a coinage already in circulation.

CUNEIFORM   literally "wedge-shaped," the writing system of Mesopotamian civilizations beginning with the Sumerians ca. 3000 B.C. and continuing through the Akkadian, Persian, and Hellenistic periods.

DIADEM   a ribbon of cloth tied around the head, with loose ends dangling; usually the insignia of a king.

DIADOCHOI   the successors of Alexander the Great.

DIE   the engraved reverse-image stamp used to manufacture the obverse or reverse of a coin.

DIE AXIS   the relative position of the obverse die to the reverse die during striking, generally expressed with arrows or clock-face numbers. If the two dies
are aligned in the same direction, this will be noted as ↑ ↑ (or simply ↑) or
12:00; if in opposite direction, then ↑ ↓ (or simply ↓) or 6:00, and so on.

DIE LINKAGE   the sharing of a die by two or more coins.

DIKAIOS   a royal epithet, meaning "Just" in Greek.

DORIKTETOS CHORA   meaning "spear-won territory" in Greek, referring to the
concept of legitimate rule by right of conquest.

DRACHM   a standard silver denomination weighing approximately 4.2 grams
on the Attic standard.

ELECTRUM   a naturally occurring alloy of silver and gold.

EPARCH   an administrator, usually a commander or governor.

EUERGETES   a royal epithet, meaning "Benefactor" in Greek.

EX-VOTO   a dedication made in fulfillment of a vow.

FABRIC   in numismatics, the general appearance of a coin.

FIELD   in numismatics, the area around the central design of a coin.

FLAN   the blank piece of metal into which the coin-type is struck, usually precast and weighed.

FOURRÉE   a plated coin, usually silver over base metal.

HEMIDRACHM   a standard silver denomination equal to half a drachm, thus
weighing approximately 2.1 grams on the Attic standard.

HIERAX   a royal epithet, meaning "Hawk" in Greek.

KAUSIA   a broad-brimmed Macedonian hat.

KHAROSHTHI   an Indian script, read right to left, derived from Aramaic and used
widely on Mauryan inscriptions and Indo-Greek coins.

KLEROS   a land grant, usually given by a king in exchange for the military ser-
vices of a soldier-settler (*kleruch*).

KYLIX   a Greek drinking cup.

LEGEND   the inscription on a coin, often identifying the issuing authority by
name and title.

MONOGRAM   a distinguishing mark on a coin (such as ⊘ or 𝍩), usually formed
by combining letters representing a supervisory mint official; also called mint
marks and control marks.

NIKATOR   a royal epithet, meaning "Conqueror" in Greek.

OBVERSE   the side of the coin struck by the lower, or anvil, die and normally
bearing the portrait of the ruler on precious-metal issues.

OCTODRACHM   a large coin equal to eight drachms, weighing approximately
33.6 grams on the Attic standard.

OSTRACON   a potsherd, often used to record tax receipts, letters, and other
documents.

OVERSTRIKE   a coin made by using an old coin as the blank or flan, often showing traces of the original coin-type (the under-type) on the surface of the new
coin (the over-type).

PALAESTRA   a Greek building with an open, sandy courtyard used for wrestling
and exercise.

PELTASTS   light infantry armed with javelins and small shields.

PETASOS   a broad-brimmed felt hat favored by ancient travelers.

PHILADELPHUS   a royal epithet, meaning "Brotherly" in Greek.

PHILHELLENE   a royal epithet, meaning "Greek-loving" in Greek.

POLIS (PL. POLEIS)   a specifically Greek city-state.

PROPYLAEA   a porch or entryway, often of elaborate size as on the Athenian acropolis.

REVERSE   the side of the coin struck by the upper, or punch, die and normally showing the patron deity and name/title of a Hellenistic ruler.

SATRAPY   a province within a Persian or Hellenistic kingdom, administered by an appointed governor (satrap).

SIGLOS   the standard silver denomination of the Persian Empire, comparable to the Greek drachm.

SOTER   a royal epithet, meaning "Savior" in Greek.

STADE   a unit of distance, approximately two hundred yards, based upon the Greek stadium.

STATER   any principal denomination of a state's coinage, especially of gold; on the Attic standard a gold stater weighs approximately 8.4 grams.

STRATEGOS   the usual Hellenistic term for a satrap (governor), meaning "general" in Greek.

STUPA   a Buddhist burial mound.

TALENT   a unit of weight, normally referring to 25.8 kilograms (56.88 pounds) of silver as an ancient accounting term: 1 talent = 60 minae = 6,000 drachms = 36,000 obols.

TETRADRACHM   a standard silver denomination equal to four drachms, thus weighing approximately 16.8 grams on the Attic standard.

THEOS   a royal epithet, meaning "God" in Greek.

Abbreviations

In addition to the standard abbreviations employed by *L'Année Philologique*, S. Hornblower and A. Spawforth, eds., *The Oxford Classical Dictionary*, 3d ed. (Oxford: Clarendon Press, 1996), and those separately listed in appendices A and B, the following abbreviations have been used in this volume:

AAASH   *Acta Antiqua Academiae Scientiarum Hungaricae*
AHB   *Ancient History Bulletin*
AJN   *American Journal of Numismatics*
AK   *Fouilles d'Ai Khanoum*
ANCW   *Ancient World*
ANSMN   *American Numismatic Society Museum Notes*
AUSTIN, HELLENISTIC WORLD   Austin, M. M., ed. and trans., *The Hellenistic World from Alexander to the Roman Conquest*. Cambridge: Cambridge University Press, 1981.
BALL, GAZETTEER   Ball, Warwick. *Archaeological Gazetteer of Afghanistan*. 2 vols. Paris: Editions Recherche sur les Civilisations, 1982.
BMC, BACTRIA   Gardner, P. *The Coins of the Greek and Scythic Kings of Bactria and India in the British Museum*. 1886; rpt. Chicago: Argonaut, 1966.
BOPEARACHCHI, MONNAIES   Bopearachchi, Osmund. *Monnaies gréco-bactriennes et indo-grecques: Catalogue raisonné*. Paris: Bibliothèque Nationale, 1991.
BURSTEIN, HELLENISTIC AGE   Burstein, Stanley M., ed. and trans., *The Hellenistic Age from the Battle of Ipsos to the Death of Kleopatra VII*. Cambridge: Cambridge University Press, 1985.
CH   *Coin Hoards*
CHI   Rapson, E. J., ed., *The Cambridge History of India*. 6 vols. Cambridge, 1922; rpt. Delhi, 1962.
CUNNINGHAM, CASE   Cunningham, Alexander. *Coins of Alexander's Successors in the East (Bactria, Ariana and India)*. London, 1884; rpt. Chicago: Argonaut, 1969.

ESM   Newell, E. T. *The Coinage of the Eastern Seleucid Mints*. New York: American Numismatic Society, 1938; rpt. 1978.

GBI   Tarn, W. W. *The Greeks in Bactria and India*. 3d ed. Edited by Frank Holt. Chicago: Ares Press, 1984.

GOUKOWSKY, MYTHE D'ALEXANDRE   Goukowsky, Paul. *Essai sur les origines du mythe d'Alexandre*. 2 vols. Nancy: Biales, 1978.

GREEN, ALEXANDER TO ACTIUM   Green, Peter. *Alexander to Actium: The Historical Evolution of the Hellenistic Age*. Berkeley: University of California Press, 1990.

HOLT, ALEXANDER AND BACTRIA   Holt, Frank. *Alexander the Great and Bactria: The Formation of a Greek Frontier in Central Asia*. Leiden: Brill, 1988.

HOLT, "PEDIGREE COINS"   Holt, Frank. "The So-Called 'Pedigree Coins' of the Bactrian Greeks," pp. 69–91 in W. Heckel and R. Sullivan, eds., *Ancient Coins of the Graeco-Roman World: The Nickle Numismatic Papers*. Waterloo, Ontario: Wilfrid Laurier University Press, 1984.

IASCCAINFB   *International Association for the Study of the Cultures of Central Asia Information Bulletin*

IGCH   Thompson, Margaret, Otto Mørkholm, and Colin Kraay, eds., *An Inventory of Greek Coin Hoards*. New York: American Numismatic Society, 1973.

IHQ   *Indian Historical Quarterly*

INN   *International Numismatic Newsletter*

JASB   *Journal of the Asiatic Society of Bengal*

JIH   *Journal of Interdisciplinary History*

JNSI   *Journal of the Numismatic Society of India*

LAHIRI, CORPUS   Lahiri, Amarendra Nath. *Corpus of Indo-Greek Coins*. Calcutta: Poddar Publications, 1965.

MITCHINER, IGISC   Mitchiner, Michael. *Indo-Greek and Indo-Scythian Coinage*. 9 vols. London: Hawkins, 1975.

NARAIN, IG   Narain, A. K. *The Indo-Greeks*. Oxford: Clarendon Press, 1957.

NUMDIGEST   *Numismatic Digest*

OGIS   Dittenberger, W. *Orientis Graeci Inscriptiones Selectae*. Vol. 1. Leipzig, 1903.

PACT   *Revue du Groupe Européen d'Etudes pour les Techniques Physiques, Chimiques et Mathématiques Appliquées à l'Archéologie*

PMC   Whitehead, R. B. *Catalogue of the Coins in the Punjab Museum, Lahore*. Vol. 1. *Indo-Greek Coins*. Oxford, 1914; rpt. Chicago, 1969.

ROSTOVTZEFF, SEHHW   Rostovtzeff, M. *The Social and Economic History of the Hellenistic World*. 2d ed. 3 vols. Oxford: Clarendon Press, 1953.

SHERWIN-WHITE AND KUHRT, SAMARKHAND TO SARDIS   Sherwin-White, Susan, and Amélie Kuhrt. *From Samarkhand to Sardis: A New Approach to the Seleucid Empire*. Berkeley: University of California Press, 1993.

TQ   Curiel, Raoul, and Gerard Fussman. *Le trésor monétaire de Qunduz*. Paris: Klincksieck, 1965.

WILL, MONDE GREC   Will, E., C. Mossé, and P. Goukowsky. *Le monde grec et l'Orient*. Vol. 2. *Le IVᵉ siècle et l'époque hellénistique*. Paris: Presses Universitaires de France, 1978.

WILSON, AA   Wilson, Horace H. *Ariana Antiqua: A Descriptive Account of the Antiquities and Coins of Afghanistan.* 1841; rpt. Delhi: Oriental Publishers, 1971.

WN   *Wiadomosci Numismatyczne*

ZFN   *Zeitschrift für Numismatik*

Select Bibliography

In addition to the items already cited above under "ABBREVIATIONS," the following works have contributed most to this study. Ancillary materials, book reviews, obituary notices, numismatic auction catalogs, and so forth, have been omitted here, but full citations appear in the notes.

Adams, W. L. "In the Wake of Alexander the Great: The Impact of Conquest on the Aegean World." *AncW* 27 (1996): 29–37.

Adcock, Frank. "Greek and Macedonian Kingship." *PBA* 39 (1953): 163–180.

Alcock, Susan. "Breaking Up the Hellenistic World: Survey and Society," pp. 171–190 in Ian Morris, ed., *Classical Greece: Ancient Histories and Modern Archaeologies*. Cambridge: Cambridge University Press, 1994.

Allchin, F. R., and N. Hammond, eds. *The Archaeology of Afghanistan from the Earliest Times to the Timurid Period*. London: Academic Press, 1978.

Allchin, F. R., and K. R. Norman. "Guide to the Asokan Inscriptions." *South Asian Studies* 1 (1985): 43–50.

Allotte de la Füye, C. "Monnaies incertaines de la Sogdiane et des contrées voisines." *RN* (1910): 6–73, 281–333.

Allouche-LePage, Marie-Thérèse. *L'art monétaire des royaumes bactriens*. Paris: Didier, 1956.

Altheim, Franz, and Ruth Stiehl. *Geschichte Mittelasiens im Altertum*. Berlin: Walter de Gruyter, 1970.

Amandry, M. "Un nouveau trésor de monnaies d'argent pseudo-athéniennes venu d'Afghanistan (1990)." *RN* 36 (1994): 34–54.

Anson, E. V. *The Attalids of Pergamon*. 2d ed. Ithaca: Cornell University Press, 1971.

Austin, M. M. "Hellenistic Kings, War, and Economy." *CQ* 36 (1986): 450–466.

Babelon, Ernst. *Traité des monnaies grecques et romaines*. Vol. 1. Paris: Leroux, 1901.

Badian, Ernst. "Alexander the Great and the Unity of Mankind." *Historia* 7 (1958): 425–444.

———, ed. *Alexander le Grand: Image et realité*. Geneva: Fondation Hardt, 1976.

Banerjee, Aloke Kumar. "Role of Coin in Agrarian Economy of Northern India during Pre-Mauryan and Mauryan Age." *JNSI* 52 (1990): 112–115.

Bar-Kochva, B. "On the Sources and Chronology of Antiochus I's Battle Against the Galatians." *PCPS* 119 (1973): 1–8.

———. *The Seleucid Army: Organization and Tactics in the Great Campaigns*. Cambridge: Cambridge University Press, 1976.

Bartholomaei, J. de. "Notice sur les médailles des Diodotes, rois de la Bactriane." *Journal de Numismatique et de Science Heraldique* (1843): 12.

Bayer, Theophilus. *Historia Regni Graecorum Bactriani*. St. Petersburg: Academia Scientiarum, 1738.

Bellinger, A. R. "The Coins from the Treasure of the Oxus." *ANSMN* 10 (1962): 51–67.

———. *Essays on the Coinage of Alexander the Great*. New York, 1963; rpt. New York: Durst, 1979.

Bernard, Paul. "Première campagne de fouilles d'Ai Khanoum." *CRAI* (1966): 127–129.

———. "Ai Khanoum on the Oxus: A Hellenistic City in Central Asia." *PBA* 53 (1967): 71–95.

———. "Deuxième campagne de fouilles d'Ai Khanoum en Bactriane." *CRAI* (1967): 306–324.

———. "Campagne de fouilles 1967 à Ai Khanoum." *CRAI* (1968): 263–279.

———. "Chapiteaux corinthiens hellénistique d'Asie centrale découverts à Ai Khanoum." *Syria* 45 (1968): 111–151.

———. "Quatrième campagne de fouilles à Ai Khanoum (Bactriane)." *CRAI* (1969): 313–355.

———. "Sièges et lits en ivoire d'époque hellénistique en Asie centrale." *Syria* 47 (1970): 327–343.

———. "Campagne de fouilles 1969 à Ai Khanoum." *CRAI* (1970): 301–349.

———. "La campagne de fouilles de 1970 à Ai Khanoum (Afghanistan)." *CRAI* (1971): 385–452.

———. "Campagne de fouilles à Ai Khanoum (Afghanistan)." *CRAI* (1972): 605–632.

———. "Ai Khanoum: Ville coloniale grecque." *DA* 5 (1974): 99–114.

———. "Fouilles d'Ai Khanoum (Afghanistan), campagnes de 1972 et 1973." *CRAI* (1974): 280–308.

———. "Note sur la signification historique de la trouvaille." *RN* 17 (1975): 58–69.

———. "Campagne de fouilles 1974 à Ai Khanoum (Afghanistan)." *CRAI* (1975): 167–197.

———. "Les traditions orientales dans l'architecture gréco-bactrienne." *JA* (1976): 245–275.

———. "Campagne de fouilles 1975 à Ai Khanoum (Afghanistan)." *CRAI* (1976): 287–322.

———. "Campagne de fouilles 1976–1977 à Ai Khanoum (Afghanistan)." *CRAI* (1978): 421–462.

———. "Ai Khanoum." *Afghanistan* 31 (1978): 15–32.

———. "La Bactriane à l'époque Kushane d'après une nouvelle publication soviétique." *JS* (1979): 237–256.

———. "Pratiques financières grecques dans la Bactriane hellénisée." *BSFN* (1979): 517–520.

———. "Campagne de fouilles 1978 à Ai Khanoum (Afghanistan)." *CRAI* (1980): 435–459.

———. "Diodore XVII, 83, 1: Alexandrie du Caucase ou Alexandrie de l'Oxus." *JS* (1982): 217–242.

———. "An Ancient Greek City in Central Asia." *Scientific American* 246 (1982): 148–159.

———. "Alexandre et Ai Khanoum." *JS* (1982): 125–138.

———. *Fouilles d'Ai Khanoum. Vol. 4. Les monnaies hors trésors: Questions d'histoire gréco-bactrienne.* Paris: Boccard, 1985.

———. "Le Marsyas d'Apamée, l'Oxus et la colonisation séleucide en Bactriane." *Studia Iranica* 16 (1987): 103–115.

———. "Alexandre et l'Asie centrale: Réflexions à propos d'un ouvrage de F. L. Holt." *Studica Iranica* 19 (1990): 21–35.

———. "L'Asie centrale et l'empire séleucide." *Topoi* 4 (1994): 473–511.

———. "Maracanda-Afrasiab colonie grecque," pp. 331–365 in *La Persia e l'Asia centrale da Alessandro al X Secolo.* Rome: Accademia Nationale dei Lincei, 1996.

Bernard, Paul, and Rémy Audouin. "Trésor de monnaies indiennes et indo-grecques d'Ai Khanoum (Afghanistan) 1: Les monnaies indiennes." *RN* 15 (1973): 238–289.

———. "Trésor de monnaies indiennes et indo-grecques d'Ai Khanoum (Afghanistan) 2: Les monnaies indo-grecques." *RN* 16 (1974): 6–41.

Bernard, Paul, and H-P. Francfort. *Études de géographie historique sur la plaine d'Ai Khanoum (Afghanistan).* Paris: CNRS, 1978.

Bernard, Paul, and Olivier Guillaume. "Monnaies inédites de la Bactriane grecque à Ai Khanoum (Afghanistan)." *RN* 22 (1980): 9–32.

Bernard, P., et al. *Fouilles d'Ai Khanoum. Vol. 1, pts. 1 and 2. Campagnes 1965, 1966, 1967, 1968.* Paris: Klincksieck, 1973.

———. "Fouilles d'Ai Khanoum (Afghanistan): Campagne de 1974." *BEFEO* 63 (1976): 5–51.

———. "Campagne de fouille 1978 à Ai Khanoum (Afghanistan)." *BEFEO* 68 (1980): 1–104.

———. "Fouilles de la mission franco-soviétique à l'ancienne Samarkand (Afrasiab): Première campagne, 1989." *CRAI* (1990): 356–380.

———. "Fouilles de la mission franco-ouzbèque à l'ancienne Samarkand (Afrasiab): Deuxième et troisième campagnes (1990–1991)." *CRAI* (1992): 275–311.

Bickerman, Elias. *Institutions des Séleucides.* Paris: Paul Geuthner, 1938.

———. "Notes on Seleucid and Parthian Chronology." *Berytus* 8 (1944): 73–83.

———. "The Seleucids and the Achaemenids," pp. 87–117 in *Atti del Convegno sul Tema: La Persia e il mondo greco-romano*. Rome: Accademia Nationale dei Lincei, 1966.

Bilde, Per, et al., eds. *Religion and Religious Practice in the Seleucid Kingdom*. Aarhus: Aarhus University Press, 1990.

———. *Centre and Periphery in the Hellenistic World*. Aarhus: Aarhus University Press, 1993.

Billows, Richard. *Antigonus the One-Eyed and the Creation of the Hellenistic State*. Berkeley: University of California Press, 1990.

———. *Kings and Colonists: Aspects of Macedonian Imperialism*. Leiden: Brill, 1995.

Bivar, A. D. H. "The Bactra Coinage of Euthydemus and Demetrius." *NC* 11 (1951): 22–39.

———. "Bent Bars and Straight Bars: An Appendix to the Mir Zakah Hoard." *Studia Iranica* 11 (1982): 49–60.

Bopearachchi, Osmund. "The Euthydemus Imitations and the Date of Sogdian Independence." *Silk Road Art and Archaeology* 2 (1991–92): 1–21.

———. *Indo-Greek, Indo-Scythian, and Indo-Parthian Coins in the Smithsonian Institution*. Washington, D.C.: Smithsonian Institution, 1993.

———. "L'indépendance de la Bactriane." *Topoi* 4 (1994): 513–519.

Bopearachchi, O., and Aman Ur Rahman. *Pre-Kushana Coins in Pakistan*. Islamabad: Iftikar, 1995.

Borza, E. N. *In the Shadow of Olympus: The Emergence of Macedon*. Princeton: Princeton University Press, 1990.

Bosworth, A. B. "Alexander and the Iranians." *JHS* 100 (1980): 1–21.

———. *Conquest and Empire: The Reign of Alexander the Great*. Cambridge: Cambridge University Press, 1988.

Braudel, Fernand. *Civilization and Capitalism, 15th–18th Century*. Vols. 1 and 2. New York: Harper and Row, 1981 and 1982.

Briant, Pierre. *L'Asie centrale et les royaumes proche-orientaux du premier millénaire (c. VIIIe–IVe siècles avant notre ère)*. Paris: Editions Recherche sur les Civilisations, 1984.

Brodersen, Kai. "The Date of the Secession of Parthia from the Seleucid Kingdom." *Historia* 35 (1986): 378–381.

Buckley, J. A. "An Analysis of Thirty-One Coins from the Hellenistic Period." *Archaeometry* 27 (1985): 102–107.

Burnes, Alexander. *Travels into Bokhara*. 3 vols. London: John Murray, 1834.

Burstein, Stanley. "Hellenistic Culture: Recent Resources (1960–1989)." *Choice* (June 1990): 1634–1643.

———. *The Hellenistic Period in World History*. Washington, D.C.: American Historical Association, 1996.

Callatay, François de. "Les trésors achéménides et les monnayages d'Alexandre: Espèces immobilisées et espèces circulantes?" *REA* 91 (1989): 259–274.

Camp, John. *The Athenian Agora: Excavations in the Heart of Classical Athens*. London: Thames and Hudson, 1986.

Canfora, Luciano. *The Vanished Library*. Translated by Martin Ryle. Berkeley: University of California Press, 1990.

Carradice, Ian, and Martin Price. *Coinage in the Greek World*. London: Seaby, 1988.

Casey, P. J. *Understanding Ancient Coins*. Norman and London: University of Oklahoma Press, 1986.

Casey, P. J., and Richard Reece, eds. *Coins and the Archaeologist*. 2d ed. London: Seaby, 1988.

Casson, Lionel, and Martin Price, eds. *Coins, Culture, and History in the Ancient World*. Detroit: Wayne State University Press, 1981.

Christol, Alain. "Les édits grecs d'Asoka: Etude linguistique." *JA* 27 (1983): 25–42.

Clain-Stefanelli, Elvira. *Numismatics—An Ancient Science*. Washington, D.C.: U. S. Government Printing Office, 1965.

Clement, A. P. "A Bibliography of the Writings of Edward T. Newell." *AJP* 68 (1947): 427–432.

Comparette, T. L. *A Descriptive Catalogue of Greek Coins Selected from the Cabinet of Clarence S. Bement, Esq.* New York: American Numismatic Society, 1921.

Cribb, Joe, ed. *Money: From Cowrie Shells to Credit Cards*. London: British Museum, 1986.

Curiel, Raoul, and Daniel Schlumberger. *Trésors monétaires d'Afghanistan*. Paris: Klincksieck, 1953.

Dagens, Bruno, M. LeBerre, and D. Schlumberger. *Monuments préislamiques d'Afghanistan*. Paris: Klincksieck, 1964.

Dalton, Ormonde M. *The Treasure of the Oxus*. 3d ed. London: British Museum, 1964.

Davis, Norman, and Colin Kraay. *The Hellenistic Kingdoms: Portrait Coins and History*. London: Thames and Hudson, 1973.

DeRomilly, J. "Les barbares dans la pensée de la Grèce classique." *Phoenix* 47 (1993): 283–292.

Descat, R., ed. *L'or perse et l'histoire grecque*. REA 91 (1989).

Diakonov, I. M., and E. Zejmal. "The Parthian Dynast Andragoras and his Coins" (in Russian). *VDI* (1988): 4–19.

Downey, Susan B. *Mesopotamian Religious Architecture: Alexander Through the Parthians*. Princeton: Princeton University Press, 1988.

Dupree, Nancy. "Museum Under Siege." *Archaeology* 49 (March/April 1996): 42–51.

Durrbach, Félix, ed. *Inscriptions de Délos*. Paris: Champion, 1929.

Durrbach, Félix, and R. Roussel, eds. *Inscriptions de Délos*. Paris: Champion, 1935.

Eddy, S. K. *The King is Dead: Studies in the Near-East Resistance to Hellenism, 334–31 B.C.* Lincoln: University of Nebraska Press, 1961.

Errington, R. M. "From Babylon to Triparadeisos: 323–320 B.C." *JHS* 90 (1970): 49–77.

———. *A History of Macedonia*. Berkeley: University of California Press, 1990.

Errington, E., and J. Cribb, eds. *The Crossroads of Asia: Transformation in Image and Symbol in the Art of Ancient Afghanistan and Pakistan*. Cambridge: The Ancient India and Iran Trust, 1992.

Esty, Warren, and Giles Carter. "The Distribution of the Number of Coins Struck by Dies." *AJN* 3/4 (1991–92): 165–186.

Farber, J. J. "The *Cyropaedia* and Hellenistic Kingship." *AJPh* 100 (1979): 497–514.

Festugière, A. J. *Etudes de religion grecque et hellénistique.* Paris: J. Vrin, 1972.

Fleischer, Robert. *Studien zur Seleukidischen Kunst.* 2 vols. Mainz am Rhein: Philipp von Zabern, 1991.

Francfort, H-P. *Les palettes du Gandhara.* Paris: Boccard, 1979.

———. *Fouilles d'Ai Khanoum.* Vol. 3. *Le sanctuaire du temple à niches indentées.* Paris: Boccard, 1984.

———, ed. *Nomades et sédentaires en Asie centrale: Apports de l'archéologie et de l'ethnologie.* Paris: CNRS, 1990.

Fraser, P. M. "The Son of Aristonax at Khandahar." *Afghan Studies* 2 (1979): 9–21.

———. *Cities of Alexander the Great.* Oxford: Clarendon Press, 1996.

Frye, Richard. *The Heritage of Central Asia: From Antiquity to the Turkish Expansion.* Princeton: Markus Wiener, 1996.

Gardin, Jean-Claude. "Les relations entre la Méditerranée et la Bactriane dans l'antiquité, d'après des données céramologiques inédites," pp. 447–460 in *De l'Indus aux Balkans: Recueil Jean Deshayes.* Paris: Editions Recherche sur les Civilisations, 1985.

———, ed. *L'archéologie de la Bactriane ancienne.* Paris: CNRS, 1985.

———. "La céramique hellénistique en Asie centrale: Problèmes d'interpretation." pp. 187–193 in *Akten des XIII Internationalen Kongresses für klassische Archäologie.* Berlin, 1988.

Gardner, Percy. "New Coins from Bactria." *NC* 19 (1879): 1–12.

———. "Coins from Central Asia." *NC* 1 (1881): 8–12.

Gerin, Dominique. "Becker et les monnaies bactriennes du Cabinet de France." *BSFN* 38 (1983): 305–309, 321–322.

Gershevitch, Illya, ed. *The Cambridge History of Iran.* Vol. 2. *The Median and Achaemenian Periods.* Cambridge: Cambridge University Press, 1985.

Glotz, Gustav. *Ancient Greece at Work.* Paris, 1920; rpt. New York: Norton, 1967.

Grainger, J. D. *The Cities of Seleukid Syria.* Oxford: Clarendon Press, 1990.

Grant, Michael. *From Alexander to Cleopatra: The Hellenistic World.* New York: Scribner, 1982.

———. *The Visible Past: Recent Archaeological Discovieries of Greek and Roman History.* New York: Scribner, 1990.

Green, Peter. *Alexander of Macedon, 356–323 B.C.: A Historical Biography.* Berkeley: University of California Press, 1991.

———, ed. *Hellenistic History and Culture.* Berkeley: University of California Press, 1993.

Greene, Kevin. *The Archaeology of the Roman Economy.* Berkeley: University of California Press, 1986.

Grenet, Frantz. *Les pratiques funéraires dans l'Asie centrale sédentaire de la conquête grecque à l'Islamisation.* Paris: CNRS, 1984.

Grierson, Philip. *Numismatics.* Oxford: Oxford University Press, 1975.

Griffith, G. T. *The Mercenaries of the Hellenistic World.* Cambridge, 1935; rpt. Chicago: Ares Press, 1975.

Gruen, Erich. *The Hellenistic World and the Coming of Rome.* 2 vols. Berkeley: University of California Press, 1984.

Guillaume, Olivier. *Fouilles d'Ai Khanoum.* Vol. 2. *Les propylées de la rue principale.* Paris: Boccard, 1983.

————. *L'analyse de raisonnements en archéologie: Le cas de la numismatique gréco-bactrienne et indo-grecque.* Paris: Editions Recherches et Civilisations, 1987.

————, ed. *Graeco-Bactrian and Indian Coins from Afghanistan.* Translated by O. Bopearachchi. Delhi/Oxford/New York: Oxford University Press, 1991.

Hackens, Tony, and Patrick Marchetti, eds. *Histoire économique de l'antiquité.* Louvain-la-Neuve: Séminaire de Numismatique Marcel Hoc, 1987.

Hadley, Robert A. "Hieronymus of Cardia and Early Seleucid Mythology." *Historia* 18 (1969): 142–152.

————. "Seleucus, Dionysus, or Alexander?" *NC* (1974): 9–13.

Hambly, Gavin, ed. *Central Asia.* New York: Delacorte, 1969.

Hamilton, J. R. *Alexander the Great.* Pittsburgh: University of Pittsburgh Press, 1973.

Hammond, N. G. L. *Alexander the Great: King, Commander, and Statesman.* Park Ridge, N.J.: Noyes Press, 1980.

————. *Philip of Macedon.* Baltimore: Johns Hopkins University Press, 1994.

Hanaway, William, Jr., "Anahita and Alexander." *JAOS* 102 (1982): 285–295.

Heckel, Waldemar, and Richard Sullivan, eds. *Ancient Coins of the Graeco-Roman World: The Nickle Numismatic Papers.* Waterloo, Ontario: Wilfrid Laurier University Press, 1984.

Herman, G. "The 'Friends' of the Early Hellenistic Rulers: Servants or Officials?" *Talanta* (1981): 103–149.

Holt, Frank L. "The Euthydemid Coinage of Bactria: Further Hoard Evidence from Ai Khanoum." *RN* 23 (1981): 7–44.

————. "Discovering the Lost History of Ancient Afghanistan: Hellenistic Bactria in Light of Recent Archaeological and Historical Research." *AncW* 9 (1984): 3–11, 13–28.

————. "Ai Khanoum and the Question of Bactrian Independence." *AJA* 88 (1984): 248.

————. "Alexander's Settlements in Central Asia." *Ancient Macedonia* 4 (1986): 315–323.

————. "Hellenistic Bactria: Beyond the Mirage." *AncW* 15 (1987): 3–15.

————. "A History in Silver and Gold." *Aramco World* 45 (1994): 2–13.

————. "Spitamenes Against Alexander." *Historikogeographika* 4 (1994): 51–58.

————. "Eukratides of Baktria." *AncW* 27 (1996): 72–76.

————. "The Autobiography of an Ancient Coin." *Aramco World* 48 (1997): 10–15.

————. "Alexander the Great and the Spoils of War." *Ancient Macedonia* 6 (forthcoming).

————. "Mimesis in Metal: The Fate of Greek Culture on Bactrian Coins," pp.

84–100 in F. Titchener and R. Moorton, eds., *Mimesis: The Reciprocal Influence of Life and Arts in Graeco-Roman Antiquity* (forthcoming).

Hopkirk, Peter. *The Great Game: The Struggle for Empire in Central Asia.* New York: Kodansha, 1992.

Houghton, Arthur. *Coins of the Seleucid Empire from the Collection of Arthur Houghton.* New York: American Numismatic Society, 1983.

Houghton, Arthur, and Wayne Moore. "Some Early Far North-Eastern Seleucid Mints." *ANSMN* 29 (1984): 1–9.

Howgego, Christopher. "Why Did Ancient States Strike Coins?" *NC* 150 (1990): 1–25.

Jacoby, Felix. *Die Fragmente der griechischen Historiker.* 17 vols. Leiden: Brill, 1926–1958.

Jenkins, G. K. "A Group of Bactrian Forgeries." *RN* 7 (1965): 51–57.

Jones, J. M. *Testimonia Numaria.* Vol. 1. London: Spink, 1993.

Jouget, Pierre. *Macedonian Imperialism and the Hellenization of the East.* London: Kegan Paul, 1928.

Kaye, J. W. *Lives of Indian Officers.* 2 vols. London: Keliher, 1904.

Kejariwal, O. P. *The Asiatic Society of Bengal and the Discovery of India's Past, 1784–1838.* Delhi: Oxford University Press, 1988.

Khazanov, Anatoli M. *Nomads and the Outside World.* Translated by Julia Crookenden. Cambridge: Cambridge University Press, 1984.

Knobloch, Edgar. *Beyond the Oxus: Archaeology, Art, and Architecture of Central Asia.* London: Ernest Benn, 1972.

Kordosis, Michael. "China and the Greek World: An Introduction to Greek-Chinese Studies with Special Reference to the Chinese Sources." *Historikogeographika* 4 (1994): 253–304.

Koshelenko, G. A. *Grecheskij Polis na ellinisticheskon Vostoke* [The Greek Polis in the Hellenistic East]. Moscow: Nauka, 1979.

Kovalenko, Sergei. "The Coinage of Diodotus I and Diodotus II, Greek Kings of Bactria." *Silk Road Art and Archaeology* 4 (1995–96): 17–74.

Kreissig, Heinz, and Friedman Kühnert, eds. *Antike Abhängigkeitsformen in den griechischen Gebieten ohne Polisstruktur und den romischen Provinzen.* Berlin: Akademie Verlag, 1985.

Kritt, Brian. *Seleucid Coins of Bactria.* Lancaster: CNG, 1996.

Kroll, John. *The Athenian Agora.* Vol. 26. *The Greek Coins.* Princeton: American School of Classical Studies at Athens, 1993.

Kruglikova, Irina, and Shahibye Mustamandi. "Résultats préliminaires des travaux de l'expédition archéologique afghan-soviétique en 1969." *Afghanistan* 23 (1970): 84–97.

Kuhrt, Amélie, and S. Sherwin-White, eds. *Hellenism in the East: The Interaction of Greek and Non-Greek Civilizations from Syria to Central Asia after Alexander.* Berkeley: University of California Press, 1987.

Lahiri, A. N. "The Diodotus Coins." *IHQ* 33 (1957): 222–228.

———. "Religio-Mythical Bearing of the Representation of Zeus on Indo-Greek Coins." *JNSI* 42 (1980): 58–65.

Lassen, Christian. *Zur Geschichte der griechischen und indo-skythischen Könige in Baktrien, Kabul und Indien.* Bonn, 1838.

Leriche, Pierre. *Fouilles d'Ai Khanoum.* Vol. 5. *Les remparts et les monuments associés.* Paris: Boccard, 1986.

Leriche, Pierre, and Henri Tréziny, eds. *La fortification dans l'histoire du monde grec.* Paris: CNRS, 1986.

Le Rider, Georges. "Monnaies grecques récemment acquises par le Cabinet de Paris." *RN* 11 (1969): 7–27.

Lewis, Naphthali. *Greeks in Ptolemaic Egypt: Case Studies in the Social History of the Hellenistic World.* Oxford: Clarendon Press, 1986.

Liebmann-Frankfort, T. "L'histoire des Parthes dans le livre XVI de Troque Pompée: Essai d'identification de ses sources." *Latomus* 28 (1969): 894–922.

Ligabue, Giancarlo, and Sandro Salvatori, eds. *Bactria: An Ancient Oasis Civilisation from the Sands of Afghanistan.* Venice: Erizzo, 1989.

Litvinsky, B. A., and I. R. Pichikyan. "Monuments of Art from the Sanctuary of the Oxus (Northern Bactria)." *AAASH* 28 (1980): 25–83.

———. "The Temple of the Oxus." *JRAS* (1981): 133–167.

———. "Découvertes dans un sanctuaire du dieu Oxus de la Bactriane septentrionale." *RA* (1981): 195–216.

———. "From the Throne of Stone." *UNESCO Courier* (July 1985): 28–31.

Litvinsky, B. A., Y. G. Vinogradov, and I. Pichikyan. "The Votive Offering of Atrosokes, from the Temple of Oxus in Northern Bactria" (in Russian). *VDI* (1985): 84–110.

Longpérier, Adrian de. "Collection numismatique du Général Court." *RN* 4 (1839): 81–88.

———. "Médailles de la Bactriane." *RN* 5 (1840): 83–84.

Lund, Helen. *Lysimachus.* London: Routledge, 1992.

MacDowall, D. W., and M. Ibrahim. "Pre-Islamic Coins in Herat Museum." *Afghan Studies* 2 (1979): 45–54.

McGovern, W. E. "Missing Die Probabilities, Expected Die Production, and the Index Figure." *ANSMN* 25 (1980): 202–223.

Mahaffy, John. *Alexander's Empire.* London: T. F. Unwin, 1887.

Majumdar, N. G. "The Bajaur Casket of the Reign of Menander." *Epigraphia Indica* 24 (1937): 1–8.

Marshall, John. *Taxila.* 3 vols. Cambridge, 1951; rpt. Varanasi: Bhartiya, 1975.

Masson, Vadim M. *Das Land der tausend Städte.* Munich: Udo Pfriemer, 1982.

Mehl, A. *Seleukos Nikator und sein Reich.* Louvain: Studia Hellenistica, 1986.

Metcalf, D. M. "What Has Been Achieved Through the Application of Statistics to Numismatics?" *PACT* 5 (1979): 3–24.

Mielczarek, Mariusz. "On the Finding of a Copy of a Bactrian Tetradrachm" (in Polish). *WN* 28 (1984): 194–199.

Momigliano, Arnaldo. *Alien Wisdom: The Limits of Hellenization.* Cambridge: Cambridge University Press, 1975.

———. *Essays in Ancient and Modern Historiography.* Middletown, Conn.: Wesleyan University Press, 1977.

Montgomery, Hugo. "The Economic Revolution of Philip II—Myth or Reality?" *Symbolae Osloenses* 60 (1985): 37–47.

Mørkholm, Otto. "The Life of Obverse Dies in the Hellenistic Period," pp.

11–21 in C. N. L. Brooke et al., eds., *Studies in Numismatic Method Presented to Philip Grierson.* Cambridge: Cambridge University Press, 1983.

———. *Early Hellenistic Coinage from the Accession of Alexander to the Peace of Apamea* (336–188 B.C.). Cambridge: Cambridge University Press, 1991.

Mukherjee, B. N. "Emergence of Coinage in the Indian Subcontinent." *JNSI* 51 (1989): 38–47.

Muller, J. W. "Estimation du nombre originel de coins." *PACT* 5 (1981): 157–172.

Nachtergael, G. *Les Galates en Grèce et les Sotéria de Delphes: Recherches d'histoire et d'épigraphie hellénistiques.* Brussels: Académie Royale de Belgique, 1977.

Narain, A. K. "The Greek Monogram ⊕ and Ai Khanoum—the Bactrian Greek City." *NumDigest* 10 (1986): 4–15.

———. "Approaches and Perspectives." *Yavanika* 2 (1992): 5–34.

Negmatov, Numan N. "Ancient Khojent-Alexandria Eschata." *Journal of Central Asia* 9 (1986): 41–48.

Newell, E. T. *The Pergamene Mint Under Philetaerus.* New York: American Numismatic Society, 1936.

Nicolet, Claude. *Space, Geography, and Politics in the Early Roman Empire.* Ann Arbor: University of Michigan Press, 1991.

Nielsen, Inge. *Hellenistic Palaces: Tradition and Renewal.* Aarhus: Aarhus University Press, 1994.

Norman, K. R. "Notes on the Greek Version of Asoka's Twelfth and Thirteenth Rock Edicts." *JRAS* (1972): 111–118.

Oelsner, Joachim. *Materiallen zur babylonischen Gesellschaft und Kultur in hellenistischer Zeit.* Budapest, 1986.

Oikonomides, Al. N. "The Temenos of Alexander the Great at Alexandria in Arachosia (Old Kandahar)." *ZPE* 56 (1984): 145–147.

Olshausen, E. *Prosopographie der hellenistischen Königsgesandten.* 2 vols. Louvain: Studia Hellenistica, 1974.

Ozols, Jakob, and Volker Thewalt, eds. *Aus dem Osten des Alexanderreiches: Völker und Kulturen zwischen Orient und Okzident Iran, Afghanistan, Pakistan, Indien.* Cologne: Du Mont, 1984.

Pandey, Deena B. "Notes on Indo-Greek Coins." *JNSI* 28 (1966): 198–200.

Paranavitana, Senarat. *The Greeks and the Mauryas.* Colombo: Lake House Investments Ltd., 1971.

Parker, R., and W. Dubberstein. *Babylonian Chronology 626 B.C.–A.D. 76.* Providence: Brown University Press, 1950.

"Parvalus." "Gold Coin of Another Bactrian Prince." *NC* 2 (1839–40): 202–203.

Petitot-Biehler, Claire-Yvonne. "Trésor de monnaies grecques et gréco-bactriennes trouvé à Ai Khanoum (Afghanistan)." *RN* 17 (1975): 23–57.

Pichikyan, I. "The Oxus Temple Composition in the Context of Architectural Comparison." *IASCCAInfB* 12 (1987): 42–55.

———. "The Graeco-Bactrian Altars in the Temple of the Oxus (Northern Bactria)." *IASCCAInfB* 12 (1987): 56–65.

———. *Bactrian Culture: Achaemenid and Hellenistic Periods* (in Russian). Moscow: Nauka, 1991.

———. "Rebirth of the Oxus Treasure: Second Part of the Oxus Treasure from the Miho Museum Collection." *Ancient Civilizations* 4 (1997): 306–383.
Posch, Walter. *Baktrian zwischen Griechen und Kuschan*. Wiesbaden: Harrassowitz, 1995.
Préaux, Claire. *Le monde hellénistique: La Gréce et l'Orient de la mort d'Alexandre à la conquête romaine de la Grèce*. 2 vols. Paris: Presses Universitaires de France, 1978.
Price, Martin. *The Coinage in the Name of Alexander the Great and Philip Arrhidaeus*. 2 vols. Zurich and London: Swiss Numismatic Society and British Museum Press, 1991.
Prinsep, James. *Essays on Indian Antiquities*. 2 vols. Edited by Edward Thomas. 1858; rpt. Varanasi: Indological Book House, 1971.
———. *Historical Results from Bactrian Coins and Other Discoveries in Afghanistan*. Edited by H. T. Prinsep. London, 1844; rpt. Chicago: Ares, 1974.
Pritchett, W. K. *Ancient Greek Military Practices*. Pt. 1. Berkeley: University of California Press, 1971.
Pugachenkova, G. A. "The Antiquities of TransOxiana in the Light of Investigations in Uzbekistan (1985–1990)." *Ancient Civilizations* 2 (1995): 1–38.
Pugachenkova, G. A., and E. V. Rtveladze. *Northern Bactrian-Tocharistan* (in Russian). Tashkent, 1990.
Pugliese-Carratelli, Giovanni. "Asoka e i re ellenistici." *PP* 33 (1953): 449–454.
Rapin, Claude. "Les inscriptions économiques de la trésorerie d'Ai-Khanoum (Afghanistan)." *BCH* 107 (1983): 315–372.
———. "La trésorerie hellénistique d'Ai Khanoum." *RA* (1987): 41–70.
———. *Fouilles d'Ai Khanoum*. Vol. 8. *La trésorerie du palais hellénistique d'Ai Khanoum*. Paris: Boccard, 1992.
Rapin, C., et al. "Les textes littéraires grecs de la trésorerie d'Ai Khanoum." *BCH* 111 (1987): 225–266.
Rawlinson, H. G. *Bactria: The History of a Forgotten Empire*. London, 1912; rpt. New York: AMS Press, 1969.
Rea, J. R., R. C. Senior, and A. S. Hollis. "A Tax Receipt from Hellenistic Bactria." *ZPE* 104 (1994): 261–280.
Reade, Julian. "A Hoard of Silver Currency from Achaemenid Babylon." *Iran* 24 (1986): 79–87.
Rice, E. E. *The Grand Procession of Ptolemy Philadelphus*. Oxford: Oxford University Press, 1983.
Robert, Louis. "De Delphes à l'Oxus." *CRAI* (1968): 416–457.
Robinson, Charles A., Jr., "The Greeks in the Far East." *CJ* 44 (1949): 405–412.
———. "The Extraordinary Ideas of Alexander the Great." *AHR* 62 (1956–57): 326–344.
Robinson, D. M., and P. Clement. *Excavations at Olynthus*. Vols. 9 and 14. Baltimore, 1938.
Robinson, E. S. G. "The Beginnings of Achaemenid Coinage." *NC* 18 (1958): 187–193.
Rochette, Raoul. *Notice sur quelques médailles grecques inédites, appartenant à des rois inconnus de la Bactriane et de l'Inde*. Paris: L'Imprimerie Royale, 1834.

Rollin, Charles. *The Life of Alexander the Great, King of Macedon*. Providence: B. Wheeler, 1796.

Romane, Julian. "W. W. Tarn and the Art of History." *AncW* 15 (1987): 21–24.

Rosenfield, John. *The Dynastic Art of the Kushans*. Berkeley: University of California Press, 1967.

Rtveladze, E. V. "La circulation monétaire au nord de l'Oxus à l'époque gréco-bactrienne." *RN* 26 (1984): 61–76.

Rtveladze, E. V., and M. Nijazova. "First Hoard of Greco-Bactrian Coins from Bukhara" (in Russian). *Obshchestvennye nauki v Uzbekistane* (1984–86): 54–58.

Sachs, A. J., and H. Hunger. *Astronomical Diaries and Related Texts from Babylonia*. Vienna: DAW, 1988.

Sallet, Alfred von. "Alexander der Grosse als Grunder der baktrish-indischen Reich." *ZfN* 8 (1881): 279–280.

Samuel, Alan E. *The Shifting Sands of History: Interpretations of Ptolemaic Egypt*. Lanham, Md.: University Press of America, 1989.

Sarianidi, Viktor. "The Treasure of Golden Hill." *AJA* 84 (1980): 125–132.

———. "The Treasure of the Golden Mound." *Archaeology* 33 (1980): 31–41.

———. *The Golden Hoard of Bactria*. New York and Leningrad: Abrams/Aurora Art Publishers, 1985.

———. "The Golden Hoard of Bactria." *National Geographic* 177 (March 1990): 50–75.

Schlumberger, Daniel, and Paul Bernard. "Ai Khanoum." *BCH* 89 (1965): 590–657.

Schmitt, H. H. *Untersuchungen zur Geschichte Antiochos des Grossen und seiner Zeit*. Wiesbaden: Historia Einzelschriften, 1964.

Schober, L. *Untersuchungen zur Geschichte babyloniens und der oberen Satrapien von 323–303 v. Chr*. Frankfurt, 1981.

Scott, David A. "Ashokan Missionary Expansion of Buddhism Among the Greeks (in Northwest India, Bactria, and the Levant)." *Religion* 15 (1985): 131–141.

Scullard, H. H. *The Elephant in the Greek and Roman World*. Ithaca: Cornell University Press, 1974.

Sedlar, Jean W. *India and the Greek World: A Study in the Transmission of Culture*. Totowa, N.J.: Rowman and Littlefield, 1980.

Sedov, A. V. *Kobadian: Facing the Dark Ages* (in Russian). Moscow: Nauka, 1987.

Seel, Otto, ed. *M. Iuniani Iustini, Epitoma Historiarum Philippicarum Pompei Trogi*. Stuttgart: Teubner, 1972.

Seibert, Jakob. *Das Zeitalter der Diadochen*. Darmstadt: Wissenschaftliche Buchgesellschaft, 1983.

Sellwood, D. G. "Some Experiments in Greek Minting Technique." *NC* 3 (1963): 217–231.

Sharma, G. R. *Reh Inscription of Menander and the Indo-Greek Invasion of the Ganga Valley*. Allahabad: Abinash, 1980.

Sherwin-White, A. N. *Roman Foreign Policy in the East, 168 B.C. to A.D. 1*. Norman: University of Oklahoma Press, 1983.

Sherwin-White, Susan. "Babylonian Chronicle Fragments as a Source for Seleu-
cid History." *JNES* 42 (1983): 265–270.
Simonetta, A. M. "Some Hypotheses on the Military and Political Structure of
the Indo-Greek Kingdom." *JNSI* 22 (1960): 56–62.
Sircar, D. C., ed. *Select Inscriptions Bearing on Indian History and Civilization.*
Vol. 1. *From the Sixth Century B.C. to the Sixth Century A.D.* 2d ed. Cal-
cutta: University of Calcutta, 1965.
Smirnova, Nataliya. "Bactrian Coins in the Pushkin State Museum of Fine Arts."
Ancient Civilizations 2 (1995): 335–352.
———. "On Finds of Hellenistic Coins in Turkmenistan." *Ancient Civilizations*
3 (1996): 260–285.
Smith, R. Morton. "The First Bactrian Coinage: An Introduction." *Cornucopiae*
4 (1979): 6–13.
Smith, Sidney, ed. *Babylonian Historical Texts Relating to the Capture and
Downfall of Babylon.* London: Methuen, 1924.
Soren, David, and Jaime James. *Kourion: The Search for a Lost Roman City.* New
York: Doubleday, 1988.
Starr, Chester G. *Past and Future in Ancient History.* Lanham, Md.: University
Press of America, 1987.
Staviskij, B. *To the South from the Iron Gates* (in Russian). Moscow: Sovetskii
Khudozhnik, 1977.
———. *La Bactriane sous les Kushans: Problèmes d'histoire et de culture.* Paris:
Maisonneuve, 1986.
Stewart, Andrew. *Faces of Power: Alexander's Image and Hellenistic Politics.*
Berkeley: University of California Press, 1993.
Stroud, R. S. "An Athenian Law on Silver Coinage." *Hesperia* 43 (1974): 157–188.
Sullivan, Richard. *Near Eastern Royalty and Rome.* Toronto: University of
Toronto Press, 1989.
Taplin, Oliver. *Greek Fire: The Influence of Ancient Greece on the Modern
World.* New York: Athenaeum, 1990.
Tarn, W. W. "Notes on Hellenism in Bactria and India." *JHS* 22 (1902): 268–293.
———. *Alexander the Great.* 2 vols. Cambridge: Cambridge University Press,
1948.
Tcherikover, Victor. *Hellenistic Civilization and the Jews.* Philadelphia: Jewish
Publication Society of America, 1959; rpt. New York: Atheneum, 1970.
Thapar, Romila. *Asoka and the Decline of the Mauryas.* 2d ed. Oxford: Oxford
University Press, 1973.
Thomas, E. "Bactrian Coins." *JRAS* 20 (1862–63): 99–134.
Thompson, Dorothy. *Memphis Under the Ptolemies.* Princeton: Princeton Uni-
versity Press, 1988.
Tiwari, J. N. "A Survey of Indian Numismatography (Pre-Muhammadan
Coinage), 1738–1950." *Numismatic Notes and Monographs* (Numismatic
Society of India) 10 (1964): 1–28.
Todd, Richard. "W. W. Tarn and the Alexander Ideal." *The Historian* 37 (1964):
48–55.
Troxell, Hyla. "Greek Accessions: Asia Minor to India." *ANSMN* 22 (1977):
9–27.

Troxell, Hyla, and W. Spengler. "A Hoard of Early Greek Coins from Afghanistan." *ANSMN* 15 (1969): 1–19.

Usmanova, Z. I. "Inscriptions from Kara-Kamar" (in Russian). *VDI* 4 (1990): 145–147.

———. "New Material on Ancient Merv." *Iran* 30 (1992): 55–63.

Veuve, Serge. *Fouilles d'Ai Khanoum. Vol. 6. Le gymnase.* Paris: Boccard, 1987.

Walbank, F. W. *A Historical Commentary on Polybius.* 3 vols. Oxford: Clarendon Press, 1957–79.

———. *The Hellenistic World.* Cambridge, Mass.: Harvard University Press, 1982.

Walbank, F. W., A. E. Astin, et al. *The Cambridge Ancient History.* 2d ed. Vols. 7 and 8. Cambridge: Cambridge University Press, 1984 and 1989.

Westermark, Ulla. *Das Bildnis des Philetairos von Pergamon: Corpus der Munzpragung.* Stockholm, 1960.

Wheeler, Mortimer. *Flames over Persepolis: Turning Point in History.* New York: Reynal, 1968.

Whitehead, R. B. "Notes on the Indo-Greeks." *NC* 20 (1940): 89–122.

———. *Indo-Greek Numismatics.* Chicago: Argonaut, 1970.

Whitteridge, Gordon. *Charles Masson of Afghanistan.* Warminster: Aris and Phillips, 1986.

Widemann, François. "Un monnayage inconnu de type gréco-bactrien à légende araméenne." *Studia Iranica* 18 (1989): 193–197.

Wiesehöfer, Josef. "Discordia et Defectio—Dynamis kai Pithanourgia: Die frühen Seleukiden und Iran," pp. 29–56 in Bernd Funck, ed., *Hellenismus: Beiträge zur Erforschung von Akkulturation und politischer Ordnung in den Staaten des hellenistischen Zeitalters.* Tübingen: Mohr, 1996.

Wilcken, Ulrich. "Alexander der Grosse und die hellenistische Wirtschaft." *Schmollers Jahrbuch für Gesetzgebung, Verwaltung und Volkswirtschaft im deutschen Reich* 45 (1921): 394–420.

———. *Alexander the Great.* Translated by G. Richards and edited by E. N. Borza. Rpt. New York: Norton, 1967.

Will, Edouard. "Le monde hellénistique et nous." *Ancient Society* 10 (1979): 79–95.

———. "Pour une 'anthropologie coloniale' du monde hellénistique," pp. 273–301 in J. Eadie and J. Ober, eds., *The Craft of the Ancient Historian: Essays in Honor of Chester G. Starr.* Lanham, Md.: University Press of America, 1985.

Will, W., and J. Heinrichs, eds. *Zu Alexander der Grosse.* 2 vols. Amsterdam: Hakkert, 1987 and 1988.

Wolf, E. R. *Europe and the People Without History.* Berkeley: University of California Press, 1982.

Wolski, Josef. "L'éffondrement de la domination des Séleucides en Iran au IIIᵉ siècle av. J. -C." *Bulletin Internationale de l'Académie Polonaise des Sciences et Lettres* 5 (1947): 13–70.

———. "Le problème d'Andragoras." *Ephemeridis Instituti Archaeologici Bulgarici* 16 (1950): 111–114.

———. "The Decay of the Iranian Empire of the Seleucids and the Chronology of the Parthian Beginnings." *Berytus* 12 (1956–57): 35–52.

———. "L'historicité d'Arsace Ier." *Historia* 8 (1959): 222–238.

———. "Les Iraniens et le royaume gréco-bactrien." *Klio* 38 (1960): 110–121.

———. "Andragoras, était-il iranien ou grec?" *Studia Iranica* 4 (1975): 159–169.

———. "Le problème de la fondation de l'état gréco-bactrien." *Iranica Antiqua* 17 (1982): 131–146.

Wood, John. *A Journey to the Source of the River Oxus*. London, 1872; rpt. Karachi: Oxford University Press, 1976.

Woodcock, George. *The Greeks in India*. London: Faber and Faber, 1966.

Yailenko, V. -P. "Les maximes delphiques d'Ai Khanoum et la formation de la doctrine du *Dhamma* d'Asoka." *DHA* 16 (1990): 239–256.

Yardley, J. C. "The Literary Background to Justin/Trogus." *AHB* 8 (1994): 60–70.

Yardley, J. C., and W. Heckel, eds. *Justin, "Epitome of the Philippic History of Pompeius Trogus."* 2 vols. Oxford: Clarendon Press, 1997.

Zejmal, E. V. *Ancient Money of Tadjikistan* (in Russian). Dushanbe, 1983.

———. "Coins from the Excavations of Takht-i Sangin (1976–1991)," pp. 89–110 in K. Tanabe et al., eds., *Studies in Silk Road Coins and Culture: Papers in Honour of Professor Ikuo Hirayama*. Kamakura: Institute of Silk Road Studies, 1997.

Coin Index

Author Index

Subject Index

Achaemenids, 31–32, 34, 39, 41, 45, 65,
  96. *See also* Persia
Adriatic Sea, 6
Adulis, inscription from, 60, 176
Aegean Sea, 17, 37–38, 44, 118
aegis, attribute of Zeus on Diodotid coins,
  75, 100, 140, 146, 148, 151, 153, 158
Aetolian League, 38
Afghanistan 10, 15–16, 26, 35, 37, 108
Afrasiab (ancient Maracanda), 174
Africa, 63
Agathocles, Bactrian king, 25, 68, 74,
  78–79, 83, 97–98
Agathocles, eparch of Persia, 59, 61, 63,
  74, 179
agoranomos, 43
Ai Khanoum (ancient Alexandria-
  Oxiana?), 17, 27, 39, 41, 50, 66,
  121, 124, 133, 140; archaeological
  finds at, 36–38, 43–46, 51–52, 54–
  55, 62–63, 65, 88n, 95–96, 106, 108,
  113–115, 117, 120, 125, 132, 135,
  169, 174–175, 177; discovery of,
  15–16; fall of, 18, 25, 123, 135
Akkad, mentioned in Babylon text, 175
Alexander of Epirus, 53
Alexander III (the Great), 10, 19–20, 27,
  41, 44, 50, 57, 65, 67–68, 79, 96,
  101–102, 106, 121–122, 124, 126,
  129, 134, 178–180, 183–184; death
  of, 1–3, 5–6, 8–9, 11, 17, 21, 23–25,
  34, 46, 130, 137, 178, 180; invasion
  of Bactria, xiii–xiv, 24, 28, 66, 178;
  policies of, 2, 11–13, 15, 18, 21–25,
  28–37, 45–47, 61, 117, 137
Alexandria in Egypt, 5–6, 12, 59

Alexandria-Exchate, city in Sogdiana, 27
Alexandria-Margiana (modern Merv),
  refounded as an Antioch, 27
Amphipolis, Macedonian mint at, 102
amphorae, Mediterranean types found
  at Ai Khanoum, 44
Amu Darya (ancient Oxus River), 10
Anahita, Persian goddess, 121–123, 136.
  See also Artemis
anchor, Seleucid symbol, 132
Ancyra, Battle of, 180
Andragoras, satrap of Parthia, 59, 61,
  63, 96–97, 180
Androsthenes of Cyzicus, official of
  Antiochus III in India, 182
Antalcidas, Bactrian king, 74, 178
Antigonids, rulers of Macedonia, 10, 134
Antigonus I of Macedonia, 65, 180
Antigonus Gonatus, Macedonian king, 53
Antimachus I, Bactrian King, 25, 68,
  73–74, 78–79, 82–83, 98, 176
Antimachus, unknown Bactrian
  mentioned in tax receipt, 176
Antioch, city in Margiana, 27, 39
Antioch, city in Syria, 12, 39
Antiochus I, Seleucid king, 89, 99, 179;
  eastern satrapies and, 25–29, 36–37,
  39, 51–52, 54, 82, 95, 102, 109, 111–
  112, 114, 117–118, 129, 174–175,
  180; India and, 53
Antiochus II, Seleucid king, 25, 179;
  Diodotid coins and, 19, 70, 76–77,
  83, 89, 95–97, 103, 109, 111–112,
  114, 117; eastern satrapies and, 58–
  59, 64, 68–72, 79, 85, 126; India
  and, 53

Compositor: Integrated Composition Systems
Text: 10/13 Sabon
Display: Sabon
Printer and Binder: Thomson-Shore

Plate 1. Ai Khanoum, looking southwest across the lower city.

Plate 2. Ai Khanoum, looking northeast across the walls and main gate.

Plate 3. Tetradrachm of Agathocles commemorating
Antiochus Nikator.

Plate 4. Tetradrachm of Antimachus commemorating
Diodotus Soter.

Plate 5. Tetradrachm of Agathocles commemorating
Diodotus Soter.

Plate 6. Tetradrachm of Agathocles commemorating
Euthydemus Theos.

Plate 7. Tetradrachm of Diodotus I, series A, group 6.

Plate 8. Tetradrachm of Diodotus I, series A, group 8.

Plate 9. Tetradrachm of Diodotus II, series C, group 1.

Plate 10. Stater of Diodotus II, series C, group 3.

Plate 11. Drachm of Diodotus II, series E, group 3.

Plate 12. Tetradrachm of Diodotus II, series B, group 1.

Plate 13. Tetradrachm of Diodotus II, series B, group 3.

Plate 14. Tetradrachm of Diodotus II, series D, group 7.

Plate 15. Drachm of Diodotus II, series D, group 8.

Plate 16. Drachm of Diodotus II, series F, group 5.

Plate 17. Bronze single, series G, group 1.

Plate 18. Bronze double, series H, group 1.

Plate 19. Bronze double, series I, group 1.

Plate 20. Bronze double, series I, group 2.

Plate 21. Bronze quarter, series I, group 4.

Plate 22. Bronze quarter, series I, group 7.

Plate 23. Reverse of bronze double (enlarged) with countermark.

Plate 24. Tetradrachm of young Euthydemus I.

Plate 25. Tetradrachm of old Euthydemus I.

Plate 26. Silver lidded vessels from Tillya-Tepe. Weight inscribed in Greek on larger example.

Plate 27. Pendant with seal of Athena from Tillya-Tepe.